THE WORD MILITANT

Preaching a Decentering Word

WALTER BRUEGGEMANN

Fortress Press
Minneapolis

THE WORD MILITANT
Preaching a Decentering Word

Copyright © 2007 Fortress Press, an imprint of Augsburg Fortress. All rights reserved. Except for brief quotations in critical articles or reviews, no part of this book may be reproduced in any manner without prior written permission from the publisher. Visit http://www.augsburgfortress .org/copyrights/contact.asp or write to Permissions, Augsburg Fortress, Box 1209, Minneapolis, MN 55440.

Scripture passages are from the New Revised Standard Version of the Bible, copyright © 1989 National Council of the Churches of Christ in the USA. Used by permission. All rights reserved.

Cover design: Brad Norr Design
Book design and typesetting: The HK Scriptorium, Inc.

Library of Congress Cataloging-in-Publication Data

Brueggemann, Walter.
The word militant : preaching a decentering word / Walter Brueggemann.
    p. cm.
Includes bibliographical references and index.
ISBN 978-0-8006-6277-6
1. Preaching. I. Title.
BV4211.3.B78 2007
251   2007033970

The paper used in this publication meets the minimum requirements of American National Standard for Information Sciences—Permanence of Paper for Printed Library Materials, ANSI Z329.48-1984.

Manufactured in the U.S.A.

11 10 09 08 07 1 2 3 4 5 6 7 8 9 10

Contents

In Gratitude to My Classmates of Fifty Years Ago
Eden Theological Seminary
Class of '58

Foreword

"Thank you for your help in the current preaching emergency." That was how Walt ended a recent letter to me. Preaching emergency? It was a characteristic Brueggemannism. I was unaware that we were in a homiletic emergency until Walt named it thus. With Walt, that which I might circumspectly describe as malaise, a temporary problem to be dispassionately considered, becomes heated, confrontational, demandingly urgent action—preaching emergency.

Walt has been heating up things for us preachers for over three decades now. I dedicated my *Peculiar Speech: Preaching to the Unbaptized* (Eerdmans, 1992) to him, though I did not say why. Now I have the opportunity. I owe Walt a great debt. The best that this poor preacher has preached in the last thirty years, I got from either Brueggemann or Barth. (Barth appears to be about the only contemporary theologian for whom Walt has much regard—yet another endearing Brueggemannian attribute.) Walt helped make an essentially cowardly, hesitant, people-pleasing preacher like me more militant. My best homiletical frontal assaults, sneak attacks, flanking movements, offensive and defensive maneuvers were done under Walt's direction.

I first encountered Walt in his early *The Creative Word* (Fortress, 1982). His was a voice any preacher would love—strong, assertive, bold, and authoritative, but still full of humor, particularly ironic humor, mixed with militancy. I had always despised wisdom literature and yawned at Leviticus until Walt foisted them upon me in *The Creative Word*.

At the conclusion of his lectures (which were eventually published as *Finally Comes the Poet* [Fortress, 1989]) a preacher next to me exclaimed, "That's the grandest testimony to the joy of being a preacher I ever heard!" In near despair of a forlorn inner-city parish in South Carolina, when I was about to throw in the towel and quit, a reading of Walt's commentary on Jeremiah made it impossible for me to resign from preaching. Once one was called by God to testify, according to Walt and his favorite prophet, one had better stand up and deliver, measurable results be damned. They may kill you for what God makes you say, but what a way to go.

In the pulpit, Walt speaks in a strong, visceral style, clutching the pulpit as if it were a raft in a storm (the preacher in *Moby Dick* comes to mind), at times assaulting the congregation, sparring with them, mocking them, yet congratulating them for having the guts to be part of Israel's and the church's conversations with a living, demanding, and loving God. Walt's is the Word made militant. One Sunday, after Walt had thundered from the pulpit of Duke Chapel as a visiting preacher (his sermon full of pathos and grandeur—David's lament for Absalom), a student referred to Walt's style as that of the "raging bull." I thought he had Walt just right. Every time Brueggemann speaks, a congregation knows that serious matters will be wrestled into their hearing, but always with a beguiling playfulness. Every sermon I've heard him preach is a model of obedience to the text, even at the cost of his listeners. His theological expectation for the power of the spoken gospel word is extravagant and unconstrained by contemporary intellectual limitations.

In these essays you will find that Walt wastes no time in taking a text and charging into the heart of enemy territory, in grabbing the reader's attention and getting down to business. I think that he is a pacifist Christian, but you couldn't tell it from the tone of his writing. He shows that he has read just about everything, that he is in conversation and in argument with a dazzling range of partners from dozens of unlikely disciplines, and that the biblical word can mix it up with the best of them. I took the better part of two full days to work through his magisterial *An Introduction to the Theology of the Old Testament: The Canon and Christian Imagination* (2003). After that mid-career reading, my biblical interpretation was forever changed. Take that, all you aging defenders of the historical-critical method.

For all these reasons and more, we preachers and hermeneuts can rejoice at this compilation of some of the best of Brueggemann on preaching. We are the ones who regularly ask, as anxious Zedekiah queried preacher Jeremiah, "Is there a word from the LORD?" (Jer. 37:17). Walt, backed up by the prophets, exuberantly responds with pushy, biblically induced testimony that is more than merely personal generativity from his fertile mind. Yes, there is a word from the LORD, and encounters with it will not leave you unscathed. He knows that our homiletical crisis is due to theological factors rather than rhetorical ones. Through a lifetime of serious engagement with the biblical text, Walt has never lost a childlike surprise and adolescent delight at what's to be discovered in Scripture. While he reads widely and is in knowledgeable, respectful conversation with a wide range of scholars, Walt always privileges, prejudices the biblical text over any other. His reports of his skirmishes with Scripture never fail to fuel and to stoke the imaginations of us preachers. He thus provokes an emergency and shames an accommodated, culture-bound, tamed, therapeutic church with his fecund prophetic re-descriptions and creative transpositions that speak the biblical word into our time and place. Unintimidated by the disestablishment of the American Protestant church, he always hears something for us to say that the world is literally dying to hear. Walt thus gives testimony to a ceaselessly interesting God who speaks, reveals, and discloses, a God who is accurately known only through God's Word, only through a gaggle of Spirit-filled, evangelical preachers whom the Word has made militant.

William H. Willimon
Bishop, Birmingham Area,
The United Methodist Church

Preface

Anybody who lives in the church, who practices ministry, and who studies Scripture must inevitably think about preaching and engage with questions about the preaching enterprise. So it is with me. I have been thinking about preaching since I first sat and listened to my father-preacher, my first instructor on the subject. In seminary I received my lowest grades in preaching classes, not being reckoned overly competent at practical ministerial tasks. Through seminary my classmates of fifty years ago and I were taught, in great trepidation on our part, about the wonder of preaching by Frederick Schroeder and Ernest Nolte. After that I was introduced to Gerhard von Rad's leading thesis on the book of Deuteronomy as early "preaching" in ancient Israel, the subject of my doctoral dissertation. The rest unfolded for me in the daring world of Karl Barth.

Preaching is such an odd, recurring, face-to-face transaction that carries with it impossible responsibilities for the preacher. And if we were more attentive to the dialogic quality of the transaction, we would recognize that there are commensurate burdens for the listening congregation. It is odd and undoubtedly true that there is almost no consensus among us about the nature of preaching, so that every preacher exercises freedom, often with quite idiosyncratic notions of preaching. What is clear is that if there is news from out beyond us, it must be *uttered aloud* and it must be *heard face-to-face*. No adequate substitute or equivalent for face-to-face utterance is available to us (see Rom 10:14-17). It is peculiarly uttered face-to-faceness that carries with it something from beyond us. This inexplicable assurance from God is transmitted by the preacher, who yields to the free gift of the gospel. Such preaching, of course, eschews both the therapeutic charm of social "chaplains" and the urgent coerciveness of conservatives or liberals.

This collection of essays has grown over time, as my thinking has developed and matured. I have tried to pay attention to recent work in Old

Testament studies and hermeneutics, and I have been engaged in what I see as the deepening crisis of the church in U.S. society as we drift toward empire. Clearly, the preacher must be as well schooled as possible in the central disciplines that concern our critical context for preaching. In the end, however, the biblical text is likely to be more pertinent and interesting and compelling than anything else we may offer.

I am glad for the company of preachers with whom I work and from whom I continue to learn. I am grateful to Neil Elliott and his crew at Fortress Press for their patience with the process of getting the collection together. I am grateful, yet one more time, to Patrick Miller for his initial counsel about the volume. I am appreciative of Will Willimon for his generous words of introduction, as I count him a comrade in these matters. And my thanks go to Tia Foley who, again, has worked my jottings into some coherence for this volume.

My own work in exegesis and preaching, like that of every preacher, is surrounded by a great cloud of sustaining witnesses. Of long-term importance to me have been my classmates at Eden Theological Seminary, Class of '58. I am glad to remember and salute them—some retired like my well-beloved brother Ed, some still active in preaching, and some deceased, notably the dearly remembered Ray Buck. To all of them I express glad thanks and congratulations for fifty years of preaching.

Acknowledgments

Preaching as Reimagination. *Theology Today* 52 (October 1995) 313–29. Used by permission.

The Preacher, the Text, and the People. *Theology Today* 47 (October 1990) 237–37. Used by permission.

Ancient Utterance and Contemporary Hearing. In *Just Preaching: Prophetic Voices for Economic Justice,* edited by Andre Resner, Jr. (St. Louis: Chalice Press, 2003), 67–75. Used by permission.

An Imaginative "Or." *Journal for Preachers* 23 (Easter 2000), 3–17. Used by permission.

That the World May Be Redescribed. *Interpretation* 56 (October 2002), 359–67. Used by permission.

The Social Nature of the Biblical Text for Preaching. Pages 127–50 from *Preaching as a Social Act,* edited by Arthur Van Seeters (Nashville: Abingdon Press, 1998), 127–65. Used by permission.

The Shrill Voice of the Wounded Party. *Horizons in Biblical Theology* 21 (June 1999), 1–25. Used by permission.

Life or Death: De-privileged Communication. *Journal for Preachers* 21 (1998) 21–29. Used by permission.

Preaching to Exiles. *Journal for Preachers* 16 (1993) 3–15. Used by permission.

Preaching a Sub-version. *Theology Today* 55 (July 1998) 195–212. Used by permission.

Truth-telling as Subversive Obedience. *Journal for Preachers* 20 (Lent 1997), 2–9. Used by permission.

Introduction

At Risk with the Text

Preaching is an audacious act. It has always been so.

I

It is audacious because the preacher stands up to make a claim that she has something new to say that the gathered listeners want to hear. That audaciousness is now acute, because it is no longer the case, as in the days of clergy monopoly, that the preacher might be the most learned person in town. Now, almost anywhere, the congregation teems with people who, in every dimension of our common life, know things well beyond the learning of the preacher. On all counts, the act of preaching is:

- *foolish* because in the congregation some know more and because in every congregation there are those ideologically committed in ways that preclude serious listening. As a result the preacher's utterance is already determined to be disputatious even before it is heard.

- *dangerous* if it is faithful, because the powers of retrenchment are everywhere among us, a passion to keep things as they were before the utterance. Ideological resistance is readily evoked in most congregations. And if not in the congregation itself, the rulers of this age keep a close eye on any proclamation that may disturb present arrangements. We have all read of the dangers of preaching in a police state where the preacher on any occasion is at risk and may be called to account. But even in our more-or-less benign democratic society such surveillance is not difficult to evoke, as witness All Saints Episcopal Church in Pasadena, which has had its "tax status" called into question because of a preacher's critique of the Iraq war policy.

1

- a *risky self-exposure of the preacher, who at best is vulnerable in the precariousness of the utterance.* Every preacher knows with some regularity that what is said and what must be said inescapably expose the preacher as something of a fraud, for good preaching must speak truth to which the preacher's own life does not always attest. The preacher, with any self-awareness, knows of such incongruity, and of course every knowing congregation can spot the slippage between utterance and utterer. But such discrepancy is inevitable unless preaching is confined to the small truths verified in the preacher's own life.

Preaching is foolish, dangerous, and exposing, because what must be said in proclamation constitutes a daring alternative to the ideological passions that may be present in the congregation, to the powers that conduct surveillance, either inside or outside the congregation, and to the preacher's own sense of self. The occasion of preaching is risky on all counts, inherently risky because something other happens in preaching besides the echo of our preferred ideologies, our studied interests, or our personal inadequacies.

II

But if preaching is such an act of risk, then we rightly ask, Why do it with such regularity? Why enter that zone of vulnerability with such predictability? Of course there are cultural and historical expectations that preaching should happen and is scheduled to happen regularly. But there are as well serious reasons for preaching well behind cultural and historical expectations. On the one hand, there is the preacher's own vocational compulsion that this must be enacted. Such a preacher under compulsion is at deep risk if the preacher reneges on that mandate. Thus, Jeremiah knows, on behalf of all preachers who come after him, about the catch-22, to preach or not:

> For whenever I speak, I must cry out,
>   I must shout, "Violence and destruction!"
> For the word of the Lord has become for me
>   a reproach and derision all day long.
> If I say, "I will not mention him,
>   or speak any more in his name,"
> then within me there is
>   something like a burning fire shut up in my bones;
> I am weary withholding it in, and I cannot. (Jer. 20:8-9)

And Karl Barth is surely faithful to Jeremiah in his dictum:

> Here we are discussing our common *situation.* This situation I will characterize in the three following sentences:—*As ministers we ought to speak of God. We are human, however, and so cannot speak of God. We ought therefore to recognize both* our obligation and our inability *and by that very recognition give God the glory.* This is our perplexity. The rest of our task fades into insignificance in comparison.[1]

That vocational imperative on the part of the preacher of course is not a private matter and does not occur in a social vacuum. Beyond the preacher's deep impulse, there is the reality of the church, an alternative community that is evoked and sustained precisely by preaching.[2] The wonder of preaching is that people show up. Of course there are all kinds of reasons for that, all sorts of mixed motives and no doubt ignoble motivations among them. The mixed motives that propel the congregation to show up match the mixed motives the preachers have for living out their vocational impulse. In the midst of all that, however, there is no doubt an unvoiced wonderment in which the gathered listening congregation is not unlike the fearful, eager, desperate last king in ancient Judah, Zedekiah:

> Then King Zedekiah sent for him, and received him. The king questioned him secretly in his house, and said, "Is there any word from the Lord?" (Jer. 37:17)

We do not ask in futility; and when we ask, we are not sure what it is we are asking. We are, I suspect, half hoping that there is no such word, because we would rather have things as they are, even if the way things are is scarcely manageable.

Given all of that, however, we do show up with wonderment and inquiry. We show up to listen, waiting and half expecting that there will be a new word. We most often have not thought this through when we show up. But if we had thought it through, we would likely recognize our sneaking hunch that we cannot stay human if we attempt to live in a closed system of reality that is sealed against new intervention from the outside. We reach out, in fear and hope, to be addressed by newness, because we know the human spirit will wither if there is no address. And we do, in our unreflective shrewdness, know that most of the verbal noise around us is no serious address and for that reason has no chance of opening our closed system of reality to newness.

We show up like Zedekiah: Is there a word from the Lord? The king showed up to ask "secretly"... not unlike Nicodemus who came "by night" to Jesus (John 3:2). The king came because his city was besieged by the Babylonians, before whom he could not stand. The king came because his conventional "support system" and his "intelligence community" had exhausted their resources and had no clue. The king came because he hoped that his present dire circumstance did not need to be his final truth. The king came because he had heard whispered around him old memories of times past when YHWH had done saving miracles, and he hoped for yet one more saving miracle (see Jer. 21:2). In the midst of his dire circumstance and his devouring anxiety, he came in timid, desperate hope. That hope is fearful, partly grounded in a faith tradition, partly grounded in deep ambiguities of lived circumstance. Such hope is partly a theological particularity and partly a generic human impulse. Either way, the king showed up. He was ready to listen, even if he found the listening nearly unbearable, so unbearable that he took pains to establish "deniability" about having come to listen at all (Jer. 37:24-28). In the same way, I imagine, we show up for preaching, not unlike Zedekiah, half hoping, half fearful, embarrassed to be there, but half believing that our present circumstance of "weal or woe" is not the last truth of our life.

III

When we gather together, half in fear and half in hope, the preacher must speak. Preachers are tempted in that moment of utterance in many directions. The preacher is tempted to moralism, to "relevance," to entertainment, to conformity, to trivialization, to moral passion about the preacher's pet project or the congregation's needy circumstance. In the service of such temptations, we have developed settled rhetorical strategies, most notably "sermon introductions" and "illustrations" that are designed, for the most part, to narcotize the congregation and assure them that nothing odd will happen in this hour of utterance. But if the analogy of Zedekiah works at all, then we have not shown up for utterance in order to be entertained or numbed or instructed in the passion of the day. We have come to find out if there is a word from outside our circumstance, from outside our closed system of reality that could open the system—personal or public or both— to fresh air and new light.

The preacher, in such a mixed congregation of fear and hope, has a moment of speech. Even in our electronically overly busy world of Attention Deficit Disorder, the preacher has a moment. Without pretense and at best without idolatrous claim, the preacher is to speak from "the other side," from out beyond our vexed or buoyant circumstance, from the ground of holy mystery, which for Jews and Christians has been concretized in Torah and in Jesus Christ. The preacher, even if too modest to say so, is authorized for this instant to say, "Thus saith the Lord," a formula that is credible only if the utterance squares with tradition, only if it is connected to lived reality, and only if it is transparently not allied with the peculiar passions and interests of the preacher.

If it is true, as now is commonly held, that the pivot point of faith in the Old Testament is the sixth-century exile, then we may take the *exile* as metaphor for the characteristic "human predicament" in biblical mode, a situation of hopelessness and homelessness, a sense of impotence about being able to change circumstance, and a bewilderment about how to be fully human now.[3] And if we take exile as characteristic context, then we may take *gospel* as characteristic utterance in exile.[4] The characteristic task and opportunity of the preacher are to assert, yet again, that the matrix of human *homelessness* is the very arena of divine presence whereby homelessness is made *home-filled*.[5] It is the presence of the God of the exodus and of creation, the God of Friday crucifixion and Sunday resurrection, who is declared to be among us who transforms exile into a livable human habitat.

That is the rhetorical transaction that occurs in the Old Testament in the sixth century among the displaced. Voices of *divine presence* are sounded in a context of *known absence*.[6] It is so in Jeremiah, the great prophet of divine absence:

> Thus says the Lord:
> The people who survived the sword
>   found grace in the wilderness;
> when Israel sought for rest,
>   the Lord appeared to him from far away.
> I have loved you with an everlasting love;
>   therefore I have continued my faithfulness to you. (Jer. 31:2-3)

It is so in Jeremiah's later contemporary, Ezekiel:

> I myself will be the shepherd of my sheep, and I will make them lie down, says the Lord God. I will seek the lost, and I will bring back the strayed, and I will bind up the injured, and I will strengthen the weak, but the fat and the strong I will destroy. I will feed them with justice. (Ezek. 34:15-16)

But it is, above all, evident in exilic Isaiah, the poet who transposes the word "news" into theological coinage. The Babylonian regime had eliminated YHWH as a force or factor in the public life of the empire by making clear to Jews that YHWH was no longer a strong power to save.[7] The defeated Jews had in large part accepted the elimination of YHWH and the dominance of Babylonian power and Babylonian gods, the power that controlled and the gods who did not care. The imaginative field of the empire, with all of its epistemological assumptions and its political-military exhibits of hegemony, had completely emptied the field of any possible action by YHWH. The memory and the hope of that God had been erased by imperial leverage. I believe that the same erasure of gospel possibility is largely in effect among us in the United States, where the domination system with its technological totalism is matched by its ideological force. There may be little "godlets" on our horizon, but any god-reference that might matter is largely erased from public awareness.

And then the poet, this vigorous, imaginative preacher so capable, found credible cadences that could break the dominant ideology; he was able to go behind imperial erasure to say something new that was apparently still recognizable to this homeless population. The only word he has for the world-shattering utterance entrusted to him is "gospel":[8]

> Get you up to a high mountain,
>   O Zion, *herald of good tidings*;
> lift up your voice with strength,
>   O Jerusalem, *herald of good tidings*,
>   lift it up, do not fear;
> say to the cities of Judah,
>   "Here is your God!" (Isa. 40:9)

The lean proclamation is, "Here is our God." The Jews had thought, if they engaged at all, that "our God" was nowhere available. But now "here," made here and made new by poetic utterance. In that moment of utterance it must have dawned on a few of the desperate faithful that if such a gospel can be uttered, then the imperial system is not as closed as we have been led to believe. The very utterance opened new possibility that the poet will present in terms of new exodus.[9] And with the hearing of new possibility, inchoate suspicion of the ultimacy of the empire begins to emerge.

This God, now on the lips of this poet in exile, can use the term "gospel" for self-announcement, which contrasts the future-creating capacity of this God with the gods of the empire, who can only maintain what was in powerless, hopeless shutdown:

I first have declared it to Zion,
   and I give to Jerusalem a *herald of good tidings*.
But when I look there is no one;
   among these there is no counselor
   who, when I ask, gives an answer.
No, they are all a delusion;
   their works are nothing;
   their images are empty wind. (Isa. 41:27-29)

Bel bows down, Nebo stoops,
their idols are on beasts and cattle;
these things you carry are loaded
   as burdens on weary animals.
They stoop, they bow down together;
   they cannot save the burden,
   but themselves go into captivity.
Listen to me, O house of Jacob,
   all the remnant of the house of Israel,
who have been borne by me from your birth,
   carried from the womb;
even to your old age I am he,
   even when you turn gray I will carry you.
I have made, and I will bear;
   I will carry and will save. (Isa. 46:1-4)

The assertion of news about YHWH's reemergence begins to expose the hegemonic delusion that has loomed so large; there are the first stirrings of faith brought back to life, stirrings intended by the God who—it turns out—refuses to be erased by a totalizing empire.

The poet, in vivid imagination, can create a scenario of a messenger, a gospeller, who can run joyously and buoyantly across the sand of the Near East with the news that the God who had been defeated is the God who is back in force:

How beautiful upon the mountains
   are the feet of the *messenger* who announces peace,
who brings *good news*,
   who announces salvation,
   who says to Zion, "Your God reigns." (Isa. 52:7)

The news is that the defeated God of Jerusalem has been restored to awesome power. The failed God of Israel turns out to be the newly enthroned king-God, God of gods, Lord of lords, God of all the Babylonian gods, king of all imperial kings. In that poetic moment—and that is all it is—there is jubilation, the release of long-held despair, the affirmation of hope that they had not dared to hope (52:8-10). This is indeed a word from the outside, a word not uttered or censured by the empire, a word not imagined by the defeated, conformist, displaced Jews, a word that comes in the way of poetry that offers no explanation, no certainty, no accommodation to the agents of surveillance. It is a moment of utterance!

The moment will soon be past, and the listeners will have to return to "the real world," which is permeated with powerful signs of imperial control. Nothing out there has been changed—except that everything has now been changed by this poetic utterance, because *the poetry cannot be unsaid*, not by all the power and all the technology of "delete" and all the intimidators. The word has been uttered and the juices of alternative possibility have begun to flow. It is so succinct and guileless, the way of words the empire has not wanted to be uttered:

Here is your God!
Your God reigns!

They did not know they could come to hear this word. They wondered ahead of time if there was a word; but they did not know what word they wanted or what was possible. They did not know what the empire would permit or what was possible for the poet. They did not know ahead of time. But when they heard it . . . they knew! They recognized that the poet who said this word (a) spoke *from a tradition* of divine kingship that goes back to the Song of Moses (Exod. 15:18); (b) *connected to the lived reality* of imperial erasure and ersatz kingship in Babylon; and (c) offered utterance that was not *in the service of any vested interest* of the poet; if anything, it surely placed him in acute jeopardy. On all counts it was a word they, the most daring among them, could credit as true. And in that moment of poetic utterance, the erosion of imperial totalism got under way. The empire is helpless before such credible gospel utterance!

The utterance of God's speech in human articulation is news. It is the assertion of something not known until uttered. It is news hoped for, but hope jaded by the erosion of possibility and the force of imperial erasure. It is hope feared, because when heard, everything settled has to be revamped. It is news that announces that the world is other than we had thought. It is an utterance, an act of human imagination rooted in divine self-giving, that describes the world anew. Out of this threefold use of the term "gospel"

(Isa. 40:9; 47:27; 52:7) the completed utterance of exilic Isaiah (chapters 40–55) twists and turns the language, appeals to old images from the tradition and utilizes new images, all in the service of redescribing the world that is, according to the news, under new management, under the governance of the home-making, home-giving God and away from the deathly power of the empire.

It is a word that is designed to *console.* Thus, the first word is "comfort" (Isa. 40:1; see 49:13); the reiterated "fear not" is an assurance that the God of homecoming has overridden and nullified all the power of fear fostered by the empire and its gods (41:8-14; 43:1-5; 44:8). It is a word of forgiveness uttered by the God who blots out transgression and permits radically new beginnings:

> I, I am He
>> who blots out your transgressions for my own sake,
>> and I will not remember your sins. (Isa. 43:25)

But the word that *consoles* is also the word that *jars.* No doubt many among the displaced who had come to listen were fully ready to accept the world of Babylonian homelessness, had accepted Babylonian rule and had signed on with Babylonian gods—perhaps the prerequisite for economic well-being. And now the same gospel word is an imperative: "Depart, depart" (Isa. 52:11). The listeners were urged (compelled?) to depart from all that was by now familiar and comfortable. Given the new world now imagined in poetic utterance, there was a vexing offer of *comfort-with-disturbance,* both required to come to terms with the strange new world offered in gospel utterance.

IV

The prophet, Isaiah in exile, stood up in exile and offered this counter-utterance, as did Jeremiah and Ezekiel in exile before him. We may ask of them, as every preacher must regularly ask, "From where do they get such words?" Certainly gospellers like Isaiah in exile are generative, imaginative personalities, capable of lining out reality from the vigor of their artistry.

These good preachers, like every good preacher, do not, however, claim that their utterances are simply the fruit of personal generativity. These preachers, like all good preachers, know there is more, even if it is not easy to specify how the words are given. In the Old Testament, three modes of "explanation" are offered for the word that is other than one's own:

1. These utterers, like all good preachers, have "a sense of call," an experience and conviction that their lives have been impinged upon in decisive ways to claim their energy and their future for purposes other than their own.[10] Good preaching is a gift that is given, and given again, by redefining divine impingement, an impingement that wrenches one out of one's own assumptions. All three of the great exilic prophets, Isaiah, Jeremiah, and Ezekiel, operate with such a claim. Most studied is the call narrative concerning Jeremiah, a call that he resisted but eventually accepted, a call that culminated with a divine assurance of support:

> And I for my part have made you today a fortified city, an iron pillar, and a bronze wall, against the whole land—against the kings of Judah, its princes, its priests, and the people of the land. They will fight against you; but they shall not prevail against you, for I am with you, says the Lord, to deliver you. (Jer. 1:18-19; see vv. 4-19)

Most bizarre is the call report of Ezekiel who is summoned to and transported by a vision that completely dislocates him (Ezek. 1-3). Most elusive is the call of exilic Isaiah, though there are suggestions that the elusive language of Isaiah 40:1-11, addressed to "the herald of good tidings" (v. 9), is deliberately modeled after Isaiah 6:1-13 wherein the call narrative of the prophet is much more explicit. In any case, life is disrupted for this poet by a new purpose.

The notion of a "call to preach" is a familiar one to us. It has, however, been greatly routinized and institutionalized in much U.S. Christianity.[11] As a result, "call" is rather like a career path that assures one of institutional support, even including a pension plan. And of course this writer is among those who have benefited from such institutional support and pension. There is no gain in pretending otherwise. It is, however, worth more attention than we give it, that the call is a divine impingement of life-changing proportion that lives always in tension with institutional routinization. We talk easily about "the freedom of the pulpit" which is something of an institutional issue. Alongside that, however, we might also speak of "the freedom of the preacher," which is primarily a theological, psychological matter of being defined by an impingement that puts one at risk and calls one to foolishness and vulnerability (see above).

2. The arena of the call is regularly "the divine council," the place where the gods, in a polytheistic world, convene in heaven to decide about the earth, and then dispatch a messenger with the divine decree to earth.[12] This

is a poetic, imaginative formulation of what we may take to be a serious attempt to reflect theologically upon God's will being done "on earth as it is in heaven." The notion of "divine council" is most explicit in Jeremiah and hardly evident in Ezekiel. More than any other prophet in the Old Testament, Jeremiah is vexed with opponents who contradict his message and claim themselves to be legitimate prophets.[13] This opposition inescapably poses the issue of authority and the matter of contested truth. Of these other prophets, Jeremiah asks a defiant question:

> For who has stood in the council of the Lord
>   so as to see and to hear his word?
> Who has given heed to his word so as to proclaim it? (Jer. 23:18)

He specifically asks if his opponents have had access to the truth of God as has he. And then he gives his answer, which is designed to discredit them:

> I did not send the prophets,
>   yet they ran;
> I did not speak to them,
>   yet they prophesied.
> But if they had stood in my council,
>   then they would have proclaimed my words to my people,
> and they would have turned them from their evil way,
>   and from the evil of their doings. (Jer. 23:21-22)

By implication Jeremiah's answer is not only that his opponents have not had access to the truth of the rule of YHWH; *he has*, and therefore he must be heeded!

In Isaiah 40:1-11, it is noticed that the beginning of the address is a plural imperative, "Comfort ye," as in Handel's *Messiah*. If we ask who is addressed in the plural, the likely answer, reflected in the several voices that speak in vv. 3-8, is that the divine council is convened to plan and articulate the comfort of YHWH to the exiles; thus, the summons of v. 1 is addressed to members of the divine council. And then in vv. 9-11, the gospeller is dispatched with news of regime change. The textual unit that introduces exilic Isaiah is parallel to Isaiah 6:1-13, where the interaction of the divine council is unmistakable. Thus, the two texts function in a twinned way for the two parts of the book of Isaiah to claim divine authorization beyond human imagination.[14] The poet-preachers are sent with a word other than their own.

3. The claim that this is a word other than one's own is encapsulated in the familiar formula, "Thus saith the Lord."[15] The formula is frequently used by the prophets to make the claim that the preached word comes from beyond the preacher. The formula is likely reflective of the way an ambassador speaks for the government she represents, a formula still often heard in the United Nations. Thus, for example, "My government urges that . . . ." A good ambassador does not speak his own word but states the policy position of the government that has dispatched him, and so speaks with the authority of that government. So the poets of the Old Testament who invoked the formula do not speak their own word, but the word of the one(s?) who send them. This means, inescapably, that the uttered word must be taken with great seriousness and must not be dismissed as the word of someone who is crazy (Hos. 9:7) or a traitor (Jer. 38:4). The word uttered is not so easily dismissed, even by those who want to stop both the consoling and jarring power of such utterance.[16]

These three formulations of authority—*call, divine council, messenger formula*—all converge into the claim that the word uttered is from out beyond the preacher. To be sure, the claim is not for that reason everywhere easily accepted. At the very minimum, however, it is crucial that the preacher herself should have some sense of that authorization and summons to a word beyond one's own word.

Now I understand fully that such a claim is not easily transposed into our contemporary preaching environment, not least because the claim so readily spills over into coerciveness and authoritarianism. The claim is exceedingly difficult, moreover, in a society that takes itself to be democratic, psychologically oriented, and prone to easy "therapeutic" communication. It is not thinkable, however, that the claim of preaching should be conformed to cultural mores, even as powerful as they are. Preaching must perforce be grounded more securely than in the easy assumptions of a consumer culture. Preaching, even if it be street preaching, is a preaching *from and in and for the church.* That means that the church, when it is faithful, is committed to being addressed by preaching that is not easily congruent with cultural assumptions; this conviction about preaching is dramatized in the more-or-less high claims of ordination that most church traditions practice.

Inside the life and faith of the church, preacher and congregation have a tacit agreement, assumed but not often enough stated, to engage in a speaking-listening interaction whereby the newness of God's purpose is made verbally explicit and available. It is for sure that many congregations have little sense of this; I think it is equally certain that many preachers have little sense of the awesomeness of the transaction, and so it is diminished into trivialization of a dozen kinds. Rightly understood, the occasion of preaching requires both preacher and listening assembly to suspend many assumptions and to entertain the possibility that there is indeed a word other than our own, a word that comes from outside our closed systems of reality. In the word other than our own, the world is re-characterized, re-narrated, and re-described, shown to be other than what we thought when we came to the meeting.

V

There is no doubt that preaching is rooted in this transcendent claim, a claim that in Scripture is often articulated in an unembarrassed "supernaturalist way." There are, to be sure, other ways in which the transcendent claim can be evoked without supernaturalist formulation. But even given that, we may still return to the question, From whence comes that word? There is no doubt that the direct, personal, intimate impingement of God upon the preacher is crucial. It is equally clear, however, that the preacher does not operate *de novo*, as though the gospel has never been uttered before; rather the preacher stands in a long line of utterance that goes back to a text tradition.

We may take Jeremiah yet again as a case in point. The editorial introduction to the book of Jeremiah states the matter carefully:

> *The words of Jeremiah* son of Hilkiah, of the priests who were in Anathoth in the land of Benjamin, to whom *the word of the Lord came* in the days of King Josiah son of Amon of Judah, in the thirteenth year of his reign. (Jer. 1:1-2)

Most remarkably, this introductory, authorizing statement makes an important distinction. On the one hand, Jeremiah is the one to whom the word of the Lord came. This word of the Lord may be related to the foregoing discussion of the divine council. Jeremiah has been directly addressed and entrusted with "the word of the lord." But on the other hand, it is asserted that the book of Jeremiah that follows these introductory verses, the actual words of Scripture, are identified as "the words of Jeremiah." This careful hermeneutical statement clearly distinguishes between *the word of the Lord* that is given to the prophet and *the words of Jeremiah the prophet* that are

available to us in written form. The distinction makes the pivotal point that
the words of Jeremiah, here the words of the book of Jeremiah, are not to
be equated or identified with the word of the Lord. At the outset, the distinction warns us against a flat biblicism that equates Scripture with the
word of the Lord. But more precisely for our purposes it is also suggested
that the proclaimed words of the preacher are not "the word of the Lord."
They are rather the words of the preacher that stand some distance from
intimate divine impingement through the divine council.

That leaves for us the important and difficult question about the relationship between the word of the Lord and the words of Jeremiah, or vari-
antly, the words of the preacher. The tradition of Jeremiah gives us no
formulaic answer to the question, but we may see how it is that the
prophet's words function in the book of Jeremiah. It seems clear enough
that the connection between the two is made by a vigorous act of imagination that is rooted in the tradition and that is reflective of a definitive personal voice.[17]

It is Jeremiah's assignment from the God who sends him to give
Jerusalem both words of judgment and of hope:

> See, today I appoint you over
>   nations and over kingdoms,
> to pluck up and to pull down,
> to destroy and to overthrow,
> to build and to plant. (Jer. 1:10)

Jeremiah enacts that twofold assignment in a variety of ways. Here I will
delineate six aspects of "plucking up and tearing down . . . planting and
building" that provide ways of thinking about the preaching task of jarring
and consoling:

1. It is clear that Jeremiah, like any good preacher, is deeply informed by
and engaged with a tradition of faith . . . in our belated case certainly textual, in his case probably textual. Broadly understood, the Jeremiah tradition can be understood as a poetic, imaginative practice of the textual
tradition of Deuteronomy that likely was shaped a century earlier.[18] The
Deuteronomic shaping of Jeremiah is well established; we may cite the use
of the text from Deuteronomy 24:1-4 in Jeremiah 3:1-5 as a specific case
in point.[19] It is clear that the extant textual tradition was used freely and
imaginatively, but there is no doubt of textual rootage.

Beyond the textual tradition of Deuteronomy, we may notice how Jeremiah utilizes and exposits particular themes from the extant tradition:

a. In Jeremiah 21:5-7 the prose text appeals to the exodus tradition, though in a quite altered form, one that William Moran terms "anti-Exodus."[20]

b. In his famous declaration concerning new covenant in Jeremiah 31:31-34, Jeremiah clearly appeals to old covenantal—likely Deuteronomic—tradition. In the earlier part of my discussion I have suggested that the covenant renewal in this text is intimately parallel to Exodus 34:9-10, also a report on a renewed covenant.

c. There is no doubt that the well-known "Lamentations of Jeremiah" are derived from and play upon the textual traditions of the Psalms.[21]

d. The "royal promises" of Jeremiah 23:5-6 and 33:14-16 appeal to an older liturgical tradition, perhaps mediated through something like Psalm 72 with its accent on "justice and righteousness."

While the data could be multiplied, this is sufficient to make clear that prophetic utterance is textually grounded and informed.

2. Jeremiah's charge to "pluck up and tear down" leads him to mobilize the textual tradition with poetic imagination in order to articulate the theme of divine judgment and, consequently, Israelite loss. He does so through a rich panoply of images including marriage and infidelity (chapters 2–3), war (chapters 4–6), illness (8:18-22), remarkable stupidity (8:4-8), and a powerful, concrete pondering of coming death (9:10-22).

3. Jeremiah's charge "to plant and build" leads him to mobilize the tradition with poetic imagination in order to articulate the theme of divine promise and, consequently, Israelite hope. He does so through a rich variety of traditional images including land promises (see Jer. 32), the resumption of weddings after the rejection of weddings (Jer. 33:11), and the steadfastness of creation, perhaps an allusion to the post-flood promise of Genesis 8:22 (Jer. 31:35-36, 37; 33:25-26).

4. The theme of judgment ("pluck up and tear down") and the theme of promise ("plant and build") are articulated through daring poetic imagination that is textually informed. By exposition of these themes poetically through textual resources, Jeremiah radically redescribes the sixth-century historical world of his listeners. His act of *prophetic redescription* inescapably and by design serves to refute the dominant description of reality that was sponsored by the royal establishment and legitimated by the liturgical claims of the Jerusalem temple. Against the immense ideological force of

the Jerusalem establishment, Jeremiah works from a *countertext* enacted through a *counterimagination* that offers a *counterdescription of reality*.[22]

The key factor in the counterdescription that is the burden of textual preaching is that Yhwh—the Holy One of Israel who is creator of heaven and earth—is a key player in the life of the world, even though Yhwh as key player had been largely excluded or domesticated by dominant descriptions of reality. That counterdescription is everywhere committed to representing Yhwh as the decisive agent in the life of Israel and in the affairs of the nations. On the one hand, that rearticulation of Yhwh as a serious agent is done in terms of *judgment*, to assert that Jerusalem will be given over to Babylon by the will of Yhwh. This countercharacterization of the fate of Jerusalem refutes the vision of the "shalom prophets," who regard Jerusalem as immune to the threats and vagaries of history (see Jer. 6:13-15; 8:11-12; Ezek. 13:9-11).

On the other hand, the rearticulation of Yhwh as a serious agent is done with the theme of *promise*, the assertion that the displacement of the Jews and the hegemony of Babylon are not the ultimate outcome of the historical process. The prophetic redescription is to assert, on textual grounds with daring imagination, that such worldly power is at best penultimate and will eventually yield to the purpose of Yhwh, which is the restoration and well-being of the covenant community.

Thus, the redescription counters, by judgment, the *denial* of Jerusalem that was fostered by an ideology of exceptionalism, and by promise that counters the *despair* of the displaced. By the end of the text tradition of Jeremiah, the world is seen to be very different from the one vouched for in the dominant narrative; Jeremiah makes clear that the political-economic institutions of the city are fragile and the ideological claims that sustain the city reflect historical arrangements that soon or late but always will yield to the governing will of Yhwh. The outcome of such proclamation, which is *tradition-infused*, *poetry-daring*, and *Yhwh-focused* is a very different world, one that encourages the *relinquishment* of what was and the *reception* of what is now to be given by the power of Yhwh.

VI

From this focus on the tradition of Jeremiah, I draw two further conclusions.[23] First, while the crisis of sixth-century Jerusalem is deep and urgent, it is astonishing that the Jeremiah tradition, for the most part, focuses not on "issues" but on the underlying reality of faith and unfaith, of trust and idolatry. This is notably true of the poetry of Jeremiah; the matter is somewhat less clear in the prose materials, precisely because prose tends to devolve into concrete issues. On the main point, however, both poetry and prose cut underneath concreteness to the more elemental, relational matters. This seems to me an urgent matter for preachers, especially in a culture that is ideologically divided on every issue and in which faith is so readily reduced, by both left and right, to manageable, passionately held "positions" on the questions of the day.

Second, while I have taken Jeremiah as a case in point, the matter of biblical text as redescription is of course not limited to the text of Jeremiah. For the most part, I would insist that the biblical text is characteristically a redescription of reality with reference to the God of the gospel. Thus, creation texts intend to counter the more familiar narrative of the threat of chaos. The ancestral narratives of promise attest a future that aims to defeat the narrative of barrenness. The sapiential texts concerning the life-giving order of creation ordained by the creator intend to counter either the notion of the randomness of the world or the autonomy of human moral agents. The texts characteristically are at the work of redescribing and thereby subverting all dominant descriptions of reality.[24] It follows that where preaching is textual, that preaching is precisely *redescription of the world as God's world, away from denial and toward relinquishment, away from despair and toward receptivity.*

VII

The point of the above is to suggest that, faithful to the prophetic tradition of the Old Testament in particular, faithful to the apostolic tradition of the New Testament in particular, and faithful to the biblical tradition in general, the task of preaching is redescription of the world, with reference to YHWH by appeal to the text through poetic imagination that is connected to particular context. This way of putting the matter relates to the conviction, stated so well by Karl Barth, that the world to which the preacher attests is "strange and new," strange because it challenges conventional accounts of the world, new because reference is to God who makes all things new.[25] The further conviction that parallels this formulation is that most "acceptable" preaching in our society is an echo of dominant culture that remains without critique, so that even in the church there is a lack of awareness that there are alternatives available and that there are choices and decisions to be made.[26]

In ancient Jerusalem the dominant description of reality revolved around the conviction that (a) the temple is YHWH's permanent residence; (b) the monarchy is YHWH's chosen agent; and therefore (c) the city is safe from and immune to the threats of history. Mutatis mutandis, the dominant description of reality in U.S. society is that (a) democratic capitalism is the wave of the future that is sure to produce peace and prosperity; (b) the United States is God's chosen agent in the spread of the gospel of democratic capitalism; and (c) the United States is by divine assurance immune to the threats of history. In both ancient Israel and the current sense of self in the United States, there is a theologically rooted *exceptionalism* that imagines privilege and entitlement of idolatrous proportion.[27] It is this religion that is broadly assumed in our culture, and broadly assumed in the church that is, for the most part ... in both liberal and conservative manifestations ... content to live and work within these boundaries, without reference to the God who "plucks up and tears down, who builds and plants." By and large all of us, preachers included, have an economic stake in the narrative of the dominant description of reality.

Now I understand that most preachers in most congregations cannot frontally attempt to subvert that dominant narrative account of reality. Most preachers in most congregations have little inclination to take on big public issues on very many occasions, because in the life of the congregation most people are preoccupied with more personal and intimate crises that demand our energy and test our faith.

But if it is true, as I take as obvious, that the large dominant narrative of reality among us spins off in terms of social alienation and commodification of the most treasured dimensions of our personal lives, then the task of redescription and subversion is not necessarily or primarily focused on public issues or events. The local crises everywhere around us concerning family and health and jobs—crises that are the consequences of greed, anxiety, drivenness, loneliness, and violence of systemic proportion—in local venues are intimately connected to the big idolatrous commitments of our society.

Thus, the sense of the essays that follow in this collection reflect my growing conviction that the church is the last place in town—in many towns—where a sub-version of reality can be articulated that holds the prospect of an alternative humanness. There are limits to what any congregation can risk and is willing to risk; and there are limits in the congregation to what the preacher can risk and is willing to risk. Of course! But we should not despair. We have, in the U.S. church, spent a very long time ceding over our evangelical voice to accommodation, to an alliance with U.S. exceptionalism and a timid refusal to say what we know most deeply.

I imagine, then, that preachers and congregations now must think again, precisely because our characteristic evangelical notions of humanness are now under assault, and the forces that assault are largely left without critique among us.[28] Preachers and congregations will have to learn again that the news entrusted to us does not conform to a fearful moralism or to a brazen globalism, does not conform precisely because the God who is near at hand is also a God who is far off (Jer. 23:23). The text entrusted to the preacher and to the congregation is indeed a sub-version of reality, a *sub-version* that intends to *subvert*. It has always been so. It was so the night that Zedekiah came to Jeremiah to see if there was a word from the Lord. It was so before that, when Pharaoh came in the night to Moses and said, "Bless me" (Exod. 12:32). It was so after that when Nicodemus came to Jesus at night and asked about a second life (John 3:4). It is always so. Preachers have that hidden text that wants daylight.

The interaction is very much, always again, like the interaction between the king and the prophet in Jeremiah 37:

- There is *an asking* if there is a word from the Lord:

  Then King Zedekiah sent for him, and received him. The king questioned him secretly in his house, and said, "Is there any word from the Lord?" (Jer. 37:17)

- There is *an awareness* that speaking or not speaking that word is painful:

  For whenever I speak, I must cry out,
    I must shout, "Violence and destruction!"
  For the word of the Lord has become for me
    a reproach and derision all day long.
  If I say, "I will not mention him,
    or speak any more in his name,"
  then within me there is
      something like a burning fire shut up in my bones;
  I am weary with holding it in, and I cannot. (Jer. 20:8-9)

- There is *a recognition* that the God who occupies the text is not user friendly:

  Am I a God near by, says the Lord, and not a God far off?
  (Jer. 23:23)

- And where spoken, where heard, where acted, *new life comes*, new life
  to the preacher, new life to the congregation, new life to the city:

> The voice of mirth and the voice of gladness, the voice of the
> bridegroom and the voice of the bride, the voices of those
> who sing, as they bring thank offerings to the house of the
> Lord:
>> "Give thanks to the Lord of hosts,
>> for the Lord is good,
>> for his steadfast love endures forever!"
> For I will restore the fortunes of the land as at first, says the
> Lord. (Jer. 33:11)

The fearful fact is that most folk do not sense how subversive the text is.
The good news is that they nonetheless expect the text to be played out in
their presence with imagination. The further good news is that folk still
show up for text time. And the more there are texts that are well rendered,
the more folk show up. In all our fear we still hope for what may be "strange
and new" among us.

> For those who know it best
> seem hungering and thirsting to hear it like the rest.

It belongs to the preacher to meet that hunger—with the bread that nour-
ishes so that we may "never be hungry" (John 6:35).

1

Preaching as Reimagination

In what follows, sixteen theses are set forth and developed, suggesting that evangelical preaching finds itself now in a quite new cultural, epistemological context.

(1) *Ours is a changed preaching situation, because the old modes of church absolutes are no longer trusted.*

It is not that the church's theological absolutes are no longer trusted, but that the *old modes* in which those absolutes have been articulated are increasingly suspect and dysfunctional. That is because our old modes are increasingly regarded as patriarchal, hierarchic, authoritarian, and monologic. The mistrust that flies under all these adjectives, however, is due to a growing suspicion about the linkage between knowledge and power. The mistrust of conventional authority, now broad and deep in our society, is rooted in the failure of positivism, positivism that is scientific, political, or theological. Many are increasingly aware that "absolute knowledge" most characteristically means agreement of all those permitted in the room.[1] Such "absolutism" in "truth," moreover, characteristically has pretensions to "absolute power" as well, surely an adequate reason for suspicion. Those at the margins of dominating knowledge will no longer permit the practitioners of dominating power to be supervisors of absolute knowledge.

(2) *Along with the failure of old modes of articulation, we now face the inadequacy of historical-critical understanding of the biblical text as it has been conventionally practiced.*

I do not say the failure or bankruptcy of historical criticism but its inadequacy, for historical criticism has become, in Scripture study, a version of modes of absolutism among the elitely educated. It is increasingly clear that historical criticism has become a handmaiden of certain kinds of power.[2] This not only refers to the control of the agenda through academic politics, but it also recognizes that the rise of criticism is deeply related to the banishment of the supernatural and to the dismissal of tradition as a form of truthfulness.[3]

One can note that in academic circles, where methodological discussions are conducted, there is a growing tension between old-line historical criticism, which serves to distance the text from the interpreter, and the emerging criticisms (sociological, literary, and canonical).[4] A generalization can probably be made that critical scholars who most resist change and who regard the transfer of social power and influence as only modes of political correctness cling most passionately to older modes of historical criticism, whereas scholars who advocate and benefit from redistributions of interpretive power engage in sociological and literary criticism. Indeed, old-line historical criticism is our particular form of positivism to the biblical, interpretive guild and so receives its share of the suspicion I have more generally noted in thesis 1. I am aware that moves away from historical criticism are easily judged to be obscurantism, advocacy, or ideology, but those labels have lethal connotations only in the context of self-satisfied positivism.

(3) *A great new reality for preaching is pluralism in the interpreting community of the local congregation.*

All but the most closed and sheltered liturgical congregations are indomitably heterogeneous.[5] That emerging pluralism, moreover, can no longer be overcome by absolute assertion. For such absolute assertion, whether by strong pastoral authority or by denominational dictum, can only serve to excommunicate those who see and take and experience reality otherwise. The more frantic our zeal to maintain the oneness and wholeness of "our truth," the more divisive does such practice become.

An honest facing of pluralism can be pastorally and usefully engaged only by an open-ended adjudication that takes the form of trustful, respectful conversation.[6] Such a conversation is joined with no participant seeking to convert the other and no participant knowing the outcome ahead of time but only entering with full respect for the good faith of others and the willingness to entertain the troublesome thought that new "truth" received together may well be out in front of any of us. While such an approach sounds like relativism, an answering objectivism is destructive not only of the community but of any chance to receive new truth together. Preaching thus must be conducted in a context where one makes proposals and advocacies but not conclusions.[7]

(4) *Pluralism as the perspective and orientation of the community that hears and interprets is matched by an emerging awareness of the polyvalence of the biblical text.*

Texts are open to many meanings, more than one of which may be legitimate and faithful at the same time. This is evident, in its most simple form,
in the awareness that many preachers on any given occasion preach many
sermons on the same lectionary texts. While not all such sermons may be
legitimate and faithful, many of them would qualify as such, without mutual
exclusiveness. Notice that such a polyvalence flies in the face of old-line
historical criticism, which tried to arrive at "the meaning" of the text.[8]

The claim of polyvalence is an invitation for Christians to relearn from
Jewish interpretive tradition.[9] Indeed, Jewish interpretation does not seek
to give closure to texts but can permit many readings to stand side by side,
reflecting both the rich density of the text and the freedom of interpretation. Such a way of reading reflects the mode of midrashic interpretation,
a Jewish affirmation that the voice of the text is variously heard and is not
limited by authorial intent.[10]

It is now suggested, moreover, that midrashic interpretation is strongly,
even if unwittingly, reflected in Freud's theory of psychoanalysis and in his
practice of dream interpretation.[11] Freud understood that dreams are endlessly open to interpretation. In this regard, the reading of dreams is not
unlike the reading of texts. At the same time, it is important to note that
dreams are no more unreal fantasies than are texts but contain a profound
truth that is available only upon a rich reading. It is unhelpful for the text
interpreter, and therefore the preacher, to give heavy closure to texts because
such a habit does a disservice to text and to listener, both of which are evok-
ers and practitioners of multiple readings.

(5) *Reality is scripted, that is, shaped and authorized by a text.*
Paul Ricoeur has done the most to show us that reality lives by text.[12] By
"text," Ricoeur means written discourse that is no longer in the control of
the "author" but makes its own testimony and insists on interpretation.
Interpretation, moreover, is "to appropriate *here and now* the intention of
the text."[13] But such intention is derived not from the "author" of the text
but from the work within the act of interpretation.

That text may be recognized or invisible. It may be a great religious classic or a powerful philosophical tradition or a long-standing tribal conviction.[14] It is an account of reality that the community comes to trust and to
take for granted as a given that tends to be beyond reexamination. This text
describes reality in a certain way and shape. In a world where there is more
than one text, that is, a world of plurality, a given text may describe, but if
another text intrudes, it is possible for that text to redescribe reality.[15]

It is important, on the basis of this thesis, for the preacher to recognize
that there are no "textless" worlds. Such an assertion may be much disputed;

at a practical level, however, it is no doubt true. People come to the preaching moment with texts already in hand that describe the world. The preacher who interprets the text, who "appropriates here and now the intention of the text," does not act in a vacuum. There are always rival and competing texts, in the face of which the biblical text may be a countertext that does not primarily describe but subversively redescribes reality.

(6) *The dominant scripting of reality in our culture is rooted in the Enlightenment enterprise associated with Descartes, Locke, Hobbes, and Rousseau, which has issued in a notion of autonomous individualism, resulting in what Philip Rieff calls "The Triumph of the Therapeutic."*[16]

It is difficult to take in the radical shift of assumptions in "world making" that occurred at the beginning of the seventeenth century.[17] The collapse of the hegemony of medieval Christianity, hastened by the Reformation, the Thirty Years War, and the rise of science, produced, as Susan Bordo has made clear, a profound anxiety about certitude.[18] It was clear that certitude would no longer be found in "the truth of Christ," for confessional divisions had broken that truth. Believers henceforth could appeal only to reason guided by the spirit, or the spirit measured by reason, clearly a circular mode of truth. Indeed, Descartes introduced his massive program of doubt as an attempt to link the new truth to the claims of Christianity. What emerged was the individual knower as the decontextualized adjudicator of truth.[19]

That autonomy in knowledge, moreover, produced autonomy in action and ethics as well, so that the individual becomes the norm for what is acceptable. The end result is a self-preoccupation that ends in self-indulgence, driving religion to narcissistic catering and consumerism, to limitless seeking after well-being and pleasure on one's own terms without regard to any other in the community.[20]

While this scripting of reality has profound critical thought behind it, the practice of this script is embraced and undertaken by those in modern culture who have no awareness of the text, its rootage, or its intention.[21] Thus, it is clear that very many folk in our culture who come to preaching events are reliant on this "text of reality" that is permitted to describe the world. The preacher perforce preaches in a world shaped by this text.

(7) *This scripting tradition of the Enlightenment exercises an incredible and pervasive hegemony among us.*

(a) In economics, this text-generated ideology issues in consumerism, which operates on the claims that more is better, that most will make happy, and that each is entitled to and must have all that one can take, even if at the expense of others. Such a value system, of course, must discredit the claims of any other who is a competitor for the goods that will make me happy. Television advertising is a primary voice in advocating this view of reality, and television is closely allied with spectator sports, which move in the same direction.[22] Witness the "show contracts" of college coaches.

(b) In political affairs, this same ideology is rooted in the privilege of European superiority and colonialism, although in recent time that political dimension of the text has found its primary expression in the notion of Pax Americana. That ideology assumes that the world works best if the United States adjudicates from a position of dominant power which, in turn, guarantees and endlessly enhances the privileged position of the United States in terms of prosperity and standard of living. Thus, the public administration of power guarantees the private capacity to consume without limit. The deepness of this claim is evident in the political requirement of a commitment to a strong America.

In political affairs, this vision of political hegemony perhaps was given authoritative voice by Elihu Root, Secretary of State under Theodore Roosevelt, and his expansionist notions. Root, in turn, was the mentor to Henry Stimson, who moved the United States, almost single-handedly through his advocacy and political machinations, to take responsibility for the world.[23] Stimson, in turn, was the patron and mentor of the "Wise Men" who guided foreign policy, produced the Cold War, and finally overreached in Vietnam.[24]

But of course the end is not yet. The United States, as the remaining superpower, can have it all its own way, so it thinks, finding itself most often on the side of the old colonial powers and allied with the forces of reactionism in order to preserve the old hegemony that goes unexamined.

(c) The Enlightenment text, as practiced in the Euro-American world, thus provides an unchallenged rationale for privilege and advantage in the world in every zone of life. This not only means political ascendancy and economic domination but also makes its adherents the norm for virtue. In turn, this shows up even in the church, where it is assumed that the Western church is the privileged norm by which to test the rest of the church. In the end, even truth is tied in some way to Western virtue.

(d) This defining text of the West is exceedingly hard on and dismissive of those whose lives do not measure up to the norms of competence, productivity, and privilege. This text has resulted in a kind of social Darwinism in which the fast, smart, well-connected, and ruthless are the "best" people.[25] And the counterpart is impatience with those who are not so competent-productive-righteous. Very many of the enormous social problems and social inequities in our society are legitimated by this text.

(e) This definitive text exercises great authority over the imagination, even of those who set out to resist its claim and power. As Karl Marx saw, it exercises a powerful attraction for those who do not share in its promised benefits but are in fact its victims. Marx's dictum is, "The ideas of the dominant class become the dominant ideas."[26] Marx, moreover, understood well that in the end, the dominant class does not need to exercise force but holds sway by "hegemonic theatre."[27] I suspect that just now the lottery is a tool of such imagination, which proposes that any may succeed in this system. Is this a great system or what?!

(8) *We now know (or think we know) that human transformation (the way people change) does not happen through didacticism or through excessive certitude but through the playful entertainment of another scripting of reality that may subvert the old given text and its interpretation and lead to the embrace of an alternative text and its redescription of reality.*

Very few people make important changes in their description of the world abruptly. Most of us linger in wistfulness, notice dissonance between our experience and the old text, and wonder if there is a dimension to it all that has been missed.[28] Most of us will not quickly embrace an alternative that is given us in a coercive way. Such coercion more likely makes us defend the old and, in general, become defensive.

Victor Turner noted that there is an in-between time and place in social transformation and relocation, which he termed "liminality."[29] Liminality is a time when the old configurations of social reality are increasingly seen to be in jeopardy, but new alternatives are not yet at hand.

What we need for such liminality is a safe place in which to host such ambiguity, to notice the tension and the unresolved without pressure but with freedom, to see and test alternative textings of reality. It is my impression that very much preaching, which is excessively urgent and earnest, does not pay sufficient attention to what we know about how we change or how anyone else may receive change when it is given. The text entrusted to the preachers of the church is all about human transformation, but the characteristic modes of presentation, in many quarters, contradict the claim of the text and are the enemies of transformation.

An inviting, effective alternative does not need to be toned down in its claim or made palatable. It does, however, need to be presented in a way that stops well short of coercion that is threatening and evokes resistance to hearing or appropriating the new text. Preaching is not only the announcement of the alternative but the practice of that very liminality that does not yet know too much.

(9) *The biblical text, in all its odd disjunctions, is an offer of an alternative*

script, and preaching this text is the exploration of how the world is if it is imagined through this alternative script.

This thesis reminds us of two important recognitions. First, the biblical text is indeed a profound alternative to the text of the Enlightenment and therefore alternative to the dominant text with which most of us came to church. For a very long time we have assumed that the "American Dream," which is our version of Enlightenment freedom and well-being, coheres with the claims of the gospel.[30] It is the United States that is God's agent in the world, God's example, and God's most blessed people. I imagine that even those of us who reject blatant forms of this claim have been schooled effectively in the notion in some lesser ways. Now we are coming to see belatedly—indeed, we are required to see—that the American Dream as it is now understood has long since parted company with the claims of the gospel. Whereas the dominant text finds human initiative at the core of reality, the gospel witnesses to holiness as the core, and whereas it is the self that arises out of the hegemonic text, in the gospel it is the neighbor. The preacher and the congregation will be much liberated for serious preaching if it is understood that all of us, liberal and conservative, are in fact conducting an adjudication between these two competing texts, between which there is diminished overlap and between which we do not want to choose. The preacher must show how this countertext of the gospel is a genuine alternative.

The second notion here is that the preacher, from this text, does not describe a gospel-governed world but helps the congregation imagine it.[31] Every text that describes and redescribes presents something that is not in hand, until the text is appropriated and all reality is passed through the text. Something like this must be the intent of Wallace Stevens in his enigmatic statement:

> Poetry is the supreme fiction, madame . . .
> But fictive things Wink as they will.[32]

The preacher traffics in a fiction that makes true. But that is why preaching is so urgent and must be done with such art. This world of the gospel is not real, not available, until this credible utterance authorizes a departure from a failed text and an appropriation of this text.

Such an imaginative act of making fiction real is expounded well by Garrett Green in his assertion that "as" is the "copula of imagination."[33] I take Green to mean that an event or object must be interpreted "as" something before it comes available. First, such a notion means that there are no available uninterpreted events or objects. They are beyond reach until interpreted, and when interpreted, they are seen or taken according to that "as."[34] Second, there is no right answer in the back of the book. Thus, formally, an interpretive "as" has as much claim as any other. What the preacher is doing is proposing that the world and our lives be seen or taken *as* under the aegis of the gospel. Such an imaginative "as" means a break with the world and our lives taken "as" under the aegis of Enlightenment construal. It is, of course, our usual assumption that the Enlightenment descriptions of reality are given.[35] They are not, according to Green, given but only a powerful, long-sustained "as," which is now to be countered by this evangelical "as."

(10) *The proposal of this alternative script is not through large, comprehensive, universal claims, but through concrete, specific, local texts that, in small ways, provide alternative imagination.*

I have no doubt that every preacher and every interpreter of biblical texts operates with something like a "systematic theology."[36] Of course. But such systematic thinking, which is essential to some provisional coherence about reality, is not the primary mode of the biblical text. In fact, our macrovision in systematic theology is stitched together selectively from little texts that refuse long-term stabilization. Of course, there is deep disagreement about this proposition. "Canonical criticism," as proposed by Brevard Childs, assumes long-term stabilization of a larger reading.[37] While there is some truth in that claim, it is equally (or more pertinently) true that continual study, reading, and reflection on the text cause that stabilization to be constantly under review and change. Thus, the insistence on concrete, specific, local presentation is parallel to the nature of the text itself, which is put together of small parts, the precise relation of which to each other is not self-evident. The interpretive act is itself a major set of decisions about how the parts relate to each other this time.

Thus, the preacher, if taking the text seriously, does not sound the whole of "biblical truth" in preaching but focuses on one detailed text to see what it yields of "as." It can be a great relief to the preacher not to have to utter a universal truth with each utterance, and it may be an assurance to the church that it is not given to pronounce universally on every issue that comes along.[38] It is enough to work with the local detail in the interest of transformation.

As examples of such "local work," we may cite almost any part of the Bible. In the powerful memories of Genesis 12–50, the action is quite local around one family, the members of which are known by name and in considerable detail.[39] Perhaps more poignantly, the parables of Jesus focus remarkably on detail of one time and place.[40] Helpful dimensions of this accent on the concrete are offered by Sandra Schneiders in her programmatic use of the phrase "paschal imagination," in which she shows how the text moves beyond the subject/object split to world construal and construction.[41] And Jacob Neusner shows how very small acts of piety and ritual are ways in which practitioners can "imagine themselves to be Jews."[42] Such detail was perhaps not necessary when Christianity recently occupied a hegemonic position in our society, and one could deal in unnuanced summaries. Now, however, with the dehegemonization of Christianity, we are back to the little pieces that in various ways make a claim against the dominant text. The preacher can understand the act of a single sermon as providing yet another detail to the very odd and very different description of reality being enacted over time in the congregation.

(11) *The work of preaching is an act of imagination, an offer of an image through which perception, experience, and finally faith can be reorganized in alternative ways.*

The alternative voiced in textual preaching intends to show that this scripting of reality is in deep conflict with the dominant description of reality, so that the scripts are shown to be in deep tension with each other, if not in contradiction. If an alternative is not set forth with some clarity and vigor, then no choice is given, and no alternative choice is available. There is, of course, a long history of suspicion about imagination going back to Aristotle and suggesting that imagination is an inferior and unreliable source of knowledge.[43] With the failure of Enlightenment notions of "objectivity," imagination has made an important comeback as a mode of knowledge. Gaston Bachelard has elaborated in powerful ways the creative function of imagination in the generation of knowledge.[44] Of his work, Richard Kearney writes that, in contrast to Sartre,

> Bachelard . . . conceives of the imagination not as privation, but as audition—an acoustics of the *other* than self. His poetical model of imagination is two-dimensional: at once a giving and a taking, a projection and a discovery, a centrifugal exodus towards things and a centripetal return to the self. This notion of an "interlacing rhythm" which spans the breach between subjectivity and being epitomizes the Bachelardian theory of poetics.[45]

According to Bachelard, it is imagination that "valorizes" an alternative, and that, of course, is what preaching intends to do. Such a mode of preaching requires a break with our more usual modes of didactic, doctrinal, or moralistic preaching.

More recently, John Thiel has argued that imagination is a reliable mode of theological knowledge.[46] He, of course, knows that imagination is available for distortion but asserts that it is no more available for distortion or less reliable for knowing than is reason, a long-trusted practice in theological reflection.

It is thus my notion that the preacher and congregation can reconstruct the time and place of preaching as a time and place for the practice of imagination, that is, the reimagination of reality according to the evangelical script of the Bible. Such preaching does not aim at immediate outcomes but, over time, intends, detail by detail, to make available a different world in which different acts, attitudes, and policies are seen to be appropriate. To aim at this "underneath" dimension of faith is consistent with Ricoeur's conclusion that the "symbol gives rise to thought."[47] I would paraphrase Ricoeur to say that "the image gives rise to a new world of possibility," and the preaching for which I contend is aimed at the image-making out of the text that may give rise to a church of new obedience.[48]

(12) *Because old modes of certitude are no longer trusted, the preaching of these texts is not an offer of metaphysics but the enactment of a drama in which the congregation is audience but may at any point become participant.*

In *Texts under Negotiation*, I have already articulated what I think is at issue in the move from metaphysical to dramatic thinking.[49] It is clear that dramatic modes of thought are more congenial to the way in which the Old Testament proceeds and in which the primal testimony of the New Testament is expressed. Characteristically, biblical faith may assume metaphysic, but it is of little interest and of little value for the generation of faith. What counts, characteristically, is the dramatic turn of affairs to which the community bears witness and responds in praise, joy, and obedience. The result is that, in the text itself, God is a character at play and at risk; in the preaching moment, the congregation may see itself as among the characters in the drama.

This means that the preacher, in the drama of the sermon, must "undo" much of the metaphysical preoccupation of the church tradition, to see whether the world can be imagined in terms of God's action in the ongoing account of the world, the nations, Israel, and the church. Such freedom and vitality as drama, which Hans Urs von Balthasar has shown to be definitive, is matched in yet another image offered by Frances Young.[50] Young proposes that the Bible is a musical score and that, in each interpretive act, the score must be "performed" with the freedom and discipline always required of good performance. Moreover, Young proposes that much interpretation is a "cadenza" in the score, which gives the interpreter (here preacher) a good bit of room for maneuverability and idiosyncrasy.

(13) *This dramatic rendering of imagination has narrative as its quintessential mode, the telling of a story, and the subsequent living of that story.*

The claim that narrative is a privileged mode in Christian preaching is, of course, not a new idea. After paying attention to the "testimony" of Israel and the early church, as in the earlier work of G. Ernest Wright, Reginald Fuller, and C. H. Dodd,[51] more recent study has considered the epistemological assumptions in the use of the genre of narrative and has concluded that, in this mode, reality itself has something of a narrative quality, that reality is an ongoing theater that has a plot with a beginning, middle, and end and has characters who remain constant but also develop, change, and exercise great freedom.[52] As Dale Patrick has shown, God in the Bible (like Jesus in the New Testament) is an ongoing character in a narrative who is endlessly re-rendered in the Bible and whom the preacher subsequently re-renders.[53] The constancy of God is the constancy of a character in a narrative who must change in order to remain constant and who necessarily violates our conventional notions of immutable transcendence.

Moreover, it is clear that the living of human life is embedded in a narrative rendering. Thus Hayden White has argued, persuasively in my judgment, that history is essentially a rhetorical activity in which past memory is told and retold in alternative ways, ways that may be intentional but that also take into account the vested interests of the narrating community.[54] And Alasdair MacIntyre has shown decisively that alternative ethical systems cannot be understood or assessed apart from the narrative world in which they are told, received, and valued.[55] Thus, narrative is not a secondary or auxiliary enterprise; it is an act whereby social reality is constituted. Amos Wilder has championed the view long held by serious rhetoricians that speech, and specifically narrative speech, is constitutive of reality, so that narrative is indeed "world-making."[56]

To be sure, there are many texts in the "script" of the Bible available to the preacher that are not narrative. Given my presuppositions, these are the most difficult to preach. It is my impression, nonetheless, that every text in any genre has behind it something of a narrative that generates it and through which the texts in other genres are to be understood. Thus, for example, the Psalms are notoriously difficult preaching material. I suspect that the preacher characteristically either presents a narrative situation that is critically recoverable (as in Psalm 137) or imagines such a context that led this speaker to speak thusly. In the case of the Psalms, some of the superscriptions, even if not historically "reliable," provide a clue for such narrative construal.[57] And in the letters of Paul, a critically recoverable or homiletically imagined narrative context serves the preaching of the letters.

Such a mode of preaching has the spin-off effect of a drama being enacted, a story being narrated, and a plot being worked out. Such a mode holds the potential of showing the congregants that their lives (and life together) also constitute a drama being enacted and a story being told, in which we are characters with work to do, options to exercise, and loyalties to sustain or alter. This mode of preaching not only reconstrues the shape of the Bible but also reconstrues human life. It moves away from an essentialist focus to see that much of life is a rhetorical operation and that we are indeed "speeched into newness."[58]

(14) *The invitation of preaching (not unlike therapy) is to abandon the script in which one has had confidence and to enter a different script that imaginatively tells one's life differently.*

The folk in the Bible are shown to be those who have often settled into a narrative that is deathly and destructive. Thus, the early Hebrews settled for a slave narrative as their proper self-presentation. That narrative is disrupted by another narrative that has YHWH the liberator as the key and decisive agent. The decision about staying in Egypt or leaving for the promise is a decision about which narrative in which to participate, whether to understand the "plot of life" according to the character Pharaoh or according to a different plot featuring YHWH.[59] Likewise, the New Testament narratives portray many folk either in a narrative of hopelessness and despair or in one of self-righteousness and arrogance. In each case, they are invited into an alternative narrative, which is the narrative of the life-giving kingdom of God.

In *Texts under Negotiation,* I have already suggested the analogue of psychotherapy.[60] I have no wish to "psychologize" preaching but only to suggest an analogue. In such a parallel, I do not understand the conversation of psychotherapy as simply one of self-discovery, but I envision an active "therapist" who, together with the one in need, conducts a conversation in which an alternative account of his or her life may emerge. And if such an alternative narrative emerges, then the needful person in therapy has the opportunity and the task of adjudicating between the old narrative long since believed and the new narrative only now available. Such a person may eventually decide that the old narrative (from childhood) is not only destructive and paralyzing but false, and a new one may be chosen that renarrates life in health. Many alternatives of one's life or the life of the world are made available in the process.

Mutatis mutandis, the task of the preacher is to exhibit this particular narrative script of the Bible and to show how and in what ways life will be reimagined, redescribed, and relived if this narrative is embraced. The old-fashioned word for this process is "conversion." In my book *Biblical Perspectives on Evangelism,* I have shown in some detail what this might mean for the study and proclamation of the Bible.[61] It is in this context that Peter Berger and Thomas Luckmann understand the social construction of reality as a process of "switching worlds."[62] Nobody can switch worlds unless an alternative world is made richly available with great artistry, care, and boldness.

(15) *The offer of an alternative script (to which we testify and bear witness as true) invites the listener out of his or her assumed context into many alternative contexts where different scripts may have a ring of authenticity and credibility.*

That is, the place wherein I know myself to be living is not the only place where I could live. That is why it is important to pay attention to the several *contexts* of Scripture texts that may be either critically recoverable or textually evoked. Thus, I know myself to be living in a crime-threatened suburb in which I hear of the poor but, on most days, do not see them. In the text of Deuteronomy (to take one easy example), however, I do not listen in a threatened suburb. My "place" is different. The claimed location of this text is the River Jordan, whereby "we" are about to enter the land of promise, a land filled with threatening Canaanite social structures and seductive Canaanite religion. As I listen, I have important decisions to make, according to Deuteronomy, mostly concerning neighbors. Or alternatively, to take the critical judgment about Deuteronomy, I live in seventh-century Jerusalem under the danger and threat of Assyria, where the temptation is strong to accommodate and compromise until one's identity is gone.[63] In listening to this text, I can be at the Jordan or in Jerusalem only for a brief period, and then I return to the "reality" of suburbia. But being transported briefly by rhetoric invites me to re-see and redescribe my own setting, perchance to act differently. Thus, the hearing of a counterscript invites to a countercontext which, over time, may authorize and empower counterlife.

(16) *Finally, I believe that the great pastoral fact among us that troubles everyone, liberal or conservative, is that the old givens of white, male, Western, colonial advantage no longer hold.*

The trust in those old givens takes many forms. It takes the form of power whereby we have known who was in charge, whom to trust and obey. It takes the form of knowledge, for we could identify the knowing authorities who had a right to govern. It takes the form of certitude, because the world was reliably and stably ordered. And those in control or authority had great finesse in conducting the kind of "hegemonic theatre" that kept the world closely ordered and coherent.[64]

No special argument needs to be made about the demise of that world, even though a lot of political and ecclesiastical mileage is available out of the claim that the old world can be sustained even longer. The demise of that hegemony touches us in many different ways, personal and public, but there is in any case a widely shared sense that things are out of control. That sense is widely shared not only by beneficiaries of the old patterns of certitude but also by many of its perceived victims. Nothing seems to be reliable as it used to be. And that sense of things being out of control invites all kinds of extreme notions of fear and anxiety that eventuate in acts and policies of brutality.

In that context, preachers are entrusted with a text, alternative to the failed text of white, male, Western hegemony, which mediates and valorizes a viable world outside that given, privileged advantage of certitude and domination. It turns out that the script we have trusted in the Enlightenment (and in the older Euro-American) tradition is an unreliable script, even though we have been massively committed to it. And now, we are wondering, is there a more adequate script out of which we may reimagine our lives? Although few would articulate their coming to worship on such grounds, I believe people are haunted by the question of whether there is a text (and an interpreter) that can say something that will make sense out of our pervasive nonsense.[65] It is my conviction that neither old liberal ideologies nor old conservative certitudes nor critical claims made for the Bible will now do. Our circumstance permits and requires the preacher to do something we have not been permitted or required to do before. Ours is an awesome opportunity: to see whether this text, with all of our interpretive inclinations, can voice and offer reality in a redescribed way that is credible and evocative of a new humanness, rooted in holiness and practiced in neighborliness.

2

The Preacher, the Text, and the People

The Bible, especially through the lens of its most vigorous interpreters, can be dangerous, subversive, and scandalous. Its scandalous quality is, of course, theological. The God mediated to us in Scripture does not fit our preferred notions but is always more odd and surprising than we can expect or anticipate. That theological scandal, however, will not be contained in formal theological categories. It spins off into other dimensions of scandal. Just now in the church, the oddness and danger of the biblical God are evidenced around socioeconomic, political questions concerning the cry of the poor, the urge of justice, and the power and possibility of real social transformation.

In Luke 7, after John the Baptist raises his christological question through his disciples whether Jesus is the Christ, and after Jesus answers with specificity that "the blind see, the lame walk, lepers are cleansed, the dead are raised, and the poor rejoice," Jesus adds, "blessed is the one who is not scandalized by me" (Luke 7:23). Or, as I would have rendered it, "Lucky are you, if you are not upset." The theological scandal of biblical faith, especially when rendered into political, economic issues, is indeed upsetting.

How is a pastor to give voice to this scandal in a society that is hostile to it, in a church that is often unwilling to host the scandal, and when we ourselves as teachers and pastors of the church are somewhat queasy about the scandal as it touches our own lives? How can the radical dimension of the Bible as it touches public reality be heard in the church? We all have our strategies about these matters. We may simply select around the dangerous texts so that the difficult passages are never voiced. Or we may interpret them away from their evident intent in a spiritualizing direction to make them mean something they clearly do not intend.[1] Or we may speak the text as it seems to stand and hope nobody notices what has been said.

There are no easy ways about these texts, either for the congregation or for pastors who are also scandalized in our own social setting. Textual conversation in the congregation is important, not only because we have powerful texts that require a hearing, but because we have entrusted to us the word of life that matters urgently in a society seemingly bent on its self-destruction. In recent biblical scholarship—which moves away both from tired scholasticism and from flat historical criticism—there are important resources for taking the scandalous texts seriously without pastors necessarily committing professional or personal suicide. These newer interpretive approaches invite us to pay attention to the processes through which people do in fact engage in transformation through their hearing of the text. In order for the scandalous texts to be voiced and heard in the church without the pastor paying all the costs of the conversation, I suggest three strategic clues that may be useful. When the pastor discerns the text differently, a different conversation in the congregation is possible.

I

In his theory about family therapy, Murray Bowen, popularly echoed by Edwin Friedman, has worked with the notion of "triangling."[2] Bowen proposes that all domestic relations, even if a family has many siblings and is multigenerational, are a series of triangles, that is, a network of relations in which there are endless patterns of "two against one." In such patterns, the exhausting work of family members is not to be the single one left alone against the other two. Bowen proposes that family therapy consists in breaking up the triangles to permit new, healthy relations that are direct and not manipulative power plays.

The notion of triangles and "triangling" has set me to thinking about the text in the church. My impression is that in controversies in the church that get the pastor in trouble, controversies about theology and ethics, that is, controversies about interpretation, we usually assume two parties in the quarrel, pastor and people (or some people). Given two parties, controversies predictably lead to win/lose situations. What has happened in many such situations is that the text has disappeared as a live, vocal partner in the conversation. The text has disappeared in the church largely, I believe, because of historical criticism, which has unwittingly served to eliminate the voice of the text as real and authoritative. And when the text is silenced as a serious theological presence in the community, the pastor has had to substitute a personal voice for the voice of the text. In the place of the text stands the voice of the pastor. That leaves the pastor vulnerable and exposed, for it is only one person's voice. People are not fooled by the substitution when they receive the word of the pastor instead of the voice of the text.

If it is not flattened historical criticism that has silenced the text, then it may be creedal scholasticism that has emptied the text of its voice and its own danger, and again we are left in a situation when the pastor must say things to substitute for the lost or silenced text.

Consider what happens in such a conversation when it is seen to be a triangle. There are, in fact, in most church situations of interpretation three voices, that of the text, that of the pastor, and that of the congregation, three voices creating a triangle. The text continues to be present, but it has been usurped by the pastor. Our standard practice is for the pastor to triangle with the text against the congregation, that is, to make an alliance so that the voice of the pastor and what is left of the voice of the text gang up on the congregation and sound just alike. This process automatically generates controversy because, completely aside from the substance of theological or ethical conflict, nobody wants to be the lone one in a triangle. Predictably the third party, the congregation, becomes a hostile, resistant outsider who will undertake reckless, destructive action in such a triangle where one is excluded by the other two.

If, however, the text is as scandalous as we suspect it is, then we need an alternative strategy. We are aware that the text is in fact more radical and more offensive and more dangerous than any of us, liberal or conservative. As a result, it is not honest to ally with the text, because the dangerous text is not anyone's natural or easy ally. I suggest, then: let the pastor triangle with the congregation against the text, so that the text is the lone member of the triangle, and then see how the text lives as the odd one in such a triangle. I believe that the textual conversation in the church could be very different if pastors were able to begin with the awareness that the text is too offensive for the people, but it is also too offensive for the pastor, because it is the living Word of God, and it pushes always beyond where we want to go or be. Such a posture honors the great authority of the text. It also acknowledges our restless resistance to the text and lets us enter into dangerous textual conversation with some of our best friends as allies.

The proposal for alternative triangling requires, however, that the text be permitted its own voice, apart from our creedal impositions or our critical reductionisms. There can be no genuine triangle unless the text is permitted a voice other than our own. Thus, this strategy calls for some visible interpretive distance between pastor and text.[3]

II

The strategy of triangling invites us to perceive the text very differently from the way we have conventionally perceived it. In order for the triangle to work, the text must have power and freedom to utter its own voice as a real voice in the conversation. This is in part a theological matter concerning inspiration, revelation, and authority. Close to home, however, it is now an issue of textual theory and literary interpretation as well. Newer literary approaches to the text, rightly handled, will let the text regain its own voice. There are important methodological developments in Scripture study, mostly concerning narrative, and mostly in Old Testament study, that can be useful in letting the text utter its own voice.

For all our prattle about "the authority of Scripture," almost all of us are schooled in silencing the voice of the text. On the one hand, well-educated liberals have utilized historical criticism largely to explain away the voice of the text, so that when we finish with the text, there is no authoritative voice left except our own. Without gainsaying or dismissing the crucial gains of historical criticism,[4] we may identify two tendencies in it that choke the voice of the text. First, we have preconceived notions concerning what could have happened. I am not urging an obscurantist approach that says, "It must have happened because the Bible says so"; rather, but that we should take the text on its own terms as an utterance, without raising the external question of whether something could have happened. The important point is the text's utterance, an utterance we ourselves are frequently incapable of making. The assertion that Moses brought water from flint rock is a textual utterance on which Israel stakes a great deal (Exod. 17:6; Num. 20:8-11; Deut. 8:15; Ps. 78:15-20; 114:8). Israel stakes much not on the flint or on the water or on Moses, but on the utterance. And that utterance and staking are not subject to our geological claims about flint rock.

Second, the text is a daring utterance that is largely uncensored, which means it is free to be ambiguous, filled with contradiction, and freighted with irony, as the text struggles through to a new utterance. Our modernist epistemology, however, cannot tolerate such ambiguity and contradiction, and our fearfulness cannot tolerate irony. We characteristically resolve such daring rhetorical acts by killing or dissolving the text by source analysis, by identifying glosses, and by various maneuvers that destroy the artistic intent of the text, as though the text could utter only one thing at a time. Elsewhere I have considered, for example, Jeremiah 31, in which scholarly analysis has dissolved the play of the text.[5] When all such reductionist settlements of the text have been made, there is nothing of interest or power left in the text. Then the pastor must fill in the silences, and that often results in pablum or ideology.

Conversely, conservatives also find the text too dangerous or problematic. In that case, the preferred way of avoiding the danger of the text is not historical criticism, but submerging the text into a theological system so that the text loses its dangerous voice and becomes either a servant or an echo for some intellectual articulation that is distanced from the dangerous utterance. Such submerging of the text is analogous to a repressed ego function, in which the untamed parts of personality must be submerged and silenced in order to make the dominant self-presentation work. Such repression in the end, however, will not work or succeed as the contained, silenced parts will break out somehow.[6] A systematic control and reduction of Scripture will not finally work, as the "less honorable parts" of the texts will insist on their honor (cf. 1 Cor. 12:23). Thus, in doing theology, the text keeps having its say in ways that do not conform to our schemes, liberal or conservative.

When the text is allowed its own voice, other than that of the congregation and other than that of the pastor, we discover that the text is not directly addressed to us, and we should not work too hard at making it immediately relevant. We are helped in this regard by the category about textual strategies proposed by Wayne Booth.[7] He has proposed that in addition to the "real author," who wrote the text and occupies all our historical questions, there is an "implied author," a literary fiction, who utters the text and who may stand at an important distance from the real author. Conversely, there is in addition to the real audience, an "implied audience" that corresponds to and is evoked by the implied author. Historical criticism has regularly tried to identify and deal with the "real author," for example, "J" or "P" or a "wisdom teacher." It follows from such an approach that the "real audience" is the one addressed by the "real author." Thus, "J" addressed tenth-century royalists, and the sage addressed young boys in a court school. When we think we know the "real author" fully enough, we seek to enter into history to imagine that we ourselves are the "real audience" to whom the text is addressed. We are in the end blocked in this attempt by our historical categories, but we keep trying. When we construe ourselves to be the real audience to whom the text is addressed, we have an inordinate passion that the text should address us directly—hence the drive for relevance, which distorts the text and sets up a destructive ideological triangle for us and the text against whomsoever.

The main voice of the text, however, is not that of "J" or "P"; and the primary addressee is not a seventh-century audience, as critical consensus has it, rather than us. Concerning the book of Deuteronomy, we all know that Moses did not write it, but it was a Levitical tradent in the seventh or eighth century addressed to Jerusalem in the face of Assyrian syncretism. We all know as well that such knowledge will not preach too well. The best preaching, then, is that the text is addressed to us in our syncretism, which is a people not unlike that of seventh-century Jerusalem.

If, however, we take seriously the implied exchange of author and audience, the text speaks otherwise. The implied author is indeed Moses, the "Lech Wałęsa" of early Israel, who has come with scars from Pharaoh, come from the forty days' rendezvous with God and two broken tablets, he of quail and manna and flint rock. And the implied audience is Israel, land-hungry and desperate, lined up at the Jordan ready to charge into the "Land of Promise" like "Sooners" at the edge of Oklahoma, with "cities you did not build and cisterns you did not hew out," ready to go into the promise that Moses thinks is dangerous. The text does not concern us at all. It does not ask us to do anything. It does not comment on abortion or aid to the Contras. Indeed, it comments on very little that pertains to us. It deliberately addresses an audience other than us, maintaining a distance from us, hardly at all interested in us.

The text is, nonetheless, an utterance. In handling the text, the task is to let the utterance of the text be uttered. It is not my utterance as a preacher, and I do not need to like it or agree with it or vouch for it. It is not the utterance of the congregation, and the congregation does not get to vote on it as the text. It is an utterance that the text insists on. The preacher may indeed triangle with the congregation against textual utterance. The congregation may, in turn, cower in the corner hoping not to be reached by the utterance. The preacher has only to let the implied author address the implied audience in its many implications and let it be. So, the utterance and its reception do not directly and immediately concern us. It is an utterance and a reception of utterance that happen out beyond us. We watch and listen, but at a distance. That distance keeps the text from being too concerned with our dogmatic questions and too insistent about our moral issues.

The text as canon insists on having its own voice, as norm, as classic.[8] It does not ask to be held to its critical situation of origin, but only to be permitted to have its own say when and where it will, even at the risk of distance and perhaps irrelevance. It does not ask for approval or action or consent. It asks only to be voiced for a moment. It asks to be voiced for a moment on its own terms, in all of its concreteness, its specificity, and its precise formulation. It does not ask to have lessons extracted or points to be scored, but only listening that may draw the "real listener" back into the implied world, that may mediate to the new members of the implied audience something new they did not know before this utterance. That is enough, because what is to be known is in the terms of the utterance itself, not our terms. That is all. But that is enough. Booth's notion of fictional author and fictional audience gives us freedom. On the one hand, it lets us come to the text with some freedom and ease, knowing that we are not going to be grabbed by the throat and coerced. On the other hand, it lets us go to the text with awed anticipation, knowing we are likely to hear a voice addressing us that we have never heard before, saying to us what we have never heard before.

III

Now what is going on in this triangle with a text that has its own voice? The conclusion drawn from this line of reasoning is that we are essentially textual creatures. We live from a text. Sometimes in the church we think that if we did not have the biblical text, we would not have a text at all. That is, we would be textless.

But there are no textless people. Everyone has a text, known or unknown. It may be a text hidden from us, powerful and authoritative, even if unrecognized. It has been suggested that Ronald Reagan's text came from Hobbes's *Leviathan,* even though Reagan probably never heard of Hobbes.[9] Or it may be a very local text, like "My Dad always said." Or it may be a narrative construal of an old ecstasy or an old hurt.[10] That old happening, however, has become a text that bears many retellings and many reinterpretations, telling and interpretations far removed from an event. That old happening has become a text that powers and shapes one's life. Most of our texts are hidden and uncriticized, and therefore exercise the persuasive irresistible power of mystification. Therapy, on one reading, is to bring to speech the hidden texts and invisible loyalties out of which we live.[11]

The psychotherapeutic notion that we are scripted people is so utterly, utterly Jewish.[12] Jews order life around script, not around ideas. In Jewish epistemology, ideas are only spin-offs from texts, but life consists in our texts, in studying, receiving, serving, criticizing, and answering our texts. What has happened in modernity is that we have abandoned our text.[13] We have abandoned it by scholastic creedalism that tends to put a cover over the danger of the text, or we have abandoned the text by historical criticism.[14] The latter we can check out by noting that in the high days of historical criticism, we did not so much study the text in seminary; we read many books *about* the text—but no text. We lost confidence in the text, thought it not adequate, and were embarrassed about it.

I am increasingly aware of the recurring inclination among seminarians, who prefer for preaching some idea, some cause, some experience, some anything rather than the text. A community without its appropriate text clearly will have no power or energy or courage for mission; it will be endlessly quarrelsome because it depends on ideology and has no agreed-upon arena where it adjudicates its conflicts. I am, of course, aware that the text is no sure source of unity, as texts can indeed be divisive. A text does, however, provide a subject of conversation that gives us space from each other. It is better to struggle together with the text than about ideologies that are the extreme voices of the community.

We are learning the hard way that when the church scuttles its text, other texts will readily intrude. We cannot tolerate textlessness very long. So now we have on our hands in the church alien texts that sound authoritative, texts of secular humanism, texts of free-market advocacy, texts of scholastic certitude, texts of moral absolutism, texts of individual subjectivity, all of which are idolatrous texts that are pitiful when contrasted with the dense, rich playfulness of our text.

IV

A text, as Walter Ong notes, creates its own community.[15] Ong's argument, congruent with Booth's notion of an implied reader, suggests that writers, even school children who write about "What I Did Last Summer," must create in imagination those to whom they are writing. A text implies its own audience and summons its audience in each hearing to become the community for which the text is voiced, and therefore the community that can sympathetically and responsively host the text. Ong states that all such implied audiences for texts are in fact fiction, for no such audiences exist, except in the intent and address of the author.

Put theologically, the biblical text creates the church, that is, the text summons a certain kind of audience to host and receive the text. Moreover, the audience cannot receive the text as its text unless it will imagine itself to be the audience intended by the text.

The drama of Deuteronomy, for example, creates the listening community at the Jordan on the Plains of Moab. The drama of the Gospel of Mark creates a community that ponders the One who is strong in utter weakness.

The Book of Revelation creates a community waiting in the presence of whore Babylon for a new heaven and a new earth and who can share in the ultimate prayer, "Come Lord Jesus." When the preacher and the congregation first come to the text, we are not folks seeking land from the Jordan, not prepared for weak strength, not waiting in the presence of Babylon. But we must be, if this is our text. In being addressed, we must yield ourselves to the requirements and expectations of the voice of the text.[16]

Our "realism" says no; we are not with Moses on the Plains of Moab, or in Rome with Mark, or on Patmos with John. And we are certainly not witness to Elisha making iron float (2 Kgs. 6:6). We are just middle-class taxpayers trying to get along. Such a realistic resistance, however, ignores the power of the implied author (Moses, Mark, John), who implies the listener, compelling an imaginative act of entry into the world of the text. Of course such self-presentation for hearing is an act of imagination. It is, however, the force and authority of the text that authorize such imagination of a counterself and a countercommunity in a counterworld reading for counterjoy and counterobedience. That is at its best what happens in the moment of the text. And then, if I have disagreement with the text (hopefully with the text and not with preacher), I can at least entertain that my disagreement is not that of a twentieth-century taxpayer, but first of all is a dispute concerning a land-hungry Israelite or a waiting, needy, persecuted Christian. The disagreement is softened; it is not so here-and-now, life-and-death, not so immediate, not so lethal, because I am invited into another hearing beyond my assumed self.

The text implies that I can be and must be someone other than I assumed myself to be prior to hearing. If the text cannot create a different community of pain and obedience, nothing can, certainly not our scholastic certitude, certainly not our historical criticism, certainly not our best theology. The text not only has a voice of its own that waits to be reuttered. That reutterance in the most practical, concrete way is reality-summoning. It is reality-summoning more radical than we expect, but a summons to the reality that is in the end our God-given true self and true community.

V

The proposal of *triangling* (Bowen) and an *implied voice* (Booth) that evokes an *implied audience* (Ong) may sound as though the text is excessively open, and as though the conversation is not very earnest. Against such an impression, I would make two points. First, this way of understanding the moment of interpretation takes the text with utmost seriousness, with more seriousness than does most historical criticism and most creedal closedness. It is the text that provides the sound and formulae and cadence of the utterance, whenever the preacher can submit and stay out of the way. Second, this playful, teasing, imaginative process is not an imposition of our interpretation, but is a characterization of what in fact happens when our interpretation has transformative force. I am not proposing something odd, but reporting on what happens when the text is permitted to be its own life self. It is the power of the text that may call us out of our presumed self to newness. It is this chance of newness we take whenever we engage in serious interpretation. If this strategy sounds odd to us, it is only because we have been too fearful, too reductionist, too coercive to respect the dynamic of newness initiated by the text itself.

This tensive text, as every preacher knows, has little chance against the closed orthodoxies of economics, politics, psychology, theology, or morality. Nevertheless, that little chance is urgent, for this text is not simply the offer of another closed orthodoxy. It is a protest against all closed orthodoxies, left, right, and center. It is the voice of holy freedom that shatters all closedness for the news; it is the voice of free holiness that refuses to let us be where we are or on our own terms.

In this textual strategy, there is no closed orthodoxy, and so no final settlement in any certainty. So what is this live text about? What do we intend to happen in the moment of the text? The moment of the text is a moment poised for transformation, a pause in our several settlements, a chance of liminality.[17] The text in its moment of liminality is not on the far settled side, as our caricatures of the Bible often pretend. The text is rather an offer of evangelical liminality that sponsors, authorizes, and invites to a regrouped, repatterned world.

In the most practical way, the text's moment of playful imagination is urgent in our church and in our society, before we destroy each other in our certitudes. If we think of liminality as a prerequisite for reappropriating life afresh, it is imperative that we identify where such textual moments may occur among us. Liminality for reappropriation is offered primarily in three ways in our society: (a) in art that gives us a text from the artist but is mostly elitist in our society; (b) in therapy that reworks our personal, hidden texts, but is expensive and a little restrictive in our society; and (c) in these textual moments that are readily available in our society. The text entrusted to us is a broad offer of freshness that in our society has enormous access, enjoyed neither by art nor by therapy.

It is this text that we know to be God's live word that utters, shatters, destroys, and creates.[18] It authorizes our rechoosing beyond all our settlements. It requires, for such rechoosing, its own utterance. We should be commonly alarmed that the text is not trusted much among us. Instead of this dangerous bread, we often give stones.[19]

This text is classic, which means it keeps generating new worlds.[20] It is not, however, "our" classic, but a classic that offends even us. To create space for this text in the church requires not certitude, not deductiveness or historical reductiveness, but a skilled capacity for its own utterance in its own cadences. When this text offends, it is not the pastor's affront but the text's own trouble.

The text, when rightly uttered, will still offend. Scandal belongs to its very character.[21] When it is trusted enough to create its own community, however, there will be those lively enough not to be upset. In that utterance that serves no consistent ideology, while the gospel is shared, the pastor becomes more marginal to the process, less exposed, and therefore less vulnerable. The pastor is not the voice of newness nor the source of trouble. It is the text, in its own utterance, that is both life-giving and scandalous. The text's own voice, without sounding exactly like the pastor, may indeed be what we mean by "Scripture alone." The scandal may continue to be acute, but it is a scandal rightly rooted in this affirmation of reality, not in quarrels too horizontal to give either light or life. When preachers reposition themselves vis-à-vis the dangerous text, congregations may also be repositioned for a listening they thought not possible.

3

Ancient Utterance and
Contemporary Hearing

The radical faith of ancient Israel in the Old Testament, perched on the lips of the prophets, continues in our own time as a particular, concrete, and urgent imperative about power, money, good, and access.

I

These prophetic voices in ancient Israel did not appear *de novo*, but were long schooled in deep traditions about the character, will, and purpose of the God who created heaven and earth.

First, the God uttered by the prophets is already known and celebrated in Israel's deepest, oldest doxologies. This is who Yhwh has been—in the purview of Israel—from the outset; it is not possible to go behind the doxologies to find a less committed God, for these cadences of praise are the deepest sounds that Israel can imagine or utter. Thus, the temple choirs, perhaps borrowing from older, pre-Israelite phrasing, sang without reservation:

> Father of orphans and protector of widows
>   is God in [God's] holy habitation.
> God gives the desolate a home to live in;
>   [God] leads out the prisoners to prosperity,
>   but the rebellious live in a parched land. (Ps. 68:5-6)

> The Lord sets the prisoners free;
>   the Lord opens the eyes of the blind.

The LORD lifts up those who are bowed down;
  the LORD loves the righteous.
The LORD watches over the strangers;
  [the LORD] upholds the orphan and the widow,
  but the way of the wicked [the LORD] brings to ruin.
    (Ps. 146:7c-9)

Imagine what it was like to hear these affirmations sung regularly! The doxologies do not doubt the immense power and large sovereignty of the God here praised.

That YHWH's power and sovereignty are mobilized in the direction of the marginal is astonishing. Both songs portray the God of Israel as actively, powerfully engaged. Both songs identify YHWH's particular attentiveness to those whom the world wants to make invisible. Both songs identify as a special concern widows who are without a male protector in a patriarchal society. Both songs reference orphans, who are vulnerable. Both songs comment on prisons because, already in that ancient world, prison was a place for the poor, who had no adequate means of self-defense and so were at the mercy of exploitation and greed. Both songs, moreover, voice a threat to "the rebellious" (68:6), "the wicked" (146:9), who do not share these passions for a reordered society.

Second, Israel's songs of YHWH's peculiar social intentions are matched in Israel's most elemental *narrative memory*, which was regularly recited as an identifying mark of this community. Thus, in the Passover narrative, Israel remembered how its own unbearable pain became the key datum of life and faith: "The Israelites groaned under their slavery, and cried out. Out of the slavery their cry for help rose up to God" (Exod. 2:23).

Israel remembered that the pain of oppression and abuse was so intolerable that it simply required out-loud expression that could not be stifled any longer in conformity. The cry of pain was not addressed by Israel to anyone in particular but simply needed to be sounded.

Israel, however, remembered more than the fact that crying was the initiating point for Israel's narrative memory of rescue. Israel also remembered who was, unexpectedly, on the receiving end of that cry as it "rose up to God." This God was remembered as the magnet that drew the cry of social pain toward God's own life, so that the cry had a decisive impact on this God and evoked in God a new, decisive response: "God heard their groaning, and God remembered [God's] covenant with Abraham, Isaac, and Jacob. God looked upon the Israelites, and God took notice of them" (Exod. 2:24-25).

This is a remembered characterization of a God who is *reachable* by voiced pain and who responds in transformative ways to such a cry. In response to the cry, "God heard, God remembered, God saw, God noticed"; in 3:7-8, moreover, added to this series of verbs is a final one: "I have come down to deliver." This exchange of cry and response sets in motion the stunning narrative drama of Exodus 3–15 whereby the slave band in Egypt is transformed into a people covenanted to YHWH; conversely, Pharaoh, emblem of rapacious power in the world, is reduced to nonpower, shown to be a hopeless bully (see 8:18 on the impotence of Pharaoh and his agents). Thus, the God celebrated in the doxologies of Israel is the one who comes to specific action in Israel's narratives.

Third, beyond the world offered in Israel's narratives that witness to an alternative God, Israel moved from narrative to commandment and assured that the same responsive concern of YHWH functions as a guarantee and sanction for law. This is evident in two early laws. First, Exodus 22:21-22 has a pair of negative imperatives:

> You shall not wrong or oppress a resident alien ... You shall not abuse
> any widow or orphan.

This is the same "widow and orphan" we have seen in the doxologies of Psalms 68 and 146. Now to these is added the "resident alien," a new category that became a third element of the socially vulnerable who must have special "entitled" protection.

But it is especially the sanction for this pair of commands that interests us.[1] After an appeal to the memory of the exodus in Exodus 22:21b, the primary sanction is that a protesting cry by the abused will indeed be heard by the God who has heard the slave cry and is mobilized by such a cry of pain. The threat from this God, commensurate with the threat to the rebellious in Psalm 68 and against the wicked in Psalm 146, is that the wives of the abusers will become widows and the children of the abusers will become orphans. That is, the status of the abuser population will become as wretched as those whom they abuse and the abusers themselves will be killed. It is clear in such an articulation that this God is no evenhanded sovereign, but rather is a deeply committed partisan in the struggle for neighborly relations. YHWH who speaks the command is the Great Equalizer who readily intervenes on behalf of the vulnerable to guarantee their well-being.

The second commandment in Exodus 22:25-27 is different in tone, but it exhibits the same concerns. It begins with two negative imperatives concerning treatment of the economically disadvantaged:

You shall not deal with them [the poor] as a creditor; you shall not exact interest from them.

This commandment insists that the relationships in the community between "haves" and "have nots" is not to be determined in economic categories. Rather, in this community ordered by covenant, those who lend and those who borrow are neighbors; the neighborly fabric of the community is not to be distorted by or administered according to the conventional economic impositions of credit and debt.

The sanction here, unlike 22:24, is not threat but affirmation. The grounding of the commandment is that YHWH is compassionate and will attend to the cry of the needy and will side with the needy. It may be that action against the abuser, spelled out in verse 24, is implicit here as well, but that is left unsaid.

The same defining concern in Israel's Torah provision is voiced in the series of specific commands in Deuteronomy 24:17-22. In every case the Torah and the God who speaks through Torah are insistent that the disadvantaged and economically marginal are to be protected. That protection, moreover, is commanded, sanctioned, and legitimated by the God who is endlessly attentive to the oppression, abuse, and disadvantage that are a product of the workings of socioeconomic, political processes that are elsewhere regarded as routine and conventional.

II

So imagine that these great prophetic figures we know so well—Amos, Hosea, Isaiah, Micah, Jeremiah—are products of this sustained pedagogy in the peculiar covenantal ethics of Israel, grounded in the peculiar character of the God of Sinai.

Imagine them as little children regularly attending Passover liturgy, hearing with regularity the particular dramatic affirmation that their community of Israel exists precisely because God hears the cries of the abused and intervenes on their behalf.

Imagine them as boys (and Huldah as a girl) in liturgy regularly, where they heard sung (or themselves sang) the great doxologies that voiced the claim that the God of Israel is precisely the one who is "father" of orphans and protector of widows.

Imagine as they grew older, in their adolescent years, that they moved through liturgy and hymn to serious instruction in the commandments and noticed even there the God who responds to the cries and needs of the vulnerable and powerless.

Doxology, narrative, and *commandment* all converging to nurture younger members of the community into a particular angle of vision! They received a particular critical perspective on social reality that managed in daring rhetoric to insist that the Holy God "in his holy habitation" (Ps. 68:5) is intimately and attentively engaged with the economic, political realities of the world. Long after, when they had departed from this pedagogy of doxology, narrative, and commandment, the cadences of attentiveness, the solidarity of God with the needy, the severity of God toward the abusers, and the readiness of God to take sides, all of that was profoundly defining for their prophetic voices. We do not know much about the psychology of the prophets or the ways in which they came to be summoned and authorized to prophetic vocation, even though a great deal has been written on the subject. What we do know, however, is that the prophets, for all their wild imagination and daring rhetoric, were not odd and inexplicable in Israelite society. Rather, they were products—in the extreme to be sure—of a community that operated with a different kind of social analysis and a different kind of social experience, both grounded in the character of the God whom they had long known from doxology, narrative, and commandment.

III

The prophets were real live human beings existing in real concrete social circumstance. They were adults (or as in Jer. 1:4-10 a soon-to-be adult) capable of seeing the world in adult ways, critical and discerning, informed by deep memory from which they did not depart. The strangeness of these prophets, now remembered and given to us through a complicated editorial process, is that they did not (and I think could not) see the world in the same way as most of their contemporaries, especially the power elite. The latter had long since decided that the old traditions of doxology, narrative, and commandment were nice for "little children" but had nothing at all to do with the "real world," for the "real world" was defined apart from God and shaped by credit, debt, mortgage, interest, surplus, and profits, without any disruptive theological footnote.

In the eighth century B.C.E., during the prosperous regimes of Uzziah in Judah and Jeroboam II in Israel, the economy grew and the prosperous prospered in exaggerated form. Into that happy scene comes the disturbing utterance of Amos, who characterizes in fine hyperbole the extravagant self-indulgence of the prosperous:

> Alas for those who lie on beds of ivory,
> > and lounge on their couches,
> and eat lambs from the flock,
> > and calves from the stall;
> who sing idle songs to the sound of the harp,
> > and like David improvise on instruments of music;
> who drink wine from bowls,
> > and anoint themselves with the finest oils. (Amos 6:4-6a)

Predictably the negative recital ends in v. 6 with the adversative conjunction *but:*

> *But* are not grieved over the ruin of Joseph! (v. 6b)

"Joseph" refers to Israel, the northern kingdom. Amos speaks of its "ruin," which was not yet visible to most. He expected that those who paid attention would see and, if they saw, would grieve; they would be sad about their future and perhaps take steps to "establish justice in the gate" (5:15).

But of course the prophet is not finished until he utters his climactic *therefore* in 6:7:

> *Therefore* they shall now be the first to go into exile,
> > and the revelry of the loungers shall pass away.

What a strange thing to say: "exile" and then an accusatory hyperbole about self-indulgence that he names "revelry of the loungers." Exile, displacement, loss, and termination were on no one's horizon . . . except for Jeremiah, the product of the doxology, narrative, and commandment. Exile (= deportation) was perhaps already known as the preferred policy of the dangerous-looking Assyrian empire. And no doubt Amos had such a reference to imperial policy in mind. In fact, however, Amos's grounding is theological: he knows in deep ways the neighborly intention of God. He can see at a glance that the luxury of vv. 4-6 is an extravagance wrought at the expense of the poor; it will not go on, moreover, because YHWH wills otherwise (see 4:1-3; 8:4-6).

In the seventh century, with Israel now gone and Amos vindicated, Jeremiah—child of doxology, narrative, and commandment—read his Judean situation and noticed how the economy was organized so that the same crowd of the vulnerable are the victims of an unnoticing social arrangement:

> They have become great and rich,
> > they have grown fat and sleek.

They know no limits in deeds of wickedness;
   they do not judge with justice
the cause of the orphan, to make it prosper,
   and they do not defend the rights of the needy.
     (Jer. 5:27d-28)

The imagery is of a hunter who traps birds. The "great and rich" have all the necessary equipment (cages, traps, nets = tax laws, mortgage arrangements, interest rates). With "no limit" on the number they can "bag," they go their way, becoming "fat and sleek" in numbering self-indulgence, undeterred by doxology, narrative, or commandment.

IV

The close discernment of the prophets and their capacity to utter what they saw and knew in clear and imaginative ways are crucial for "just preaching." In my judgment one other factor belongs alongside such an assessment of the prophets. Especially in the oracles of Hosea and Jeremiah, but also in the prayer of Amos 7:2-6, it is clear that the God to whom they bear witness is not an outsider who stands over against failed Israel and who takes glee in harsh judgment. The articulation of God's pathos—God's suffering solidarity—indicates that the failure to care for the "little ones" in Israel is not only disturbing to God but hurtful to God's own life, because of God's intense solidarity.[2]

God's pathos concerns the suffering of Israel, as in Hosea 11:8-9 and Jeremiah 31:20. From that, however, we may extrapolate that God is hurt whenever God's dearly beloved—the widow, the orphan, and the alien—are hurt. It is God's capacity for solidarity in pain and grief that gives resonance and depth to the severity of prophetic judgment. The distortion of the world causes grief and dismay to this one who dearly loves the world, so that the prophetic utterance, bespeaking God's own inclination, is characteristically a mix of anger and anguish. Any prophetic utterance that lacks the anguish that qualifies the anger is less than a full voicing of this God as presented in the prophetic tradition.

V

The script of the prophet is a script for our own "just preaching." The text provides a skeleton and spine for contemporaneity in our preaching, a text that invites, generates, and authorizes imaginative linkages between what they uttered and what we may utter after them. A caveat, however, needs to be entered. There is a long tradition of so-called prophetic preaching that is filled with anger, indignation, and condemnation, so that the preacher's own juices of anger can run loose in the process.

I suggest that we need to unlearn that common notion of prophetic preaching on two counts. First, it is clear that some of the most effective "prophetic preaching" in our time by such dazzling voices as Desmond Tutu, Daniel Berrigan, and Jonathan Kozol—to name three choice cases—has the power of indignation but comes across as utterances of hope-filled, compassionate truth-telling largely free of rage. I suggest that we have misread the prophets to think them voices of simplistic rage, for hard truth can be told quietly if it intends to evoke a response rather than simply be an imposition of rage on the listener.

Second, it is clear that most pastors (who have at best precarious tenure, who are administratively responsible for program and budget and institutional maintenance, and who worry about their pensions) are not free-floating voices who can simply emote. Thus, I suggest that "just preaching" may well be done by *scribes* who attend to prophetic *texts,* for what scribes characteristically do is to preserve, value, and interpret old scrolls.[3] To think of one's self as a scribe "trained for the kingdom" may deliver one from the excessive "righteous indignation" that is connected to conventional notions of "prophetic preaching" (Matt. 13:51-53). A scribal notion may suggest that the prophetic chance is to help the listening community discern differently through the lens of the old tradition of oracles presented in treasured scrolls (see Jer. 36:32; Neh. 8:1). Seeing differently and imaginatively through such a "scrolled" lens leaves a choice for changed attitude and policy; the work of the scribe, however, is to let the prophetic text authorize the difference.

Such scribal work, mediating the text of Amos and company,

- can prevent *effective social analysis,* for it is still true that "haves and have nots" are in it together, with a growing gap in our time between them because of the manipulation of taxes, interest, loans, and so forth; the church is characteristically weak and timid about social analysis, but without it there is no effective prophetic utterance;

- can make visible and prominent the "widows and orphans" among us, *the vulnerable marginalized* who lack clout, who are deficient in health insurance, for whom it is not easy to focus on the education of children, and who live pitifully and meanly on $7 an hour;

- can make the connection that the failure of the life of the "have nots" eventually will destroy the life of the "haves," because there are no "safe houses" outside *the common fabric* of lived humanity.

Beyond the social analysis, the scribe can also lift up texts

- that witness to the terrific loss that comes on the community that in prophetic parlance is *judgment,* but judgment communicated with more sadness than rage;
- that testify to the *pathos* of God, to the pathologies of human community that contribute directly to God's own pain, a pain that reaches an extremity in the cross;
- that find around the edges of failure *new beginnings,* new social possibilities that are given here and there in the midst of the deathliness as the prophets watch for and discern signs of newness.

The work of the scribe in *judgment,* in *pathos,* and in *hope* is to invite the congregation to come outside the narcotic of consumerism to rediscern the world as a place where issues of life and death are at work, not because of a God angry without pain, but because life is not sustainable without intentional investment in a human future.

VI

The scribe does not read the prophetic scrolls and rearticulate prophetic oracle in a vacuum. If the scribe is the pastor of a congregation, prophetic proclamation—judgment, pathos, possibility—are made credible by a context of intentional pastoral, liturgical, and educational work.

All around the prophetic assertion are *cadences of doxology* that tell of God's wondrous abundance as the bottom truth of creation, an abundance not cheapened even by cunning tax and mortgage arrangements.

All around the prophetic assertion are *many retellings of the narratives* that attest to the reality of God in the life of the world, an attestation that calls the congregation away from the narrativeless life of consumerism to the dramatic narrative of covenantal engagement that issues in health, liberation, and well-being.

All around the prophetic assertion are the rich probing and teaching of *old commandments* as the nonnegotiable condition for the life of the world. Many church people do not know the commandments, either to probe deeply into "the Big Ten" or to face texts that are completely unknown in the church, commandments of neighborliness and compassion, of holiness and justice.

A sustained offer of doxologies concerning the miracles of abundance, of narratives of the give-and-take of covenantal mutuality, and of commandments as preconditions for life in the world make room for prophetic analysis and articulation. When done in context, the scribe may not need to raise her voice or exude indignation. It is enough to see differently and to imagine alternatively, for such posturing of hearers permits and evokes different action.[4] Neither a scribe nor a prophet can dictate or coerce. It is enough to line out the world differently, to resist the phony reassurance of therapeutic consumerism, and to show insistently that the first command of loving God is always followed quickly and with equal insistence by the second command, the imperative to love one's neighbor (Mark 12:28-34). Giving voice to the neighbor command in a context of satiating consumerism is a stark *either/or* that requires great courage, especially if it is linked to the characteristic prophetic agenda of tax, mortgage, and interest arrangements.[5] "Just preaching" is about voicing the either/or alongside (a) pastoral candor about the terrible ambiguity about which we all know and (b) the wondrous chance for choosing again, differently, obediently, freely, hopefully, gladly . . . again. When the scribe works the *either/or* in a context of doxology, narrative, and commandment, there may arise, through long seasons of listening, another prophet or two for the next age of the church. In the meantime, being a faithful scribe for the kingdom is, I do not doubt, more than enough.

4

preaching to a decision

An Imaginative "Or"

Perhaps the assigned theme, "preaching from the Old Testament," is intended to raise the sticky christological issue about finishing up Old Testament texts with Jesus. The question is difficult, and I should say where I am. I believe the Old Testament leads to the New and to the gospel of Jesus Christ. It does not, however, lead there directly, but only with immense interpretive agility. It does not, moreover, lead there singularly and necessarily in my judgment, because it also leads to Judaism and to the synagogue with its parallel faith. I shall bracket out of my consideration the christological question with the recognition, put in trinitarian terms, that in the Old Testament we speak of the Father of the Son.[1] As we confess the fullness of the Father manifest in the Son, so we may confess the fullness of God manifest to Israel in the Father. This is a question of endless dispute, but I owe it to you to be clear on my own conviction.

I

Rather than the christological question, I shall focus on the ecclesial question. I understand preaching to be the chance to *summon and nurture an alternative community with an alternative identity, vision, and vocation, preoccupied with praise and obedience toward the God we Christians know fully in Jesus of Nazareth.* (This accent on alternative community resonates with the point being made in current "Gospel and Culture" conversation, much propelled by Lesslie Newbigin's focus on election, that God in God's inscrutable wisdom has chosen a people whereby the creation will be brought to wholeness).[2] Two other beginning points make the community-forming work of the Old Testament peculiarly contemporary for us.

First, it is crucial to remember that the Old Testament is zealously and

pervasively a Jewish book. Jews, and Israelites before them, are characteristically presented and understand themselves to be a distinct community
with an alternative identity *rooted theologically and exhibited ethically*—alternative to the Egyptians, the Canaanites, the Philistines, the Assyrians, the
Babylonians, the Persians, and the Hellenists—not only alternative but
always subordinate to and under threat from dominant culture.[3] Thus I
understand the intention of the Torah and the Prophets—and differently I
believe also wisdom—to be insisting on *difference* with theological rootage
and ethical exhibit. The God question is decisive, even if backgrounded, but
the urgency concerns maintenance of communal identity, consciousness,
and intentionality.

Second, with the disestablishment of Western Christianity and the collapse of the social hegemony of the church, the formation of a distinctive
community of praise and obedience now becomes urgent as it had not been
when the Western church could count on the support and collusion of
dominant culture. If the church in our society is not to evaporate into an
ocean of consumerism and antineighborly individualism, then the summons
and nurture of an alternative community constitute an emergency. Thus,
with a huge mutatis mutandis, I propose that, as the Jews lived in a peren-
nial emergency of identity, so the church in our time and place lives in such
an emergency.[4] In both cases, moreover, a primal response to the emergency
and a primal antidote to assimilation and evaporation is the chance of
preaching. In reflection upon the Old Testament and the ecclesial emergency, I will consider three theses.

II

The summons and nurture, formation and enhancement of an alternative
community of praise and obedience *depends upon the clear articulation of an
either/or, the offer of a choice and the requirement of a decision that is theologically rooted and ethically exhibited, that touches and pervades every facet of the
life of the community and its members.*[5] The choice is presented as clear. I
believe that this *either/or* belongs inevitably to an alternative community,
because an alternative identity requires an endless intentionality. For without vigilance the alternative cannot be sustained. I have reflected upon Old
Testament texts around this theme; my impression is that there are only
rare texts that are "holding actions." Everything in Israel's text urges an
alternative.

The alternative that must be embraced in order to be Israel includes the
summons to Abraham and Sarah to "go," for without going there will be

no land and no future, no heir and no Israel. The summons to slaves in
Egypt through Moses is to "depart," for if there is no "departure" there is
no promised land. Moses worries, moreover, that if Israel does not believe,
it will not depart and will not be Israel (Exod. 4:1).[6] Less instantaneous
but certainly pervasively, the prophets endlessly summon Israel to an alternative covenant ethic, lest the community be destroyed. And even in the
wisdom traditions, the restrained advocacy of wisdom and righteousness
is in the awareness that foolishness will indeed bring termination. Perhaps
the most dominant statement of *either/or* that belongs characteristically to
the faith perspective of the Old Testament is the context at Mt. Carmel
where Elijah challenges Israel: "How long will you go limping with two
different opinions? If the Lord is God, follow him; but if Baal, then follow him" (1 Kgs. 18:21). We are told first, "The people did not answer him
a word" (v. 21b). But at the end they said, "The Lord indeed is God; the
Lord indeed is God" (v. 39). This text knows that Israel, in order to be the
people of YHWH, must be endlessly engaged in an intentional decision for
Yahwism, a decision that fends off the powerful forces of the dominant
culture.[7]

I wish now to consider in some detail two classic formulations of *either/or*
that occur at pivotal points in Israel's life. The first of these is Joshua 24, a
much discussed text that von Rad regarded as an ancient credo that is situated as the culmination of the Hexateuch.[8] The meeting at Shechem over
which Joshua presides is set canonically just as Israel is situated in the land.
Joshua 1–12 concerns control of the land, albeit by violence, and Joshua 13–
21 concerns division of the land among the tribes. I read this moment as
Israel's arrival at security, well-being, affluence, and rare self-congratulations.
The text is presented as a *bid to non-Israelites* to join up.[9] I shall consider
that a fictional staging, so that the text is in fact a *bid to Israelites* in their
new affluence to reembrace the faith of the Yahwistic covenant. The text
(and Joshua) know that there are indeed attractive alternatives, alternatives
that Israel must resist.

As von Rad saw most clearly, vv. 2-13 is a recital of Israel's core memory.[10] It includes the ancestors of Genesis (vv. 2-4), the Exodus (vv. 5-7a),
the wilderness sojourn (v. 7b), and the entry into the land (vv. 8-13). This
latter theme ends:

> I gave you a land on which you had not labored, and towns that you
> had not built, and you live in them; you eat the fruit of vineyards and
> oliveyards that you did not plant. (v. 13)

It is all gift!

After this recital, the speaker (here Joshua the preacher) makes his bid for allegiance to this particular narrative construal of reality: "fear and serve Yhwh in completeness and in faithfulness." Negatively: "put away the other gods." Positively: "serve Yhwh." *Choose:* If Yhwh ... if not then, option (a) is the gods of the Euphrates valley, option (b) is the Amorite gods in the land. Choose! Then says the preacher, "those in my household will serve Yhwh," and will put our lives down in the Yhwh narrative just recited. But if you refuse this narrative, then put your life down somewhere else and live with the consequences. No doubt the entire Hexateuch has been pointed to this moment. The Pentateuch consists of the live narrative of Yhwh that generates a world of gift and liberation and demand about which decisions must be made.[11]

Then follows in vv. 16-24 a dialogue about church growth. The exchange of Joshua and the community is a negotiation about the *either/or.*

People (vv. 16-18): Far be us from us to serve other gods ... we will serve Yhwh;[12]

Joshua (vv. 19-20): You cannot do it. It is too hard and Yhwh is more ferocious than you imagine (No growth seduction here).

People (v. 21): No, we are committed. We will serve Yhwh.

Joshua (v. 22a): You are witnesses ... you are on notice.

People (v. 22b): Yes we are.

Joshua (v. 23): with an imperative:

Negative: put away foreign gods.[13]

Positive: extend your hearts to Yhwh.

Conclusion (v. 25): Joshua made a covenant with Torah demands.

This particular crisis of *either/or* is negotiated and Israel comes to be, yet again, an intentional alternative community, alternative to the gods of the land.

The second case of *either/or* that I cite is in Second Isaiah. This wondrous text is situated in the exile. That is, the context is exactly the opposite of Joshua 24. There it was excessive security in the land. Here it is complete displacement from the religious, cultural supports of Jerusalem, set down in an ocean of Babylonian seductions and intimidations, with effective Babylonian economics and seemingly effective Babylonian gods. No doubt many deported Jews found it easier to be a Babylonian Jew, and for some that status was only a transition to becoming Babylonian. The lean choice of remaining Jews embedded in YHWH depended upon having the *either/or* made plain, for without the *either/or*, cultural accommodation and assimilation go unchecked.

It is precisely the work of Second Isaiah to state the alternative, so that Jews tempted by Babylon have a real choice available to them. The text of Second Isaiah is well known to us (unfortunately Handel reworked it so that the *either/or* is not at all visible). The recurring accent of Second Isaiah is that it is now the emergency moment when Jews may and must depart from Babylon. In our historical criticism, we have focused much on Cyrus and the overthrow of Babylon by the Persians, so that the emancipation of the Jews is a geopolitical event. No doubt there is something in that. But I suggest not so much, because the primal departure from Babylon is not geographical but imaginative, liturgical, and emotional: imagine Jewishness, imagine distinctiveness that has not succumbed to the pressures and seductions of the empire. From this familiar poetry of departure and distinctiveness, I will mention four characteristic elements.

1. The initial announcement, "comfort, comfort," is an assertion to Jews displaced by YHWH's anger that caring embrace by YHWH is now the order of the day: "For a brief moment I abandon you, but with great compassion I will gather you" (54:7). The Jews in exile are addressed as the forgiven, as the welcomed, as the cherished. They had pondered, for two generations, rejection by YHWH. But to be forgiven, welcomed, and cherished invites the reembrace of Jewishness. The poet, moreover, draws out the scenario of wondrous, jubilant, victorious procession back to Jerusalem, back to Jewishness, back to alternative identity (40:3-8). It is in this reassertion and reenactment of Jewishness that the glory of YHWH is revealed before all flesh. These Jews in this uncommon identity, moreover, are surrounded by the God who leads like a triumphant general and the God who does the rearguard pickup in order to salvage the dropouts:

> See, the Lord comes with might,
> and his arm rules for him . . . .
> He will feed his flock like a shepherd;
> he will gather the lambs in his arms,

and carry them in his bosom,
and gently lead the mother sheep. (Isa. 40:10-11)

The purpose of the poetic opener is to permit the community to reexperience the embracive quality of Jewishness welcomed in its peculiarity.

2. In order to create imaginative space for Jewishness, the poet employs two kinds of rhetorical strategies.[14] First, it is important to debunk the vaunted powers of Babylon. This is done by teasing and mocking the gods of the empire. In Isaiah 46:1-2, the gods are mocked as dumb statues that must be carried around on the backs of animals, like so many meaningless floats in a May Day parade. The ridicule is like the old humor at the chiefs of the Soviet Union or the mocking of "whitey" that black people have had to do for their own health and sanity. Or the poet holds a mock trial in order to show how weak and ineffectual are the imperial gods, who are passive, silent, and dormant—all failures who can do neither good nor evil (41:21–29). The intention of such speech is to dress down the powers of domination, to exhibit courage in the face of power, to show that the choice of Babylon that looks so impressive is in the end sheer foolishness.

3. This debunking is matched by the vigorous reassertion of Yhwh as the most reliable player in the struggle for the future. In the salvation oracles, this poet has Yhwh repeatedly saying to terrified Jews, "Fear not." "Fear not, I am with you." "Fear not, I will help you." "Fear not," be a Jew. The poet knows that the empire traffics in fear and intimidation with its uniforms, its parades, its limousines, its press conferences, its agents with dark glasses, and its intrusions in the night. All is for nought, because Yhwh is the great Equalizer who creates safe space and overrides the threat of dominant claims.

4. Finally, looking back on the highway of Isaiah 40 and the fearless safe return that the dumb Babylonian gods cannot stop—nothing can stop resolved Jewishness—the poem announces the departure: "Depart, depart, go out from there" (52:11)! They could remember the ancient "departure" from Egypt. They remembered every Passover by means of unleavened bread. The lack of leavening recalled that they left in a hurry, with no time for the yeast to rise. This is a like emergency and a like departure.

For you shall not go out in haste,
and you shall not go in flight;
for the Lord will go before you,
and the God of Israel will be your rear guard. (Isa. 52:12)

No rush. Leave at your convenience. First class passengers may board at their leisure for the journey back to full, alternative Jewishness: "For you shall go out in joy, and be led back in peace" (55:12).

They might not depart from the emotional grip of Babylon on the day they first hear the poem; but the poetry lingers. Alternative identity, even in places of threat and seduction, is embraced as the invitation does its proper work.

III

The *either/or* of distinctive identity for praise and obedience is not self-evident in the nature of things, but *depends completely and exclusively on the courageous utterance of witnesses who voice choices and invite decisions where none were self-evident.* My accent on the urgency of preaching the *either/or* is grounded in my conviction that Israel lives by a certain kind of utterance without which Israel has no chance to live. It is for this reason that I have insisted in my recent book on Old Testament theology that Old Testament claims for God finally do not appeal to historical facticity or to ontology, but rely on the utterance of witnesses to offer what is not self-evident or otherwise available.[15] This is indeed "theology of the word," by which I mean simply and leanly and crucially *utterance.*

I take as my primary case Second Isaiah, admittedly an easy case; but I would extrapolate from Second Isaiah to claim that the entire Old Testament is utterance expressing *either/or* that is not self-evident.[16] The massive hegemony of Babylon—political, economic, theological—had, so far as we know, well nigh driven Jewishness from the horizon; and with the elimination of Jewishness it had vetoed YHWH from the theological conversation. It is the intention of every hegemony to eliminate separatist construals of reality that are endlessly inconvenient and problematic—and certainly a separatism as dangerous as Jewishness, which endlessly subverts. The tale of Daniel, perhaps later but clearly reflective of the Babylonian crisis, tells the tale of how Nebuchadnezzar is enraged that Jews should refuse imperial allegiance and hold to their odd alternative claim (Dan. 3:13-15).

This power of hegemony, moreover, matched the exiles' own sense of things, for they also had concluded that YHWH was not engaged or worth trusting:

Why do you say, O Jacob,
and speak, O Israel,

"My way is hidden from the Lord,
and my right is disregarded by my God"? (Isa. 40:27)

But Zion said, "The lord has forsaken me,
my Lord has forgotten me." (Isa. 49:14)

Is my hand shortened, that I cannot redeem?
Or have I no power to deliver? (Isa. 50:2)

It is in such an environment of hegemony-*cum*-despair that the utterance of *either/or* takes place. It is the utterance of *either/or* that shapes the perceptual field of Israel anew, to become aware of resources not recognized, of dangers not acknowledged, and of choices that had not seemed available. I shall consider this new, subversive voice of *either/or* in two waves. First, Second Isaiah himself, perhaps someone who had risen out of a continuing seminar on the text of First Isaiah, is now moved to generate and extrapolate new text. "Moved," I say, because some think that it was by an out-of-the-ordinary confrontation in "the divine council"; when the voices say, "Cry . . . what shall I cry . . . get you up on a high mountain, herald of good tidings," the one moved by divine imperative is none other than Second Isaiah, who moves out from this theological experience to reshape the lived emergency of Israel.

It is this poet who gives to the rhetoric of the synagogue and the church the term "gospel."[17] Indeed, I suggest provisionally that gospel is the offer of an *either/or* where none seemed available. So in Isaiah 40:9:

Get you up to a high mountain,
O Zion, herald of *gospel tidings,*
lift up your voice with strength,
O Jerusalem, herald of *gospel tidings,*
lift it up, do not fear.

The gospeler is twice named. The gospeler, moreover, is given the utterance to be sounded: "Behold, your God," or in the NRSV, "Here is your God." It is the exhibit of YHWH as God of the exiles in a context where Babylon had banished the God of the exiles so that there were only Babylonian gods available. The news is that YHWH is back in play, creating choices. YHWH is back in play on the lips of the one moved to new utterance.

That text in Isaiah 40:9 is matched in 52:7 in a better-known utterance:

> How beautiful upon the mountains
> are the feet of the *gospel messenger*
> who announces peace,
> who brings *gospel news,*
> who announces salvation,
> who says to Zion, "Your God reigns."

Again the term "gospel" is twice used, and again the lines are given: "Your God reigns," or better, "Your God has just become king." The line is a quotation from the Psalms (see 96:10), but the utterance here is an assertion that in the contest for domination, the gods of the empire have been defeated and the God of Israel is now the dominant force in creation. The poet creates an environment for choice, for decision, for homecoming, for new, faithful action, none of which is available or choosable without this utterance.

It is, however, the second layer of utterance in this poetry that interests me, namely, that the Israelites are summoned by the poet to be witnesses, to give testimony about the Yahwistic alternative about which they did not know and which the Babylonians certainly could never tolerate. In 43:8-13, the poet offers a contest among the gods. Negatively he invites the Babylonians to give evidence for their gods: "Let them bring forth their witnesses" (v. 9). Then in v. 10: "You are my witnesses," you exiles. You are the ones who are to speak my name, confess my authority, obey my will, accept my emancipation, tell my miracles. The exiles who themselves had thought there was no *or* to the Babylonian *either* are now called to testify to this Yahwistic *or.* There are two quite remarkable features to this poem authorizing Israel's testimonial utterance about an alternative that the empire cannot tolerate.

First, the summons and authorization to testify are interwoven with *the substance of testimony* that is to be given:

> Before me no god was formed,
> nor shall there be any after me.
> I, I am the Lord,
> and besides me there is no savior . . .
> I am God, and also henceforth I am He;
> there is no one who can
> deliver from my hand;
> I work and who can hinder it? (Isa. 43:10b-11, 13)

What is to be said is that YHWH is the alpha and the omega, the first and the last, the creator, the one who is utterly irresistible. Note well that this extravagant claim allows no room for any Babylonian gods. In the statement of the *either/or*, the Babylonian *either* is dismissed as an irrelevant fantasy. There is only the Yahwistic *or* as an option.

Now we might suspect that this is a frontal assault to convince the Babylonians. Perhaps so. But the second feature I observe in v. 10 is this:

> You are my witnesses, says the Lord,
> and my servant whom I have chosen,
> so that you may know and believe me
> and understand that I am he.

Notice: You are my witnesses ... in order that ... *you may know, believe, understand!* The giving of testimony is to claim the ones who testify. Israel is to enunciate the Yahwistic option so that they themselves should trust and embrace that option. This is surely the most direct claim I know concerning Paul's assertion that faith comes from what is heard (Rom. 10:17); where there is no speaking and hearing of an alternative world, there is no faith, no courage, no freedom to choose differently, no community of faith apart from and even against the empire.

The other remarkable text is Isaiah 44:8, followed by the negative of 44:9. It is clear that vv. 8 and 9 belong to quite different literary units; they are joined together perhaps to make the point about utterance. Verse 8 asserts yet again, "You are my witnesses." The last two lines of the verse, just as we have seen in chapter 43, outline the utterance that is to be uttered: "Is there any god besides me? There is no other rock; I know not one."

The testimony is not only that there is a choice outside Babylon, but it is the only real choice. The new feature here, after chapter 43, is the first line of the verse to the witnesses now being recruited: "Do not fear, or be afraid." One can imagine a lawyer briefing a witness, perhaps a witness who is a whistle-blower against a great corporation, who must say in court what the company cannot tolerate: "Do not be afraid." Or one can imagine a woman in a rape trial who must give evidence, but is terrified both of the shame and of the continuing threat of the rapist: "Do not fear." The lawyer must encourage and reassure. Every witness, every serious preacher, every exile who speaks against hegemony knows the fear. And YHWH says, state the *or*, because it is true. Many witnesses discover, of course, that YHWH in the end has no "witness protection program," but the witness is often compelled to give evidence nonetheless.

The negative of v. 9 is surprising. Verses 9-20 constitute an odd unit that mocks the makers of idols, the Babylonians who manufacture powerless gods. Verse 9 speaks of idols and then of witnesses, that is, the Babylonian gods and the Babylonians who champion them or Jews who trust those imperial gods too much. The idols are, with the NRSV, "nothing." The term looks like a simple rejection. But the Hebrew *tôhû* means "chaos." The Babylonian gods are embodiments of chaos, forces of disorder. This is a remarkable claim, for the empire had claimed to be a great sponsor of order and well-being. But here it is clear: the spiritual force of the empire is against *shalôm,* against peace and order and well-being. The *tôhû* of Babylon, of course, is to be contrasted with the power of the true creator God, YHWH. Finally it is asserted that the witnesses who champion the gods of *tôhû* neither see nor know. They are so narcotized and mesmerized by the empire that they cannot see what is going on. The contrast is total, no overlap between these two god offers. The exiles can choose either *the gods of the empire* who will never deliver the well-being they claim to sponsor, or *the God of the news* who stands against all things fearful. The battle for Jewishness in exile is acute, a battle now replicated in the battle for baptism in an ocean of military consumerism that generates endless layers of chaos in the name of prosperity.

To be sure, Second Isaiah is an easy case for *either/or* through utterance. But I would argue that the theme is pervasive in the text of this people always struggling for its identity. Perhaps you noticed in my longish comment on Joshua 24 that Joshua and his counterparts finally get serious precisely about testimony. He says to them: "You are witnesses against yourselves that you have chosen the Lord, to serve him" (v. 22). The answer, "Witnesses." The Hebrew is terse, without a nominative pronoun. My point is a simple one. Everything depends on utterance. The dramatic occasions of teaching and preaching, where the *either/or* is spelled out and sometimes embraced, are serious occasions, serious not simply because of formal oaths or because we claim to be speaking true, but serious elementally because *what we say* and *how we say it* are the world we receive. Israel's serious oath is to choose the *or* of YHWH and to hold to it (see also v. 27).

It would be nice if the *either/or* were simply out there in the landscape. Israel, however, knows better. It is here, in speech. If it is not uttered, it is not available. If it is not uttered, it is not. This point, that human possibility resides in utterance, it seems to me, is crucial not only for preaching, but more generally in a technological society.[18] Our technological mind-set wants to thin, reduce, and eventually silence serious speech. The urgency of preaching and all the utterance of the church and the synagogue, I suggest, are that we know intuitively that where there is not face-to-face truth telling, we are by that much diminished in the human enterprise. And Joshua insists, Israel must stand by its utterance.[19]

IV

While the *either/or* may be uttered frontally, the *or* of Yhwh is characteristically spoken in figure, because it is a possibility "at hand" but not yet *in* hand.[20] The *either/or* of Yahwism is directly utterable, and I have cited cases of such direct utterance. Characteristically, however, it is not done tersely and confrontationally, because such utterance is too lean and gives the listeners few resources for the tricky negotiation between options, and because the *either/or*, having no one shape or form, is always different with different folk in different circumstances. Moreover, while the *either* of hegemony is visible and can be described in some detail, the *or* of Yhwh does not admit of flat description because it is not yet visible, not yet in hand, always about to be, always under construal, always just beyond us. Indeed, if the *or* of Yhwh could be fully and exhaustively described, the prospect is that it would become, almost immediately, some new hegemonic *either*, as is often the case if creeds are heard too flatly, if liturgies are held too closely, if ethics is turned to legalism, if piety becomes self-confidence and pride. It is this open act of imagination in the service of a demanding, healing *or* that is the primary hard work of the preacher and the wonder of good preaching that is communicated in modes outside hegemonic certitude.

I will return to my two major cases and then in conclusion note three other places where one can see some playfulness at work in utterance.

1. I have characterized Joshua 24 as a primary model of *either/or* in which testimonial utterance is evident. That utterance of either/or in solemn assembly by Joshua culminates in v. 25: "So Joshua made a covenant with the people that day, and made statutes and ordinances for them at Shechem." The verse tells us almost nothing of what constitutes the new obedience to which Israel is pledged after this hard-won decision to embrace Yhwh's *or*. I suggest that because Joshua 24 is about the immediate settlement in the land, the Torah of Deuteronomy is the figurative articulation that fleshes out the *either/or* announced in Joshua 24. For the sake of that connection, I make two critical observations. First, it is generally agreed that Deuteronomy constitutes the norm for the "history" offered in Joshua, Judges, Samuel, and Kings, the "Deuteronomic" account of Israel's life in the land.[21] Thus, the linkage between Deuteronomy and Joshua 24 is entirely plausi-

ble; Joshua 24:25 alludes to that Torah. Second, because Deuteronomy is "Deuteronomic," we are free to say that its framing is fictive, that the staging of the speech of Moses at the Jordan is an invitation for Israel that has embraced the Yahwistic *or* against the Canaanite *either* to conjure what the land of promise would be like were it alternatively organized and practiced in covenant. This delivers us from needing to insist that Israel enacted all these laws, but it also permits us to see the "laws" as acts of imagination in which each successive generation of *or* is to explore how to take this text into its own concrete life and practice.

I shall comment on three texts from Deuteronomy. The ones I have selected are perhaps easy cases, but the point will be more generally clear. Joshua counts on the clear *either/or* worked in detail by Moses:

Deuteronomy 15:1-18. Either let the economy work unfettered so that the rich become richer, *or* read Deuteronomy 15:1-18 on the "Year of Release."[22] Moses, in this text, anticipates and imagines that the economy of the land of Canaan does not need to be organized in exploitative "Canaanite" ways, but could be reorganized in neighborly Israelite ways. He offers a scenario for a society in which poor people must work off their debts (no doubt at high interest rates), but a neighborly ethic proposes that at the end of six years, the debt is canceled and the poor person is invited back into the economy.

- Moses said, "There will always be poor people," so you must take this seriously and keep doing it all the time (v. 11).
- Moses said, If you do it effectively, you can eliminate such demeaning poverty and "the poor will cease out of the land" (v. 4).
- Moses said, "Do not entertain mean thoughts and begin to count toward the seventh year and act in hostility" (v. 9).
- Moses said, do not only cancel the debt but give the poor a generous stake so that they can reenter the economy viably, not from the bottom up (vv. 7-10).
- Moses said, If this seems outrageous to you, remember that you were bondservants in Egypt and you were released by the generous power of Yhwh your redeemer who brought you out (v. 18).

This is the most radical *or* in the Bible, insisting that the economy must be embedded in a neighborly human fabric. Almost all of us choose the *either*, imagining that Joshua's *or* is not relevant to an urban, postindustrial economy. But there it sits, always a summons, always a reminder, always an invitation. And Joshua had already said, "I tried to talk you out of this *or*; I told you it was too difficult for you."

Deuteronomy 17:14-20. Either let legitimate authority run loose in self-serving acquisitiveness, *or* read Deuteronomy 17:14-20 on monarchy. It is the only law of Moses on kingship. Moses agrees only reluctantly to let Israel have a king; he thinks kingship is a bad idea and that all available models of centralized power are bad. Then he says, but if you must, your king, your Israelite, covenantal, neighborly king shall be different. This king, embedded in covenant, must not accumulate silver or gold or horses or chariots or wives. Moses knows the three great seductions are money, power, and sex, all of which make community impossible if they are accumulated. And so he offers an *or*. The king, when in office, shall sit all day, every day, reading Torah, meditating day and night on what YHWH intends, on how covenantal community can curb raw power.

Israel, like every government since, has found it difficult to choose this *or*. The kings of Israel characteristically took the *either* of raw power, as has every kind of power . . . priests, parents, teachers, deans, bishops, corporate executives. In Israel, the primal example of the power of greed is Solomon, gold, gold, gold, three hundred wives, seven hundred concubines, and later it was said, "Do not be anxious, even Solomon in all his vast royal apparatus was not as well off as a bird."[23] The *or* is about power and governance and greed; in the end, however, it is about anxiety, getting more, keeping more while the land is lost in dread, terror, and devouring.[24]

Deuteronomy 24:19-22. Either it is every man [*sic*] for himself at the expense of all the others, *or* read Deuteronomy 24:19-22. It is about the triangle of *landowner, land,* and *landless,* and how they will live together. The *either* of Canaanite agriculture is just a "labor pool" of those nameless ones without any leverage or fringe benefits, who work but fall farther and farther behind, until they drop into welfare and then out of welfare into drugs, alcohol. They are sometimes a threat to us, often an inconvenience, always a nuisance and an embarrassment. *Or,* says Moses, in your economic operations, leave enough for *the alien, the widow, the orphan.* Leave the sheaves of wheat when you are "bringing in the sheaves," for *the alien, the widow, the orphan.* When you beat your olive trees, leave enough for *the alien, the widow, the orphan.* When you gather grapes, leave some for *the alien, the widow, the orphan.* The triad is like a mantra for this *or* of covenant because Moses knows that the powerful are in common destiny with the powerless.

The haves are linked to the future of the have-nots. Moses had already said, "Same law for citizens and undocumented workers" (Lev. 19:34). Moses knew that in a patriarchal society women without husbands and children without fathers are lost to the community, as bad off as outsiders.

The *or* requires a break with the orthodoxy of individualism. It requires a rejection of the notion of the undeserving poor. It requires a negation of all the pet ideologies whereby unburdened freedom is the capacity to disregard neighbor. And it is all there in the deep command of YHWH . . . not socialism, not liberalism, not ideology, just an alternative life.[25]

Our Christian strategy for disposing of the Mosaic Law is to dismiss it as legalism, certain that we are justified by grace alone, except that this obedience belongs to the center of an alternative community. The *or* is demanding but not obvious. The mantra of this community is endlessly "love God, then love neighbor, neighbor, neighbor."

2. I have characterized Isaiah 40–55 as a primary model of *either/or* testimonial utterance for this special community almost succumbing to Babylon. It was to this little community without confidence and almost without conviction that the poet declared on YHWH's behalf:

> because you are precious in my sight,
> and honored, and I love you,
> I give people in return for you,
> nations in exchange for your life. (Isa. 43:4)

Second Isaiah, however, only provides the trigger for liturgical, emotional, imaginative, perhaps geographical homecoming. When the Jews did come back to Jerusalem in 537 or 520 or 444, Second Isaiah gave little guidance. But then, Second Isaiah never comes without Third Isaiah. I propose that Third Isaiah, chapters 56–66, is the figurative articulation that fleshes out the *either/or* of Second Isaiah.[26] There is now a great deal of ferment about the book of Isaiah. It is increasingly likely, in scholarly judgment, that the old, deep separation of Second and Third Isaiah cannot be sustained. And therefore in its canonical shaping, one may see Isaiah 56–66 as an attempt to enact the glorious vision of Second Isaiah, but enactments must always come to detail.

Isaiah 56:3-8. Either be a community of like-minded people who are convinced of their own purity, virtue, orthodoxy, and legitimacy, excluding all others, *or* read Isaiah 56:3-8. There were all around the edges of restored Judaism inconvenient people who had no claim to purity, virtue, orthodoxy, or legitimacy. There were latecomers, not good Jews with pedigrees, who had jointed in, drawn to the faith, perhaps Samaritans or whatever, but surely not "qualified." Worse than that, there were people with marked, scarred, compromised genitals, people who had sold out to Babylon in order to become willing eunuchs with access to power. Of these Moses long ago in Deuteronomy 23:1 had declared that people with irregular sexual disposition were excluded. It is there in the Torah. All around were hovering people not like us, claiming and pushing and yearning and even believing ... What to do?

Says the *or* of Third Isaiah, have a generous spirit and a minimum but clear bar of admission. Tilt toward inclusiveness with only two requirements: that they keep covenant, that is, submit to the neighborly intention of YHWH; that they keep Sabbath, rest from the madness of production and consumption as a sign of confidence in YHWH's governance. That's all! It is the *or* of inclusiveness, no other pedigree, no sexual transposition, no other purification, an *or* that says the community is not made in the image of our strong points. The community teems with people who score irregularly on every Myers-Briggs notion of how we are and how we ought to be.[27]

Isaiah 58:1-9. Either become a punctilious community of religious discipline, engaging in religious scruple with amazing callousness about the real world of human transaction, *or* read Isaiah 58:1-9 and consider an alternative religious discipline of fasting that is not for show or piety or self-congratulations. Practice fast that commits to the neighbor, specifically the neighbor in need, the neighbor boxed in injustice and oppression. Break the vicious cycles of haves and have-nots that produce hungry people and homeless people and naked people, the most elemental signs and gestures of exposure, vulnerability, and degradation, produced by a system that does not notice.

Conventional religious disciplines that feel like virtue are disconnected. The practitioners of such self-congratulation, all the while, exploit and oppress and quarrel; they are uncaring, unthinking, unnoticing. And now the *or* of engagement moves to solidarity with the exposed and the vulnerable. The NRSV says "they are your kin," but the Hebrew says 'flesh,'" your own flesh of flesh and bone of bone, self of self. That is who they are.

When the lines of separation between haves and have-nots are broken by true fast, then, says Third Isaiah, then, only then, not until then:

Then your light shall break forth like the dawn,
and your healing shall spring up quickly;
your vindicator shall go before you,
the glory of the Lord shall be your rear guard.
Then you shall call, and the Lord will answer;
you shall cry for help,
and he will say, "Here I am." (Isa. 58:8-9)

Then, then, then, then . . . it is the *or* of communion. There is, however, no communion with YHWH until there is community with neighbor.[28]

Isaiah 65:17-25. Either cling to the old status quo of social arrangements and miss God's newness, *or* read Isaiah 65:17-25. The *or* of poetic imagination asserts that the old heaven and the old earth and the old Jerusalem, the old holy city and every old holy city and every old city and every old power arrangement is on the way out and is being displaced. The *or* of world renewal and urban renewal is a fantasy. The community of *or* engages in a strong act of vision: "We have a dream." It is a dream of joy and well-being, a dream in which there are no more cries of distress, no more infant mortality, no more social dislocation when people build houses and lose them by taxation, war, ethnic cleansing, or Olympic committees, where people do not plant gardens and have to move before harvest time. In the world coming there is no more anguish in childbirth. And to top it all, there is reconciliation of creation, lions and lambs, immediate communion with and attentiveness from YHWH, who answers before we call.

The poet offers a breathtaking *or*. He has been radical in chapter 56 on eunuchs and chapter 58 on poor people. But now in chapter 65 he no longer has time for the conventions of reality; he is off on a poetic, evangelical fantasy of what might be and what will be and what is at hand, but not in hand. He imagines, against the lovers of the old city who had felt but not yet noticed the brutal dysfunction of the old city. All will be changed. The poet can scarcely see its shape, but he has no doubt that its coming shape is a healing of all old abrasions and despairs. This *or* will never happen among us while we are bound to what was. Thus the poem is more like a parable than a blueprint, but a parable to be ingested by reforming Judaism, a parable,

about a banquet,
about a rich man and a barn,

about a man with two sons,
about a neighborly foreigner who paid the bills,
about a nagging widow,
about day laborers who get full pay.[29]

None of that is visible yet. Indeed none of that is possible . . . yet—except for those who depart from the way things are for the One who will make things new.

V

I am taking an ecclesial agenda because for too long, so it seems to me, christological certitude in the church has much of the time been permitted to silence, trump, and give closure to the Old Testament. I have wanted to suggest that faithful Christian exposition could do otherwise. I regard the preacher's engagement with the Old Testament as urgent:

- because the *or* of faith, so deeply pondered by ancient Israel, is needed in the face of our dominant *either;*

- because in a technological society, it is mostly left to the preacher, who labors at it locally, to voice the human options in a crisis of flatness;

- because preachers, more than any others, have endless opportunity for the tease of detail whereby the *or* of the gospel may be received and embraced.

The *or* is an impossible possibility. Both Israel and the church have always known that. That is what makes preaching both foolish and urgent.[30]

5

That the World May
Be Redescribed

The biblical text is itself a sufficient cause for wonder. By using an exegetical method that focuses resolutely on the texting, teachers can help people find themselves addressed and reimagined by this "strange new world" of the Bible.

My natural habitat for teaching is a theological seminary and the church constituency around that seminary. I am thus in a happy circumstance where the requirements of my teaching converge with my own passion about teaching. The task of such teaching is obvious but no less tricky: to enable the church to discern the world anew according to the script of the Bible with particular attentiveness to the character of the Bible, and thereby to accept the world as a place of joyous missional obedience. The task of rediscerning must affirm the biblical text as warranting a full, faithful response without diminishing the text to flat theological certitude. At the same time, it must engage the Bible critically (i.e., by historical criticism and ideological criticism) without ending in skepticism. This task leads teachers and students fully into the issue of "faith and reason" or, as I hope, "faith seeking understanding," which also requires faith for sense-making. Give or take a nuance, this double task of faith and criticism is inevitably the work of a Scripture teacher in the church.

Beyond Historical Explanation

In my own experience, a pedagogical approach to the biblical text must initially work against one of two inclinations. On the one hand, when the text is taken as a set of closed certitudes, attention must be given to the profound complexities that lie just beneath the surface. On the other hand, and more likely in my own teaching context, students have been taught in a modernist society to raise historical questions to such an extent that the text is overlooked. A detailed lining out of historical context usually receives a good deal more attention than the text itself. When attention *is* given to the text, there is a recurring temptation either to focus on isolated words or phrases taken out of context or to extract an idea at first glance. Such focus on either theological certitude or historical explanation is likely to miss the richness, thickness, and complexity of the text, that is, to miss both the problematic nature and the subtle interiority of the text. Given such initial propensities, it is paramount in exegetical study to see the text whole as a system of interrelated signs, to recognize that there is a lot going on in the text that pushes beyond historical explanation and at least postpones theological certitude for a spell.

Focus on the Text

In general, my pedagogical approach is to engage in "close reading," to invite students to slow down and pay attention to the artistic detail of the text. It is not easy to counter the charge that close reading is entirely subjective, but there are methods and disciplined practices that can be learned in apprenticeship and replicated from one text to another. Thus, a measure of methodological self-awareness is important. It goes without saying that a historical-critical perspective on a text provides a frame of reference for students for whom the text is relatively undifferentiated. Most of the time, this can be done rather quickly and does not need to be labored. Moreover, if sustained work is done on a biblical book, the historical-critical data can be assumed without excessive reiteration.

The two emerging methods in Bible study that move the discussion through and beyond historical-critical questions are enormously helpful. First, *sociological criticism* helps students see that texts characteristically act as advocates within a contested field; that is, they reflect vested interests that are likely rooted economically and politically. Such texts—every text?— seek to produce a certain version of reality that is in dispute with other versions of reality that may or may not be available to us. Such texts, moreover, continue to advocate as they are situated in the canon and as they function as canon in the ongoing work of the reading community. An important outcome is the discernment that there are no "innocent" texts, just as there are no "innocent" interpreters, even among those who claim they are doing "objective" reading. Such a perspective offers a mildly deconstructive corrective to "absolutes" that have arisen too quickly or too easily.

Rhetorical criticism is a second emerging method of enormous importance. Because I am educated as a rhetorical critic, it may be no surprise to the reader that I find this way of approaching a text not only fruitful but faithful. This approach focuses not on the "cognitive outcome" of the text (though there finally are cognitive outcomes) but on the artistic processes that operate in the text and generate an imagined "world" within the text. Such artistic attentiveness takes seriously the exact placement and performance of words and phrases, of sounds and repetitions that give rise to an alternative sense of reality that was not available without this particular configuration of words and images. What may emerge from such a study is an awareness that the text does not and does not intend to "match" what "happened back then." Rather, the text is a careful act of artistic imagination whereby what is "back there" is given in a trope, a reality affected by its phrasing in a certain form, shape, and tone. While texts are not endlessly indeterminate, the recognition that texts are generative acts of artistic imagination suggests that interpretation requires and evokes rooted, emancipated imagination in every subsequent reading.

While there is good literature on both sociological and rhetorical perspectives, characteristically *the text itself* becomes the focus of attention as we learn to ask fresh questions of the text.[1] Such a focus is quite different from the much older historical study, which seldom got around to the text but focused rather on books about the text. Focus on *the text itself* is not without discipline, nor is it anti-intellectual or uncritical. It is, however, democratic in contrast to older methods that encouraged a kind of expert consciousness. In these newer approaches everyone can look at the text and see something. These methods enable readers to look in informed and disciplined ways.

The Rudiments of Exegesis

Every teacher of exegesis has a guideline of methods for students, some complicated and exacting. I have been working for a long time on such a guideline with the intention of streamlining it, so that even busy pastors can engage in careful reading without being bogged down in excessive steps that are not doable in reality but merely produce a sense of inadequacy. I admit that my brief guideline is thin, but it is thick enough for pastoral interpreters, who must cope with the reality of vocational pressures. After the brief but essential matter of the text's historical location, I invite students to take three steps in interpretation.[2]

First, I ask students to do a *rhetorical analysis* of the text, to notice what words are where, how they function together to create a "world." It is often difficult to pay attention to words in an intricate, intentional design, for our wont is to take words in isolation from each other, or to look for larger meanings without reference to the concreteness of the words. The point of rhetorical criticism is to notice that the text—and the text-maker—is not only saying but *doing* something, generating a "world" that exists in rhetorical presentation. I find it most helpful to have students produce a chart showing the interconnectedness of words in the text. While it is preferable to work with Hebrew, a great deal can be done with an English translation. With attentiveness to the text and with modest skills in Hebrew, a student's chart tends to be a mix of English and some key Hebrew terms.

Second, students are asked to do a *word study,* to focus on the freight carried by particular words that emerge as important in rhetorical analysis. This task is often not easy for students, for the temptation is to find the term in a concordance and write down all the other uses. That, of course, is by itself a useless activity. A concordance is indeed the right tool, but the task is to locate, through a process of examining many uses, one or a few uses that show the term of the text being used elsewhere in ways that relate to, parallel, or illuminate the text under consideration. Such a search is frustrating, for it means not only checking many uses but also reading enough of other uses to find viable points of contact.[3]

Word study is a way of entering into "intertextuality," whereby wording, phrasing, or imagery in one text alludes to another, perhaps quoting or being quoted or perhaps offering a less precise correlation.[4] The outcome is to situate the text in a network of other texts, so that while the text is the point of singular attention, it is not isolated.

Third, when rhetorical analysis has noticed the *artistic imagination* in the text and its generative work, and when word study has uncovered the text's *intertextual* relations, I ask students to ponder the question, *What vested interest is operative in this text?* I intend the question to be taken in a quite open way. The answer may be a truth claim offered in good faith, or it might be a theological conviction stated with passion, or it might be a bad-faith assertion serving political, economic interest. The purpose of the question is to help students consider the ways in which *ideological forces* are at work in our best theological claims and in our most faithful interpretation. Of course, the answer may not indicate any vested interest. Even so, pursuing the question is a gain. For if the text is in any way an advocate, one can most often imagine its foil, the counterurging that the text opposes. And if one can locate urgency and imagine counterurgency, then one can also anticipate what function a text might perform in contemporary usage, perhaps to comfort the afflicted or afflict the comfortable, perhaps to comfort the comfortable or afflict the afflicted. In the end, the text is seen as an effective social force and not merely an innocuous statement.

All these elements of study—the *force of imagination,* the *hosting of intertextuality,* and the *pondering of ideology*—focus on the concrete text as such. Indeed, I ask my students as they focus on a particular text to imagine that this is the only text we have. If this *were* the only text, what would we have disclosed of God, or world, of church, or self? The text needs to be entertained in its own starkness before rushing to more general claims that inevitably tone down its particularity. Only after such an exercise do I ask students to reposition the text in the larger scopes of canon and ongoing confessional traditions. The intention of such a strategy is to encourage the most radical nonfoundational possibility, to engage the text without reference to protective universals.

A Text Case

I cite the poetic unit of Jeremiah 5:14-17 as an example of what I do with students—seminarians, pastors, laypeople—in pursuing my three-step interpretive procedure.

Rhetorical analysis. In prophetic rhetoric, the initial "therefore" (v. 14) indicates a prophetic sentence now to be pronounced on the basis of the indictment offered in vv. 12-13. Judah has declared God to be passive and irrelevant and so has made the prophets of Yhwh irrelevant as well. The sentence of judgment is the decisive self-assertion of Yhwh, who, according to prophetic conviction, is never passive or irrelevant. The one who speaks, the "God of Hosts," is capable of two powerful "I" statements, "I am making . . . I am bringing," each introduced by the attention-getting particle "Behold" (*hinneh*). These two statements correlate with the two indictments of vv. 12-13. The God who *brings* is not passive; the prophet who *speaks* is not "wind." The oracle of punishment contradicts and gives the lie to both preferred assumptions, for which Jerusalem stands condemned.

The two self-announcements of Yhwh lead to the term "nation" (the leitmotif of the poem), an aggressive, inscrutable historical-military force on the horizon of weak, helpless Judah, appearing at the behest of the self-announcing God. The term "nation" (*gôy*) occurs four times in v. 15, each modified by a powerful, ominous qualifier: "far away," "enduring," "ancient," with an unrecognized language. Inserted between the first and second uses of the term "nation," moreover, is the vocative "House of Israel," a pregnant contrast between the unnamed nation, so ominous, and the named House of Israel, as bereft of adjectives as it is of staying power.

After the divine "I" of v. 15, YHWH appears no more in the poem. Now the definitive player is the "ancient, enduring nation" that acts aggressively against the "House of Israel" at the behest of YHWH. The full attention of the listener is focused on this nation, given a characterization of threat and awe not unlike the Joban monsters (Job 40:15-24; 41:1-34). In the face of that coming threat, "House of Israel" does not know (yd^c) and does not understand ($šm^c$). That is, Israel is a helpless recipient of the threat, unable to make a serious response and offer serious resistance.

Now the dominant rhetorical accent is on "they/their"—nothing of YHWH, nothing of the House of Israel. Verse 16 characterizes military power, and v. 17 details the certain effect of that military power: they shall "eat up" (four times). The imagery is of a marauding, destroying, reckless invading force. The fourfold verb is matched by a series of four word pairs—harvest/food, sons/daughters, flocks/herds, vines/fig trees—that concretely characterize the rapacious action of an occupying army and that together picture everything on which the community depends—its food supply, its economy, its security, and indeed its children. The rhetorical effect of the fourfold statement is cumulative. Each word pair intensifies the previous statement of loss, until all is lost, all is helpless, all is confiscated.

After the fourfold "eat up" in v. 17, the poem turns abruptly to a different verb in v. 18, which the NRSV renders "destroy" but is better rendered "forcibly seize and occupy."[5] Before the savage sword, even the fortified cities of Judah are helpless because of their false trust. The penultimate positioning of "trust" in the poem before the concluding "sword" is a remarkable move, because the term "trust" reintroduces the theological dimension of allegiance to YHWH that has been absent in vv. 15-17. Israel is helpless, not because of poor military preparation but because of its dismissal of YHWH (v. 12), for which Judah stands indicted. The term "trust" at the end of the poem points to false trust, the theological frame in which the coming military threat is to be interpreted.

A rhetorical analysis of the passage is readily reducible to a chart so that the entire system of signs can be seen together.

Therefore: YHWH, God of Hosts
    Because. . .

Behold (*hinneh*) . . . I am making
　Behold (*hinneh*) . . . I am bringing
　　gôy from afar . . . O House of Israel
　　gôy enduring
　　gôy ancient
　　gôy you do not know
　you do not understand (*šmᶜ*)
　　Their quiver . . . like a tomb
　mighty warriors (*gibbôrîm*)
　　They devour . . . harvest and food
　　They devour . . . sons and daughters
　　They devour . . . flocks and herds
　　They devour . . . vines and fig trees
　　They destroy (*yrš*) with a sword . . . fortified cities in which you
　　　trust (*bṭḥ*).

It is difficult at the outset to give students freedom to exercise their read-ing capacity, to assure them that there is no right way, to allow them enough imaginative latitude to articulate what they see and hear in the text. In a pedagogical situation I invite students to present, share, and comment on their charted analyses, and then to pay attention to other student presen-tations. In the process students begin to notice not only the peculiar nuances but also the constants that recur in the text.

The process of rhetorical analysis is not completed until a student reflects on what is seen through the analysis. In this case, two observations arise from my analysis.

1. The subject of the oracle moves from YHWH, God of Hosts, to the unnamed nation. This poetic articulation of double agency (God and his-torical agent) makes clear that God's work is done in and through histori-cal processes. Such double agency, accomplished so easily in the poetry, connects YHWH's purposeful governance to a concrete political-military force, a quite particular reference but one left open in the poetry for other particularities by remaining unnamed.

2. The oracle is dominated by the fourfold "eat up," which may corre-spond to the fourfold *gôy* and be further reinforced by the four word pairs of v. 17. The life of Judah, in all its treasured materiality, will be profoundly diminished until the life of the community is terminated.

Linguistic analysis. The second step is to *focus on words* that arise through rhetorical analysis and are found to be crucial for the text. In this case, a beginning point might be an investigation of "eat up" (*ʾkl*). It is, of course, impossible in a streamlined study to consider all uses of the term. Nonetheless, a quick scan of the concordance suggests that the fourfold usage of "eat up" in our text is situated in a tradition whereby the verb is employed to speak of historical destruction credited to YHWH. The verb frequently appears with "devouring fire," as in Jeremiah 17:27, but often enough as a "devouring sword," as in our text. Rootage may be found in the stylized curse element of Leviticus 26:38. The usage is prominent in prophetic oracles where the verb variously has as subject YHWH, the nations, foreigners, aliens, or more specifically Assyria or Babylon (see Hos. 7:9; 11:6; Isa. 1:7; Jer. 10:25; 12:12; 50:7, 17; 51:34). Such usage includes particular reference to the temple in Psalm 79:7. Most important, beyond the particular scope of our oracle of judgment, the verb also speaks of YHWH's judgment on the nations, so that the God who judges Israel is the same God who reverses field against Israel's enemies (Isa. 31:8; Nah. 2:13; 3:14 [13]; Jer. 30:16). The sum effect is to characterize YHWH's devastating capacity in the historical process, most often (but not always) through human agency.

A second term worthy of study is "trust" (*bṭḥ*) at the end of the poetic unit. I have suggested that the term functions as an indictment but also implies the alternative of trust in YHWH that was previously available to Judah. The most spectacular use of the term occurs in the mocking speeches of the Assyrian Rabshakeh in Isaiah 36:4-10 and the related passages where the NRSV translates the term "rely." The Assyrian asserts that Israel can choose whom to trust, even though Assyria proposes a bad candidate. The same issue is evident in the doxological contrast of Psalm 146:3-5, where the same term appears. Our text affirms that Israel opted for a poor loyalty when it could have chosen otherwise and thereby chosen life.

While the verb "eat up" is a sign of YHWH's decisive governance, "trust" is a reminder of Judah's distorted loyalty. Attention might then be given to the four word pairs that indicate what is at stake (v. 17). Of the four word pairs, the first is least familiar. The others, sons and daughters (Isa. 43:6; 56:5; Jer. 7:31; 16:2; 29:6; 32:45; Joel 3:8; Amos 7:17), flocks and herds (Gen. 33:13; Jer. 31:12; Jonah 3:7; Hos. 5:6), and vines and fig trees (1 Kgs. 4:25; 2 Kgs. 18:31; Ps. 105:33; Hos. 2:12; Joel 1:12; Mic. 4:4; Hag. 2:19; Zech. 3:10), occur frequently, most often as an *inclusion* bespeaking totality. In the tradition of Jeremiah, attention can be given to Jeremiah 3:24, which contains two of these word pairs with the verb "devour," indicating huge loss. The other text to which I am drawn is 1 Samuel 8:10-17. The word pairs are not listed here, but the enunciation of what is to be confiscated by the anticipated monarchy is not remote from our list of losses to the invading empire.

These three forays into specific words help to intensify our sense of the judgment pronounced in Jeremiah 5:17. The verbs and the four word pairs together communicate the loss that is to come in radical and concrete ways, and the term "trust" roots the coming military disaster in theological reality.

Ideology. Finally, students are urged to ask of the text, *Whose vested interest is voiced here?* We may accept, for our immediate purpose, that in Jeremiah 5 the voice is that of the prophet named Jeremiah, that his oracle is offered and taken as divine utterance. Our question, however, requires us to think more broadly about the location of the prophet. We may say that the voice sounded through the prophet reflects an opinion deeply critical of royal policy (and its social by-products), an opinion that is provisionally sympathetic to Babylonian imperial policy, which threatens Judah and is seen as a vehicle for Yhwh's sovereign intention. Such public opinion may be concretely situated in the family of Shaphan (see Jer. 26:24; 36:10-12) or critically in the circles of what became "the Deuteronomists." In any case, such a social location identifies the poetic oracle as one side of a deeply contested political dispute in Jerusalem.[6]

It is easy enough to see how this expression of political opinion, which views the destruction of Jerusalem as a result of self-indulgent socioeconomic policy, came to be accepted as a normative, theologically decisive judgment in the canonizing process. The canonizing community accepted this political position as a theological verity, one matched by later texts in the tradition of Jeremiah itself, suggesting that the radical judgment against Jerusalem voiced here is penultimate. Ultimately—in the tradition of Jeremiah—it is the *gôy* far away that is devoured according to the will of Yhwh (see Jer. 30:16).

Conclusions

This reading exercise, typical of the pedagogical practice, is doable without great technical competence or a host of tools. It requires only a concordance and is genuinely democratic, for in my experience, with a bit of instruction and encouragement, those who are willing to look at a text are able to begin the process of seeing alertly what is happening in the text.

This procedure is streamlined and does not argue every interpretive point into the ground. A closer, more exacting exegesis is also possible. I am convinced, however, that what is needed is a way in which the text can be seriously engaged by busy people who will do nothing if the outcomes of technical exegesis are seen to be no match for the costs entailed. My three-step pedagogy intends to be pragmatic in the service of those who will do something discerning with the text, but not everything.

Some readers will notice that I have not spent much time or energy on historical-critical matters. I believe that the pertinent data for the tradition of Jeremiah concerning the impending threat of Babylon, the failure of the Davidic dynasty, and consequently the "rolling corpus" of Jeremiah under the aegis of the Deuteronomists can be handled quickly and summarily, because what counts is what is going on in the text itself. In this particular text, historical-critical interpretation has traditionally been preoccupied with the "Scythian" question, an endless, fruitless effort to identify the enemy referenced here.[7] In retrospect it is clear that the "Scythian" definition of the interpretive question has been not only unproductive but completely wrongheaded. It is important that the enemy in the text remain unnamed, even if concretely intended, making it possible to reuse the poem in many crises involving many enemies. My judgment is that a quick historical-critical orientation is enough, because the text itself is more interesting than any such question.

The student is now ready to let the text be a script to inform contemporary, faithful imagination. With Scripture, our work is not what the text "meant" but what it "means." If interpretation is formed around what the text "means," students—seminarians, pastors, laypeople—are willing and able in various ways to let the text guide a redescription and reimagination of the public world in which they practice faith. Everybody can see the "devouring" that now happens in the global economy. Everybody can enumerate the "treasures" always at risk in a devouring world. Everyone can entertain the question about trust and misplaced trust. And with the text, everyone can for an instant take the world as an arena of Yhwh's purposes. How odd and how wondrous that in the midst of *gôy* and "eating up" and vines and fig trees, we are privileged to have a poem of illumination, confrontation, and redescription that we take to be God's own utterance. The text itself is cause enough for wonder. A second wonder is that teachers can help people find access to the text—and, given access, we find ourselves addressed and reimagined by this "strange new world" of the Bible.

6

The Social Nature of the Biblical Text for Preaching

The preacher stands midway in the process of the biblical text. The process of forming, transmitting, and interpreting the biblical text is a creative process at its beginning, midpoint, and ending. The creative dimension of the process means that the text and its meanings are always being produced. They never simply exist. They are not just "there," but the community is continually engaged in a willful act of production of meaning. That is what is meant by "the social nature" of the text. It is the community at work with the text.[1]

The Textual Process

The textual process has three identifiable points, each of which is creative, that is, productive. First, it begins in *the formation of the text,* that is, the way in which the text has reached its settled canonical form. Historical-critical methods of study are concerned with the ways in which the community, through editors, redactors, scribes, and traditionists, has put the text together. Whatever view we have of the creation of the text, we know that human hands and hearts have been at work in its formation.

Second, the end of the textual process is *the reception and hearing of the text* which is done by the congregation. We know that such listening is a complex matter, because communication in general is exceedingly complex, and reception of the text is a specific moment of communication. No one can any longer imagine that the preaching of the text is heard by members of the community just as it is spoken, or just as it is intended by the preacher. The listening is done through certain sensitivities that may distort, emphasize, enhance, or censor, depending on the particular situation of the listening community. The listening community is engaged in a constructive act of construal, of choosing, discerning, and shaping the text through the way the community chooses to listen.[2] The text thus construed may or may not be the text that is the one offered by the speaker. That is, the text heard may be quite different from the one proclaimed.

It is the third identifiable point, *the midway process of interpretation,* that interests us in this paper. Interpretation is all the action between formation and reception that seeks to assert the authority and significance of the text. This interpretive step includes the classical creeds and commentaries, the long history of theological reflection, contemporary scholarship, and contemporary church pronouncements. Above all, it includes the interpretive work of the preacher in the sermon. It is in the sermon that the church has done its decisive, faith-determining interpretation. The sermon is not an act of reporting on an old text, but it is an act of making a new text visible and available. This new text in part is the old text, and in part is the imaginative construction of the preacher, which did not exist until the moment of utterance by the preacher.[3] Like a conductor "rendering" Beethoven so that that particular music exists only in that occasion, so the preacher renders a text so that it only exists in that particular form in that particular occasion of speaking.[4]

These three dimensions of the textual process—*formation, interpretation, reception*—are all creative acts in which the text and its meaning are not only an offer made to the community, but are a product generated in the community. Interpretation and listening, as well as formation, are creative acts of construal. This creative aspect of the text is unavoidable and should be welcomed as an arena in which faith is received, discerned, and made pertinent. Some may think such creative possibility in interpretation is an aberration to be avoided. It cannot be avoided. Nor should it be avoided, because it is the way in which God's Word is alive among us. Interpretation can and must be creative and imaginative if it is to be interpretation and not simply reiteration. Listening is inevitably an imaginative act of response in which the listener does part of the work of rendering the text.[5]

This entire creative process consists of two factors that are in tension and that make our topic both important and difficult. The textual process is at every point *an act of faith.* In faithful interpretation, the entire process is governed by the work of God's Spirit of truth. It is this that permits interpretation to be an act of faith. The promise of faith is the conviction that in its formation, interpretation, and reception the text is a word of life that makes a difference. No part of this process is undertaken on the pretense that this is objective or neutral or a matter of indifference.

Those who formed the text did so because they knew the traditions to be important and they judged them to be true and urgent for the ongoing generations of the community. That is the theological meaning of the canon. The subsequent interpreter who received the text has labored diligently over the text, as does the contemporary interpreter, because faith requires interpretation. Interpreters in every generation, even those who have exercised enormous freedom, have intended their work as an effort in fidelity. Finally, those who receive the text, the assembled community of listeners, gather in an act of faith. The church gathers around the text because it takes the text seriously. It listens eagerly (and therefore imaginatively) to try to hear the nuance in the text that is God's live Word now. Participants at every point of the textual process are unembarrassed about the premise of faith. All parts of the textual process are undertaken primarily to ensure the powerful, authoritative presence of the Word among members of the community.

It is also the case, however, that every part of the textual process is *an act of vested interest*. Exegetical study is now learning this insight from sociological criticism.[6] The textual process does not proceed objectively or neutrally, but always intends to make a case in a certain direction. Just as there is no "exegesis without presuppositions,"[7] so there is no textual activity that is not linked to a vested interest. The formation of the text itself has been an act of vested interest. Certain pieces of literature are selected, gathered, shaped, and juxtaposed in different ways to argue certain points. We know, for example, that the early community around Moses authorized certain texts that served the interest of liberation.[8] The exodus narrative is surely put together by proponents of a radical liberating faith. In the time of Solomon, other texts were celebrated because they legitimated the concentration of power in the monarchy and served to enhance the inequality of the status quo.

In like manner the interpretive act is notorious for being an act of vested interest. There is no doubt that "liberation communities" in the third world approach every text with an inclination that tilts interpretation in a specific direction. We are coming to see that even what we regarded as the objective scholarship of historical-critical method has not been objective but has served certain social interests and enhanced certain epistemological biases.[9] We are coming to see that what we thought was objective has in fact been the "class reading" of male Euro-American theology. Richard Rohrbaugh has offered stunning and convincing evidence that many of the great American preachers of the last generation handled texts so that the sharp and disconcerting social dimension that questioned our economic commitments was ignored. As a result, the text was interpreted in other directions that probably were serious distortions.[10] This was not intentional distortion on the part of the preacher. It is simply that our faith is regularly embodied in a vested interest that we ourselves are not always able to discern.

Finally, listening to the text and its interpretation is an act of vested interest. Over time we select the mode and substance of interpretation that we want to hear. We select our interpretive tradition. We read certain books, subscribe to certain journals, even join or avoid certain churches in order to find a textual interpretation congruent with our vested interests which we can receive and hear and to which we can respond.[11]

The textual process of formation, interpretation, and reception is therefore always a mixture of faith and vested interest. To study "the social process" is to pay attention to that vexed combination. That the textual process is skewed by interest requires a hermeneutic of suspicion.[12] That the textual process is an act of serious faith permits a hermeneutic of retrieval. Despite the identification of these two hermeneutics, the matter remains complicated and problematic because we cannot practice one hermeneutic first and then the other. We cannot first sort out vested interest and then affirm faith, because vested interest and faith always come together and cannot be so nicely distinguished. We must simply recognize the fact that the two always come together, even in the midst of our best efforts of discernment and criticism.

The creative act of formation-interpretation-reception *produces a text*. As it produces a text, it forms an imaginative world in which the community of the text may live. That production of a text is a willful, intentional act generated by faith and vested interest. That the text is "produced" means a *different* text could have been formed, interpreted, or received. This means that the produced text is never innocent or disinterested. But it is this text, never innocent or disinterested, that we take as the normative text for our faith. The text that has been produced and made canonical is the only one we have. It is to that text we must obediently and critically attend.

When the community has thus produced a text, it is the task of the community to *consume the text*, that is, to take, use, heed, respond, and act upon the text. The entire process of the text, then, is an act of *production and consumption* whereby a new world is chosen or an old world is defended, or there is transformation of old world to new world.[13] The purpose of using the categories of production and consumption is to suggest that the textual process, especially the interpretive act of preaching, is never a benign, innocent, or straightforward act. Anyone who imagines that he or she is a benign or innocent preacher of the text is engaged in self-deception.[14] Preaching as interpretation is always a daring, dangerous act, in which the interpreter, together with the receivers of the interpretation, is consuming a text and producing a world.

The world so produced is characteristically a world made possible by faith, but it is a world mediated through vested interest. Thus, the text never only says, but it does. What it does is to create another world of perception, value, and power that permits alternative acts. Great attention must be paid to vested interest and its impact on perception, value, and power, because vested interest has an enormous power to guide the textual process in certain directions. It is this dangerous, inevitable drama of the text that is referred to under the rubric "social nature." As both member and leader of the community, the preacher is necessarily involved in this dangerous, problematic production and consumption of texts through which worlds are chosen and life is transformed.

The Classic Tradition of Sociology

The classic tradition of sociology illuminates the lively shaping action of the community on the text.[15] It is important to recognize that sociology arose as a distinct discipline in response to a specific social crisis. That is, sociology is not simply the general study of human community, but from its beginning was a discipline preoccupied with a particular set of awarenesses and problems.[16] The startling changes in human consciousness that came in the seventeenth, eighteenth, and nineteenth centuries, which are associated with the Enlightenment and modernity, have made us aware that the world in which we live is a social contrivance that carries with it important costs and gains. Sociology is essentially a critical discipline that has exposed the deceptive notion that the social world is an absolute given arrangement, by bringing to visibility the ways in which society continually constructs itself. At the outset sociology as criticism continually constructs itself. (At the outset sociology as criticism was aimed against traditional notions of the absolute givenness of social life that were legitimated by religious orthodoxy. These notions, as sociological study made clear, also brought with them the legitimacy of an absolutist economic and political orthodoxy.[17])

Sociology was therefore initially addressed to the mystification of a religion that claimed and pretended the world was a given. At the same time, however, sociology tended to be blind and inattentive to a scientific orthodoxy that posited a new social given; this time, objective, rational, neutral, and technological—all the things we have come to label as positivistic.[18] Critical sociology emerged to deal intentionally with the naïve positivism of much social science; it has become clear that the new "objective" world is as confused as the old religious world, and as incapable of seeing as operative its own ideology.[19] Critical sociology can help us see that the vested interests and ideological defenses of "scientific objectivity" are as dangerous and dishonest as the old absolutes of religion.

This shift from the old world of religious tradition and convention to the new world of technical control is a theme that has preoccupied the classical tradition of sociology. This theme has been articulated in various forms. We may mention its appearance in the three progenitors of the classical sociological tradition.

1. Karl Marx addresses the social alienation caused by capitalism and the role of religion in legitimating social structures that are exploitative and dehumanizing.[20] Marx's great insights are that economic arrangements are decisive for all social relationships and that religion functions primarily to legitimate economic arrangements. Clearly Marx was preoccupied with the shift in economic relations that tore the economic dimension away from the general fabric of social life.[21] He saw that this shift was deeply destructive of the possibility of human community. The emergence of alienation as a central product of the modern world is at the center of Marx's analysis. The textual tradition entrusted to the preacher has as a task the discernment of that alienation and the consideration of alternatives to it. The preacher must pay attention to the ways in which the text and its interpretation participate in the process of alienation.

2. Max Weber sought to provide an alternative to Marx that did not identify economics as the cause of everything.[22] Weber paid particular attention to the new forms of social control and administration and the emerging power of bureaucracy. It would be a mistake, however, to interpret Weber (against Marx) as a friend of modernity. Like Marx, Weber saw the heavy toll that the structures and values of modernity would continue to assess against the possibility of humanness. The emergence of new forms of rationality preoccupied Weber. The emergence of destructive forms of rationality is also a struggle in the Bible, where covenantal modes of rationality are regularly offered against the temptations of naturalism and nationalism. In our present social situation, the connections Bellah has made concerning managerial rationality offer a suggestive critical insight for the preaching office.[23]

3. In a more conservative mode, Emile Durkheim was interested in the requirement of social cohesion for the survival of society.[24] In his classic study of suicide, Durkheim observed what happened in societies where the fabric of value and cohesion is exhausted and persons must live in a context of normlessness.[25] Durkheim's critique can cut two ways. Ours is a society that lives at the edge of normlessness, and on the other hand, we are a society that reacts to normlessness with a heavy-handed emphasis on

conformity. The crisis of normlessness and conformity in our culture sounds strangely reminiscent of the Mosaic crisis about freedom and obedience and the problematic of the law as Paul understood it. The preacher is cast in a social role as a voice of normativeness, in a society bereft of norms.

There are great differences among these three spokespersons for social possibility and pathology, but they all focus on the fact that societies have ways in which to articulate and distort certain kinds of truth that make human life possible or problematic. Social structure, order, and value are not objective givens. But they also are not simply connections that can be willfully and artificially wrought. They are, rather, the slow, steady work of formation, creation, and transformation by which a community orders its life of perception, value, and power.[26]

Responsive ← Interpretation → assertive

Interpretation as Social Construction

The act of interpretation takes seriously both the old treasured memory and the new demand of the situation. Interpretation seeks to mediate between tradition and situation. On the one hand, interpretation is always *responsive* to the situation, that is, commenting on the new social realities that are already established. On the other hand, interpretation is always *assertive*, saying something genuinely new and challenging the community to rethink and reperceive the newly established reality in light of the tradition. In modes of both response and assertion, interpretation is an imaginative act that articulates reality in a new way that had not been possible until the moment of speech. It is the speech that creates the possibility.

Sociology shows us that society is constantly reconstructing itself. While great attention therefore needs to be paid to the manipulation of power and the management of economic and political forces, we know that the primary mode by which a community reconstitutes itself is by its interpretation, by its reflection on ancient memory and tradition, and by its recasting of that memory and tradition in new ways that are resonant with the new situation.[27] All communities are always engaged in the process of interpretation. This is what ideology, propaganda, mass media, and civil religion are about. They are responses and assertions that are more or less creative, which seek to mediate a newness juxtaposed between tradition and situation.

In order to arrive at a better understanding of interpretation as a social act of reconstruction, several dimensions of critical exposition are particularly important.

1. Interpretation is unavoidably a communal activity. The whole community is involved in the process. Interpretation must take place if the com-

munity is to live and continue. Interpretation inevitably does happen because it is a main activity of the community. Sociology has helped us see that communities are always engaged in interpretive acts of reconstitution and reconstruction. That act of interpretation is characteristically a mixture of faith and vested interest.

With the coming of the Enlightenment and the rise of modernity, many have failed to understand the inevitability of interpretation. The fascination with so-called objectivity led to the mistaken notion that reality did not need to be interpreted. As reality did not need to be interpreted, it was mistakenly concluded that the biblical text could be read in a straightforward manner without interpretation. This is also the mistaken notion of those who want the U.S. Supreme Court to be "strict constructionists," that is, not to engage in interpretation. The kind of interpretation that denies it *is* interpretation is the most dangerous kind, because it is not then available for criticism.

2. The interpretative act of social reconstitution is what the biblical text itself is all about. That is, the text is not simply a factual reporting about what happened. In each of its statements it is an act of interpretative mediation whereby ancient Israel and the early church seek to reconstitute the community in the face of a new danger or crisis.[28] In ancient Israel the new situation is characteristically the new concentration of power and knowledge in the monarchy or the loss of monarchial power and knowledge in the exile.[29] In the New Testament the characteristic new situation is the interface between Jewish and Gentile Christians and the derivative problems of ethics and organization. In each case the new situation requires a total recasting of the memory in order to sustain the identity of the community.

The texts are not only response, however. They are also bold assertions in the face of the new situation. For example, in the Old Testament the Yahwistic theologians do not simply conform to the new social reality, but make a strong case that in the new situation Israel must understand itself as the bearer of a blessing.[30] In the New Testament, for example, Luke-Acts offers bold suggestions about how the church must understand itself and order its faith. That the Old and New Testament texts are both responsive and assertive means that they are deeply imaginative. They proclaim a social reality that did not exist until that moment of articulation. Moreover, because the text is deeply imaginative, it is probable that each such requesting of social reality is a mixture of faith and vested interest. Thus, the J writer is concerned to maintain a human vision against a monarchial enterprise of self-aggrandizement. Luke seems to have been concerned lest the early church become a sect aligned against the empire. The community over time has judged the vested interests of the texts (for example, J and Luke) to be faithful vehicles for faith and not acts of distortion. As a result, these specific texts have been judged authoritative and designated as canonical.

In the Pentateuch the documentary hypothesis of JEDP has been much misunderstood and maligned. It is an attempt to characterize the ongoing interpretive act of mediation that was under way in ancient Israel.[31] The J material, according to the dominant hypothesis, is an attempt to mediate the old memory in the affluent situation of Solomon. Similarly, the P tradition is an attempt to mediate the old memory in the despairing situation of exile.[32] These two moments, united monarchy and exile, require fresh interpretative acts or the old tradition will have been in vain. In the cases of both J and P, one can detect that this interpretive act is indeed a response to a social crisis, is an assertion in the face of the crisis, and is a remarkable act of imagination. It takes very little insight to see that in each case the mediation is a mixture of faith and vested interest.

In like manner the Synoptic Gospels are mediations of the old memory of the early church.[33] The Gospel of Mark faces the challenge of Roman imperialism; Matthew takes up the question of the relationship between Christians and Jews, or perhaps Jesus and the Jewish tradition; and Luke struggles with the Gospel in a Gentile world. These Gospel statements are clearly not theological absolutes (or we would not have these three variants), nor are they factual descriptions of what happened, but they are mediations that make available a new world in which the community may live joyously and faithfully.

3. In the creative, imaginative act of construction of reality, the interpreters, those who process the text, are dangerously engaged in two ways.[34] On the one hand, they are so engaged because they inevitably make responsive, assertive mediations in the midst of their own mixture of faith and interest. Interpreters are never interest free but always present reality in partisan ways and, indeed, cannot do otherwise. On the other hand, in the act of interpretation they also have their own world remade. They do not stand outside this process but are being self-interpreted in the very act of biblical interpretation. In this act of mediation, hermeneutics then make a new world possible. In hermeneutics as mediation, we thus bring together the "process of the text," which includes formation, interpretation, and reception, and the sociology of world-making through which the community reconstructs itself.

The key hermeneutical event in contemporary interpretation is the event of preaching. The preacher either intentionally or unintentionally is convening a new community. This recognition will help us see why preaching is such a crucial event not only in the life of the church, but in our society.

We must interpret to live. There is almost no other voice left to do interpretation on which society depends that is honest, available, and open to criticism. Most of the other acts of interpretation that are going on in our midst are cryptic and therefore not honest, not available, and not open to criticism. The preaching moment is a public event in which society reflects on what and who it will be, given the memory of this church and given a postmodern situation in society.[35]

4. In the handling of the text by the preacher as interpreter and by the congregation as receiver, the hermeneutical work of world-constitution is going on. The interpretive work is done through the preacher's mixture of faith and interest while the congregation is listening and responding in its mixture of faith and interest. All parties to this act of interpretation need to understand that the text is not a contextless absolute, nor is it a historical description, but it is itself a responsive, assertive, imaginative act that stands as a proposal of reality to the community. As the preacher and the congregation handle the text, the text becomes a new act that makes available one mediation of reality. That new mediation of reality is characteristically an act of fidelity, an act of inventiveness, and an act in which vested interest operates. Moreover, the preacher and the congregation do this in the midst of many other acts of mediation in which they also participate, as they attend to civil religion, propaganda, ideology, and mass media. They are incessantly involved in a complex of various interpretive, constructive acts, while claiming the interpretive act authorized by the Bible to be the normative one.

The Congregation and the Crisis of Modernity

The congregation that engages in interpretation (and with the interpretation embraces a certain refraction of the text) is not a contextless, undifferentiated unity. The congregation, as a community in crisis, gathers to decide one more time about its identity and its vocation. The people gathered have been bombarded since the last gathering by other voices of interpretation that also want to offer an identity and a vocation. In what follows I am focusing broadly on the typical mainline North American congregation, either Protestant or Catholic. I assume such a congregation, because that is the context in which I characteristically do my interpretation. Certainly other congregational settings could be assumed, and I do not imagine that this one is normative, or even preferable.

A different statement might be made in a different context, such as in post-Christian Western Europe, in totalitarian East Germany, or in oppressive El Salvador, but our congregation is not yet post-Christian, not in a totalitarian context, or faced with direct oppression. This congregation is a gathering of people who have been largely enveloped in the claims of modernity. It is a community with a memory and with a present reality. In the midst of this memory and this reality, the act of interpretation is undertaken one more time.

The memory is the memory about God and God's people, about the summons of ancient Israel and the baptism of the early church, about Jesus and the people of Jesus from his time until our time. That memory is about births given to barren women, bread given to desperate peasants, shepherds given to scattered sheep, forgiveness given to those immobilized by guilt. It is about deep inversions and strange power for daring obedience. This memory and the text that conveys this memory are the source and subject of our preaching.

But the memory around which the congregational gathering takes place is also somewhat distorted. In my own work I have studied the memories of David to show how those memories have been variously cast and how they have been articulated to accommodate various social settings and social possibilities.[36] The memory may be enmeshed in a nostalgic longing for normalcy and "the good old days," when life was simple and agrarian, settled, and well-ordered. That nostalgia is all intertwined with evangelical memory, so that the nostalgia has a vague religious feeling about it. There is a need to sort out the normative memory from this other vague yearning.

The present situation of the congregation needs careful attention. It is usually a situation of considerable affluence (even if some present are not affluent). The affluent ones are the ones who are competent and know how to generate income and move through the chairs to the seats of power. But the affluence and competence we treasure so much are matched by a profound fear—that the dollar will collapse, that the bomb will explode, that the Communists will attack. The affluence-competence factor invites us to "stand tall" and be secure; the fear syndrome undermines our confidence and we live our days in an inarticulate uneasiness. This interface of affluence-competence and fear distorts public issues. The matters of compassion and "justice for all" that are embedded in our public conscience have become shriveled. Our fear drives us to selfishness, greed, and vengeance. Along with public failure, we find an erosion of our personal sense of life, a restlessness that generates anxiety that drives us to greed, and finally to despair that it won't really work out. Our actual experience of our common life is not remote from the alienation of Marx, the technical rationality of Weber, and the normlessness of Durkheim.

There are many things to celebrate in this new world of competence and technical security. It boggles the mind to think how different we are from our grandparents and how much better off we are. But we are dimly aware that this new mode of life we value so much has caused us to jettison much that we previously valued. It is odd that the old festivals of solidarity wane, yet there is a persistent hunger for such occasions of solidarity. Old patterns of familiar and liturgical gatherings are less and less compelling in our society. Our young people ask about roles and careers, but vocation seems like an obsolete idea. We surprise ourselves when we entertain brutality as a policy option in the world, and vengeance now seems acceptable if aimed at the right people. We have become people we did not intend to become, and we are not fully convinced that this is who we want to be. Given our perception of the world, however, that is who we need to be if we are to "succeed" according to the norms we have embraced.

Such a community gathers for the act of interpretation. Even if we have never heard of the word "modernity," we sense in inarticulate ways that we embody much that is "modern." Much has been lost to us, even if much is gained. We gather to see if we can hold the gain and yet recover what is lost. We gather to see if the world of vocation and tradition, of birth and bread, of shepherds and forgiveness can be mediated to us in the midst of our disproportionate affluence and fear. We do not want to discard the old memory, as our modern world wants to do, but we do not want a flat reiteration of the old memory that pretends we are not affluent and not afraid. We do not want simply a nostalgia that does not touch any of the real problems, the ethics of our affluence and the moral dilemma of our fear. We yearn for a responsive, assertive, imaginative act of interpretation that recasts the memory in bold ways that will transform our situation.

Our discussion thus far suggests a convergence of four major factors in the act of interpretation. These reflect, on the one hand, our present general intellectual situation and, on the other hand, the specific situation of the church. I find it remarkable that these four factors, which are drawn from very different aspects of contemporary thought and life, should so powerfully intersect in relation to our interpretive responsibility.

1. The *textual process* itself is an act of regular recasting that includes both faith and vested interest.

2. The *sociological tradition* in its classic presentations concerns the problem of alienation (Marx), the problematic of rationality (Weber), and the emergence of normlessness (Durkheim). All of these conditions are part of the modern world, and we know them all firsthand.

3. The *task of interpretation* is the task of the community to mediate the tradition in ways that construe a new world, that permit a new ethic among us.

4. The *congregation is gathered* to see if the old memory can be articulated in ways that reconfigure our present social reality of affluence and competence, of fear and brutality, of restlessness and despair.

The preaching moment is a moment of great complexity, great danger, and great possibility. Present in that moment are the textual process, the sociological realities, the act of interpretation, the waiting congregation. Such a moment requires a strategy through which a new community might be summoned to a fresh identity and a bold vocation.

Options in Social Construction

The preacher in the act of interpretation and proclamation of the text is engaged in world-making. I find it most helpful to appeal to the phrase of Peter L. Berger and Thomas Luckmann, "the social construction of reality."[37] The community authorizes special persons to head and oversee the process of social construction. In our context, the minister (usually ordained) is authorized to lead the community of faith in its construction of reality. Such an act is an ongoing process of education and nurture, especially in liturgy.[38] This liturgical articulation is presented as objectively true. When it is also received in this way, this liturgically presented world may be internalized by members of the community as "mine." Thus, the process of appropriation includes the public action of the community and the personal internalization by the individual members who participate in the liturgy.

The second awareness from Berger and Luckmann is that the "life-world" so constructed is always under way and must be modified. New data, fresh perspectives, new experiences, and changed circumstances require recasting the life-world to keep it credible. If it is not regularly recast, the "old world" becomes disengaged from experience so that it either must live in protected, uncritical space (where it will be irrelevant), or it will be jettisoned as dead. It is the ongoing act of interpretation that recasts the life-world to keep the text credible. The preacher is engaged with the biblical texts in both elements, to sustain *the act of appropriation* and to engage in the ongoing *recasting* to keep the text credible.

This means that the purpose of interpretation and preaching is to present a life-world that is credible, that can be appropriated, out of which the community is authorized and permitted to live a different kind of life. As the text itself is a responsive, assertive, creative act, so the interpretation of the text is also a responsive, assertive, creative act. The purpose of the sermon is to provide a world in which the congregation can live. Indeed, the preacher is intentionally designated precisely to mediate a world that comes out of this text which endures through the generations. That world which the preacher mediates is one possible world out of many that could be offered. The offer of this world competes with other offers made by capitalism, by militarism, by psychologies of various kinds, by health clubs, by automobiles, by beers, and so on. Moreover, it is a possible world among many that might be articulated out of the Bible, so it makes a difference if the text mediated is a Mosaic or a Solomonic text.

Scholarship has found it helpful to speak of a typology of interpretative postures. We may speak of a primary decision, so that the interpretive act is either transformative or stabilizing, in the service of discontinuity or in the service of equilibrium.[39] The basis for that model is rooted in the social history of ancient Israel and is evidenced textually in the Old Testament tension between the transformative vision of Moses, which belonged to the earliest voice of liberated Israel, and the stabilizing tendency of royal theology, which sought to build institutions and establish a reliable social structure.[40] When the texts are read sociologically, this interpretive issue of transformation-equilibrium is enormously helpful. This Old Testament paradigm (as Gottwald has shown)[41] has important parallels to a Marxist class analysis, to Weber's construct of charisma and bureaucracy, and, I should suggest, also to Ferdinand Toennies's typology of *Gemeinschaft* and *Gesellschaft*.[42] The text itself in the Old Testament reflects this tension. The radical vision of Mosaic faith is in deep tension with the royal enterprise subsequently developed.

The tension exists between texts with different social locations.[43] The act of interpretation can and inevitably must deal with the ways in which the text destabilizes and transforms, or the way in which the text stabilizes and gives equilibrium. How the text is interpreted by the preacher and how the text is received in the congregation may depend on the vested interest of both preacher and congregation, which may or may not adhere to the position of the text itself. Texts may transform *and* stabilize. Sometimes the same text may function either to transform *or* stabilize, depending on context, interest and interpretation. Text and/or interpretation offer a world of transformation or equilibrium that enhances or diminishes a particular view of social reality. It is in the nature of the act of interpretation and therefore

of preaching to participate in these world-making acts, either knowingly or
unwittingly.

In what follows, I am presenting a typology of texts through which various texts will be interpreted. It is, of course, the case that the texts themselves are never as clear and unambiguous as is the typology. The typology
is useful only to the extent that it helps us see specific texts afresh; it should
never be imposed on texts.

The text can be an act of good faith, because both transformation and
stabilization are faithful acts of God and both meet deep human yearnings,
but the mediation of either comes through the vested interest of the
preacher. Whether the preacher will mediate a world of transformation or
equilibrium depends on many things, including what the preacher reads,
with whom the preacher eats, the economic history of the preacher, and
much else.

The texts will be received by the congregation as an act of faith. People
do come to church to hear and respond. The reception of a mediation of
either transformation or equilibrium happens through the interpretive
receptivity of the congregation. What happens, what the text can "do,"
depends on the propensity of the congregation. That will be determined by
many factors, but they include where and how the congregation is socially
situated, what travels have been taken, what part of the world has been seen,
how many members have experienced poverty, unemployment, crime, and
all sorts of social disruption—or conversely how strong is the social equilibrium in the experience and horizon of the congregation. All of these factors impinge in powerful, subtle, and complex ways upon the interchange
of text, preacher, and congregation. In the midst of the interchange, a new
world may be mediated.

In presenting the world of the text to the congregation, the preacher has,
according to this typology, four possible strategies. The typology assumes
that the text may be an offer of transformation or stability and that the congregation is likely to be in a situation of transformation or stability. The
available strategies in establishing an interface between the text-world and
the congregation are these:

1. To present "a world of transformation" to those who yearn and hope
   for transformation. This is done when oppressed or marginalized people are invited to hope for the basic changes of social reality that are
   given in the texts of transformation.

2. To present "a world of equilibrium" to those who wait and yearn for
   transformation. This is done when oppressed or marginalized people

are invited to accept and participate in the present regime as their proper duty and their only hope. The present order is then presented as the best chance for any change, but it will be change within that order that is accepted as non-negotiable.

3. To present "a world of transformation" to those who value the status quo and do not want the world changed. This is when those who benefit from present social arrangements are called, in the face of that benefit, to submit to change as the will and work of God.

4. To present "a world of equilibrium" to those who crave equilibrium and regard the present social world as the best of all possible worlds, a world decreed by God. This is done when religion becomes a comfortable endorsement of the status quo.[44]

Each of these strategies is possible, and each reflects a decision about the thrust of the biblical text and how that thrust is to be related to the actual situation of the church.

Each of these four strategies is possible, and on formal grounds each is biblical. It is equally clear that the gospel gives criteria to sort out the various strategies and to see that all the possible strategies are not equally legitimate for genuine evangelical proclamation. The preacher is summoned by the gospel to present an imaginative Word that lives "out beyond" and challenges the taken-for-granted world of the congregation.

In presenting this typology, I am aware that the actual situation of any congregation is enormously complex. In every congregation there are those who welcome change, those who resist change, and those who are unsure. Moreover, there are various kinds of changes, each of which needs to be critically assessed. In addition, various preachers and pastors are inclined either to welcome or resist change, and that helps shape interpretation and preaching. My discussion intends not to deny or disregard all of that complexity, which must be honored and taken seriously.

For purposes of clarity, however, in what follows, I have chosen to deal only with the third and fourth elements of this typology. My sense is that these dimensions of interpretation bear particularly on the typical North American congregation. A church that does not want the world changed will either be offered a text-world of transformation that calls the present into question (#3 above), or a text-world that celebrates equilibrium (#4 above). To be sure, there are times in such a congregation when equilibrium is legitimate and a genuine offer of the text, but for now we have posed the question in another way. The preacher thus may appeal to texts that offer either equilibrium or transformation and in doing so must pay attention to the possible hearing of the gospel that will occur in the congregation if the text is heard as an abrasion or as an assurance.

The important interpretive point is that the text should be kept in conversation with what the congregation already knows and believes. At times, the purpose of interpretation is to evoke fresh faith for another world from that which the community already knows and believes. In the typical North American situation, it is often the case that the text should be interpreted to make available an imaginative world out beyond the one to which the congregation now clings. More often this is so because such congregations tend to be ideologically trapped in a social world at odds with the gospel. But this interpretation that calls for newness may, nevertheless, appeal to the deep and serious faith latent in the church.

In a world of war and violence, for example, equilibrium is not objectively true but is in fact an imaginative act of interpretation that has been established and accepted as true. The interpretive issue is whether to ally the gospel with that already accepted mediated world or to propose an alternative that may "ring true" but also will surely evoke conflict.

The strategy of the preacher, then, is to use texts in ways that legitimate the present perceived life-world, or to present a life-world that puts people in crisis by offering a challenge to their present view and posing an alternative. Both are needed, but different emphases probably need to be made in various circumstances.

Whatever strategy is undertaken, it is most important that the preacher—and hopefully the congregation—is aware that good preaching (which is an act of inventive world-construction) is fundamentally opposed to two tendencies in our culture. It is opposed to a false kind of objectivity that assumes the world is a closed, fixed, fated given. That assumption of objectivity is a great temptation to us, whether the claim is given in the name of religious orthodoxy or in the name of technological certitude. An evangelical understanding of reality asserts instead that all of our presumed givens are provisional and open to newness, a newness that may be enacted in the event of preaching.

The other tendency to which good preaching is opposed is a kind of subjectivity that assumes we are free or able to conjure up private worlds that may exit in a domesticated sphere without accountability to or impingement from the larger public world. Such a powerful deception among us seems to offer happiness, but it is essentially abdication from the great public issues that shape our humanness.

The preaching task is to be critical and challenging in ways that expose our present life-world as inadequate, unfaithful, and finally flat. This is to be done, however, in ways that neither become ideological nor simply terminate the conversation. Preaching is aimed not simply at this or that ethical issue, but seeks to cut underneath particular issues to the unreasoned, unexamined, and unrecognized "structures of plausibility" that are operative in the congregation. Such preaching is also to offer reassurances about the coherence of reality, but a reassurance that is not a legitimation of present arrangements, but an act of hope about another life-world available in the gospel. That life-world could offer the joy for which we yearn, which the present life-world cannot give. This offer of another world is the primary work of the gospel, for the gospel is news of another world. The articulation of that other world is unavoidably a critique of and a challenge to every present world. This "other world" that is announced in and mediated by the gospel is not "otherworldly" in the sense that it is in the remote future, in heaven, after death, or "spiritual." Rather, the "other world" is now "at hand" (Mark 1:15). It refers to the present rule of God, which calls us to a new obedience now and releases us from every other obedience in the here and now, for the sake of God's sovereign rule.

Texts of equilibrium are important to the formation of a new life-world. The creation narrative-liturgy of Genesis 1:1—2:4a is such a text. It asserts that the world is ordered, good, belongs to God, and is therefore reliable. When according to critical study, that text is set in the exile as an affirmation to Israelites and a polemic against Babylonian imperialism and Babylonian gods, the social function of that equilibrium emerges. The Genesis text asserts that the world belongs to God and therefore not to Babylon, not to their gods or their rulers. Moreover God rests, and Israel is mandated to rest. In that mandate it is asserted that Israelites in exile need not be endlessly anxious and frantic to become secure or to please Babylon, but can rest in God's sure rule. Thus, the text offers a world of well-ordered stability and equilibrium, in which Israel is invited to live. That well-ordered stability is not neutral, however, but is a counterequilibrium that invites Israel to break with seductive Babylonian offers of stability and equilibrium that cannot be true because the world does not belong to them. The community that lives within this text is given stability but also is summoned to a freedom outside Babylonian definitions of reality. That is, by an act of imagination, creation theology becomes a warrant for what the empire would regard as civil disobedience.[45] The capacity of exiled Israel to act freely depends on its acceptance of the world of this text. The text responds to exile, asserts against Babylon, and imagines an alternative world of faith in which life is possible. The congregation may be invited to sense what an

uncommon act of imagination this text is which dares to say that the world
belongs to YHWH, who is a God of rest and order, dares to say it even to
exiles whose life is disordered and restless.

Texts of transformation are equally important for a new life-world. The
healing-feeding narrative of Elijah in 1 Kings 17:8-24 is such a text.[46] It is
a text of disruption. It tells about this strange formidable man of inexplicable power who comes into the life of a poor widow. He deals with her
poverty by giving her food. He deals with death by raising her son to life.
He is perceived by the widow, by the narrator, and finally by us, as a bearer
of the power for life. This text evokes a question about this power, where it
is available, and on what terms. The narrative asserts that power for life is
not given through the royal regime but by this uncredentialed outsider.

This story destabilizes. It shatters the poverty-stricken, death-ridden
world of the widow. It breaks her assumptions and her habits. If we listen
attentively to the story when it is well told, it will also break our conventional assumptions, for it announces that the world is not the way we
thought it was. The critical effect of the narrative is to delegitimate the king
and his deathly rule and to invite us to another rule under the God of life.
But the story of disruption also turns out to be a story of affirmation. It
asserts that power is available, that life can be given, that food is offered.

Thus, the story responds to the failure of Ahab and his governance. It
asserts an alternative reality against Ahab's world. By an act of imagination,
a story of feeding and a story of healing have been mobilized as vehicles for
a different life-world. The narrative invites the listening community into a
new arena of existence in which God's power for life has enormous vitality
for new possibility, even though it is untamed and unadministered and we
cannot harness and manage it on our terms.

Every text proposes a life-world that may counter ours. Texts of equilibrium are needed to give people a sense of order, but such texts as Genesis 1:1—2:4a turn out to be invitations to transformation. Texts of
transformation are needed to give people hope that there is possibility outside present circumstances. But such texts as 1 Kings 17:8-24 turn out to
be invitations to a new equilibrium wrought only by the gospel. Texts of
both equilibrium and transformation are needed. In both cases it requires
not only the capacity to respond and assert but also the capacity for imagination in order to let these texts become truly effective. Characteristically
they invite the listening community out beyond the presumed world to a
new world of freedom, joy, and obedience.

Scripture: Sin & consequences

challenges: A. 3 Party (Yahweh)
[Exodus]
B. [Gen 2-3] Born
into a fallen world

Challenge
in
Scripture to the (Dominant
Read.)   C Lament Psalms
to
D. Job
E. God is Gracious
* Job is the challenge within
Scripture to Scripture

7

The Shrill Voice of the Wounded Party

I

The community that both generated and lived through the Old Testament was a community of intense moral passion. In its powerful theological rhetoric, it managed to hold together two insistent ethical claims. First, it bore ①witness to a sovereign God whose announced purposes aimed to bring every element and detail of the world under God's own sovereign purpose. This sovereign purpose included the *purity* of holiness and *justice* in the neighborhood. The God who enunciated this purpose did so with clarity and solemnity, and with severe sanctions for those who refused this purpose. That is, Israel's moral passion is rooted in the character of God.

Second, this community bore witness to the moral shape and moral reli-②ability of the world that is God's well-ordered creation. The world, they claimed, is not chaotic, anarchic, or nonsensical. It holds together not by sheer power or domination but by a moral order that can be known and honored. Those who live inside this moral order, which is willed by God, benefit from the blessings of God—security, dignity, prosperity, fruitfulness—all the blessings of a good life. Conversely, those who refuse this moral order or violate it are subject to sanctions and thereby receive all the threats of destructiveness—disease, disorder, abandonment, sterility, poverty, and a bad death.

This is a world, so the Old Testament affirms, that is beneficent to its adherents but severe to its violators. Israel arrived at clarity about a way of life and a way of death, and did not confuse the two. Moreover, Israel understood that there is no compromise or concession about this moral order that is intrinsic to God's creation. Such a characterization of God, world, and

103

human life may evoke in us a sense of the severity of this order, and of God who sanctions it. In the first instance, however, one should observe not the severity of this moral passion, but its reliability. This is a world that can be counted on. It is, moreover, a world into which one will want to bring children through narration, a world that can be trusted and lived in well. This is a world in which there is no caprice, and in which power or willfulness cannot overturn its moral shape. The fact that this God-ordered world allows no slippage is, of course, part of its problem. But the lack of slippage, before it is a problem, is precisely what commends to us this moral vision.

Israel articulated this God-authorized moral shaping of reality in two ways. First and most obviously, it is the commandments of Mt. Sinai (Exod. 20:1-17; Deut. 5:6-21), which articulated the most elemental norms for Israel's moral world. Of the encounter at Sinai, we notice three factors. First, the commands are on God's own lips. These are not the commands of the king or any other human agent. Second, the theophanic prelude of Exodus 19:16-25, according to the witness, assures that the commands are rooted and grounded in God's own holiness, out beyond human contrivance. Third, for these commandments, there are no sanctions. They are absolute, and disobedience to these commands is not even entertained as thinkable or possible.

Clearly the originary enunciation of moral purpose—behind which one cannot go for explanation—in the Ten Commandments received rich and sustained interpretive expansion in the Old Testament. In every generation, we may suppose, the foundational commands of YHWH, the God of Israel, needed to be applied, interpreted, and updated.[1] All of these elaborations are assigned in the Old Testament text to Moses, but it is commonly believed that the role of Moses was occupied in each generation by authoritative interpreters, who claimed to be extrapolating what was intended by and contained in the initial commands.[2] This expansive interpretation extended, especially in the tradition of Leviticus, to every zone of Israel's worship life, concerning laws of purity, priests, and acts of sacrifice. Correspondingly, in the tradition of Deuteronomy, interpretation expanded into every sphere of "civic" life—political, economic, judicial, and military.

It is evident that two sorts of things happened in the interpretive practice of on-going Israel. First, every detail of life is brought under the rubric of obedience. There is no facet of life in which the God of Sinai does not have a specific will and purpose. Second, severe sanctions are added to the laws, especially in the curse recitals of Leviticus 26:14-33 and Deuteronomy 28:15-68. In each of these collections, a recital of blessing is given for those who obey (Lev. 26:1-13; Deut. 28:1-14). But the positive sections of these two chapters are much briefer than the negative sanctions, and ongoing energy clearly applied primarily to the negative sanctions of curse. In the end, this tradition of commandment came to be summarized in a simple formula of obedience and life, disobedience and death:

> See, I have set before you today life and prosperity, death and adversity. If you obey the commandments of the Lord your God that I am commanding you today, by loving the Lord your God, walking in his ways, and observing his commandments, decrees, and ordinances, then you shall live and become numerous. But if your heart turns away and you do not hear, but are led astray to bow down to other gods and serve them, I declare to you today that you shall perish. (Deut. 30:15-18)

Israel also devised a second rhetorical system that articulated the moral coherence of the world under the rule of YHWH. In contrast to the commands of Sinai, the wisdom tradition was not so severe in its articulation, but it was as uncompromising in its teaching. The tradition of sapiential reflection, especially given in the book of Proverbs, does not appeal directly to the authority of God, nor to explicit religious sanctions.[3] The teachers of the wisdom tradition, rather, reflected on the experiences of life, whereby parents, teachers, elders, scribes, and sages had noticed the kinds of behavior that cause good things to happen and conversely, over a long period of time, the sorts of conduct that produce bad results. That is, no rewarding or punishing agent (God) needs to intervene in the process of ethics, for the choices people make seem to produce by themselves certain outcomes that come along with the choices.

Following Klaus Koch, scholars have hypothesized that there was in ancient Israel a theory of moral order that noticed a very close connection between "deed and consequence," so that the linkage between the two, over time, is predictable and inescapable.[4] Thus, for example, laziness results in poverty, having bad friends produces trouble. These linkages, moreover, are not mere happenstance, nor can they be understood simply in utilitarian ways. Scholars suggest that this moral linkage is reflective of creation faith.[5] The creator God has ordered the world so that all of life is a series of interrelated components, each of which carries inescapable moral implications. The sapiential tradition is not so heavy-handed as the tradition of command in enunciating the dangers of destructive behavior. It is nonetheless as insistent as the tradition of command in asserting that consequences of choices and actions are inevitable and non-negotiable.

Thus, Wisdom, as a personified voice, speaks in an appeal to its listeners, who are presumed to be children being inculcated into Israel's deposit of moral observations:

And now, my children, listen to me:
happy are those who keep my ways,
Hear instruction and be wise,
and do not neglect it.
Happy is the one who listens to me,
watching daily at my gates,
waiting beside my doors.
For whoever finds me, finds life
and obtains favor from the Lord;
but those who miss me injure themselves;
all who hate me love death. (Prov. 8:32-36)

The one who accepts the guidance of accumulated wisdom and acts accordingly is himself/herself wise. The one who violates this deposit of guidelines to right conduct is not a sinner but a fool. Action that violates wisdom is not wrong—it is stupid. The outcome nevertheless is the same as with the violation of the commands of Sinai: death!

These two instructional traditions likely emerge from very different social situations with different agendas, assumptions, and intentions.[6] It is, moreover, very late before the traditions of Torah and wisdom are merged, though one can see the tendency toward convergence much earlier.[7] Erhard Gerstenberger, however, has proposed that the two kinds of formulations of moral requirement and moral sanction, for all the difference in their developments, may have the same point of origin. He proposes, moreover, that the sapiential tradition is antecedent to the Sinai tradition.[8]

Thus, it may be the voice of the *paterfamilias* who says to the young, "Thou shalt not" (Jer. 35:6-7).[9] And it is the "Thou shalt not" of conventional family nurture and discipline that becomes the preferred form of command in the mouth of YHWH at Sinai. In the end, the communal instruction of Proverbs and the theological insistence of Sinai do converge. Both enunciate moral requirement, without acknowledging any suspicion or reluctance about the moral requirement, its source, its ideological interest, or its intention. Both traditions recognize and insist on unavoidable sanction, whether imposed by a punishing agent (God), or intrinsic to the act itself. And so both traditions create a world in which the one who violates the commands or departs from established wisdom is clearly in the wrong. That person, in effect, brings down trouble upon himself or herself and upon the community, from which there is no escape. It matters little whether one receives *curse as a sinner* or *consequence as a fool*. The order that promises life is unflinching in meting out deathliness to those who violate, disregard, or mock its requirements.

This account of moral coherence is indeed the stuff of Old Testament faith. It can be given different nuance, but the main line of argument is not in doubt. It is inevitable that such a plot of moral coherence will boldly locate fault, assign blame, and be unblinking in its administration of "justice" to violators. I do believe that in its main force, this cannot be denied. And there is no way to articulate a "doctrine of sin" concerning the Old Testament apart from this heavy, unaccommodating threat without cheating.

II

Having said that, it is clear that the community that both generated and lived through the Old Testament had to live in the real world. The real world that they inhabited, the same moral world we, their belated heirs inhabit, is not so neat and clean and one-dimensional as these dominant lines of moral coherence might suggest. As a result, one can detect a variety of literary-rhetorical strategies that intend either to open the moral arena of Israel beyond the tight traditions of command and wisdom to allow for the slippages that are inevitable in lived reality, or to destabilize these high, starchy claims in order to permit less severe ways of thinking. Here I will consider four such strategies, none of which in the end prevails, but all of which persist in the text of the Old Testament and, by their existence, de-absolutize the clean "either/or" of Deuteronomy 30:15-20 and Proverbs 8:32-36.

The first of these alternative strategies is found in the exodus narrative (Exod. 1–15).[10] This narrative functions as Israel's founding act of liturgical imagination.[11] In this well-known, oft-repeated narrative, there are three players, YHWH, who wills freedom for Israel; Pharaoh, who resists the freedom YHWH intends; and Israel, who is represented by Moses (and Aaron). The fact that there are three players (instead of the usual two of Sinai and wisdom) already indicates a more complicated plot with much more maneuverability in the moral conclusions that can be drawn.

In this plot our interest concerns the third party, Israel. About that player in the narrative, we will ask to what extent Israel is sinner and to what extent "sinned against." Israel is represented in the narrative by Moses, who is only a modest actor in the key transactions that take place between YHWH and Pharaoh. Israel is in a situation of wretchedness, being ruthlessly abused and helpless to extricate itself from the situation. What interests us is the fact that Israel is in this miserable situation through no fault of its own. Israel is not said to have sinned. Indeed, in Genesis 47:13-26, we are given a review of the economic-political processes by which such a marginated people as the Hebrews became slaves, inured to the imperial production system by the brutality of supply and demand, and by the manipulation of mortgages and taxes.

It is evident that Pharaoh and his agent, Joseph, have acted against the radical notion of justice fostered in Israel and have reduced the Israelites to pawns in the service of imperial projects. As long as the social struggle of the Israelites involves only two parties, Israel and Pharaoh, Israel is a hopeless, hapless victim of the enormous, ruthless power of Pharaoh, who obeys no law but his own. Thus, Israel is indeed a victim of a social circumstance that happened through no fault of its own, but it nonetheless suffers mightily at the hands of the perpetrator, Pharaoh.

The exodus narrative proper, however, does not get under way until Exodus 2:23-25. It is remarkable that in Israel's normative narrative, YHWH the God of Israel does not initiate the process of rescuing the salves. The initiatory act is taken by the slaves themselves, who "cry out." They do not cry out to anyone in particular. They simply give public voice to their unwarranted pain, and thereby evoke the interest of YHWH and mobilize the energy and authority of YHWH on their behalf. Throughout the remainder of the narrative that issues in Israel's freedom (Exod. 15:12-18, 20-21), the primary action is a struggle between Pharaoh and YHWH. Pharaoh is cast as the resolute victimizer of Israel, and YHWH is the champion and advocate of Israel, who, through no fault of its own, is in deep trouble.

There is indeed a sinner in this tale, but it is not Israel. It is Pharaoh. The sin of Pharaoh is to imagine that he is autonomous, that is, not subject to the moral restraints of YHWH and therefore free to act in his own arrogant, unrestrained self-interest (cf. Ezek. 29:3-7; 31:2-9; 32:2-16). In the exodus narrative, Pharaoh is the historical-political embodiment of evil, or in the creation language, Pharaoh is the power of chaos, the power that seeks to undo the orderliness of creation.[12] Pharaoh is "the power of sin," which has the capacity to work evil, suffering, and death upon the victim Israel. YHWH, conversely, is portrayed as the one who actively and powerfully intervenes against this Egyptian embodiment of evil on behalf of Israel.

Everything depends, in this narrative, on having three parties to the plot. And everything for Israel depends on YHWH demonstrating that he is stronger than Pharaoh. No doubt there were those moral teachers, in the service of Pharaoh, who did not reckon with YHWH as a character in the plot, who thought that the political drama of the empire included only two characters, Pharaoh and Israel. And when there are only two characters, it is simple enough to imagine, with ideological deftness, that Pharaoh is in the right and Israel gets what it has coming to it. In such a scenario, Israel suffers because it sins against Pharaoh. Everything depends on the third character, in order for the exodus event to be dramatically visible. The exodus narrative exists in order to assure that YHWH will be a palpable and available third party in the life and imagination of Israel. It is this third party that makes it possible to see Israel not as sinner but as sinned against by Pharaoh. What Israel requires as sinned against is not guilt, punishment and repentance, but an intervening advocate who can and will work justice and extricate Israel from this unwarranted suffering.

In important ways, the great prophets of Israel continue with the three-character plot of the exodus. To be sure, the prophets often simply "condemn Israel" as an undifferentiated entity. But more often, they make important social differentiations within Israel. More often they recognize that society is not uniformly bad and under judgment. And so they characteristically address the leadership, the urban elite of the Jerusalem establishment who prey upon the ordinary folk of peasant stock, and who by economic exploitation and juridical manipulation deny a livable life to the marginated, those pushed to the margins of power and dignity.[13]

Robert R. Wilson has suggested that some of the prophets, situated as they are among the socially "peripheral," are indeed advocates for the socially marginalized against the monied interest.[14] Thus Isaiah can rail, in sapiential rhetoric, against those

who join house to house,
who add field to field,
Until there is room for no one but you,
and you are left alone
in the midst of the land! (Isa. 5:8)

Clearly the charge made by the prophet is not aimed at everyone in Israel. For every house that is confiscated there is a displaced family of unprotected people who are sinned against. And Amos can speak to the powerful in Samaria:

Hear this word, you cows of Bashan
who are on Mount Samaria,
who oppress the poor, who crush the needy,
who say to their husbands,
"Bring something to drink!" (Amos 4:1)

In the purview of the prophetic poet are the poor and the needy, who have not sinned but are sinned against. Thus, the social drama staged by the prophets, perhaps a miniature replication of the drama of the exodus, consists in the ruthless, who sin in their acquisitive arrogance; the sinned against, who suffer at the hands of their exploiters; and YHWH, who is an advocate for the sinned against, against the sinners. Again, what is required is enough social differentiation to see that the social drama is a three-player plot. In the exodus narrative Pharaoh wanted to exclude YHWH as a third player, without whom there would be no exodus narrative. In the prophets, one propensity is to ignore the sinned against and then to assume that there are only two parties, YHWH and sinners. The social differentiation is manifest in the text, but our conventional reductionism tends to collapse the drama. And when such reductionism is practiced, the sinned against disappear from the plot. The prophets were evoked in Israel, as was the exodus narrative evoked in Egypt, precisely by the presence of the sinned against, who stand at the center of the drama. Israel regularly celebrates the willingness of YHWH to stand in transformative solidarity precisely with the sinned against. That is what justice is about in Israel's prophetic tradition.

III

We turn now to a second, more difficult, more crucial means whereby the witness of the Old Testament destabilizes the central ethical structures of "sin–punishment" and "deeds–consequences." Any consideration of sin in the Old Testament must of course take on issues rooted in the story of the garden in Genesis 2–3, and the subsequent interpretive history of that chapter.

The conventional reading of this subtle narrative directly reinforces the "sin–punishment" structures of the book of Deuteronomy. The core story is not difficult, when taken on its surface reading. The "first couple" is placed in the loveliness of paradise. They sin by disobeying God's command concerning the tree of knowledge (Gen. 3:6). and so they are, perforce, banished from the garden as punishment. This simple story line has been reinforced by the assignment of the word "Fall" to this narrative, suggesting that this brave act of disobedience has a universal dimension, whereby all human persons are guilty, merit punishment, and stand in need of pardon.[15]

It is a truism that this reading of the narrative as "Fall" plays no role in the Old Testament itself. But in the post–Old Testament period, this "strong reading" (misreading?) of the text is evident. Thus, in 4 Ezra there is a profound lament over the "human predicament" of sin, and of course in Romans 5:12-21, Paul escalates the claim of universal guilt that arises from this narrative. This reading of the text goes well beyond the claim of the text itself, but it has become the dominant Western reading of the text, so as to establish that sin is, in "Christian realism," definitional for the human person, who is intrinsically guilty.[16]

This reading of Genesis 2–3, rooted in Paul, and derivatively in Augustine and Luther, which asserts human culpability at the root of reality, received its most popular and enormously powerful articulations in John Milton's *Paradise Lost* I, 1–4:

> Of man's first disobedience, and the fruit
> Of that forbidden tree, whose mortal taste
> Brought death into the world, and all our woe,
> With loss of Eden . . .[17]

It is difficult to overestimate the power of this utterance on Western Protestant spirituality, with its inordinate accent on guilt. It is clearly the human person and nothing else, not God, not Satan, who has brought the wretchedness of sin and punishment into the world.

This claim by Milton, however, was a claim barely made by the poet. In *Paradise Lost* I, 27–37, Milton writes:

> Who first seduced them to that foul revolt?
> The infernal serpent; he it was, whose guile
> Stirred up with envy and revenge, deceived
> The mother of mankind, what time his pride
> Had cast him out from Heaven . . .[18]

In *Christian Doctrine*, however, Milton had written,

> This sin was instigated first by the devil. . . . Secondly it was instigated by man's own inconstant nature, which meant that he, like the devil before him, did not stand firm in the truth.[19]

Robert Crosman makes the important observation that Milton uses in one place the word "seduced" and in the other "instigated" but never "caused," for "cause" would preclude choice and responsibility. Arthur Sewell has suggested that these several articulations reflect Milton's own conflict with the High Calvinism that yielded such a severe God.[20]

The important point for us, however, is that Milton, in the midst of his classic and influential statement of human sin, guilt, fall, and responsibility, was able to entertain an alternative view. There was on the horizon of

Milton a counterview of sin, in which the cause of sin "cannot logically stop until it reaches back to the First Cause, God Himself."[21] Milton does not take that step, but he is within an ace of it. (It is worth observing that in 2 Samuel 24:1, in a context very different from that of Genesis 2–3, the Old Testament itself approaches that affirmation, only to draw back in 1 Chronicles 21 to relieve God of such a burden.) The notion of this tension in Milton suggests that his popular rendering, which finally overrides such a possibility, is not as settled as it might be. There is more going on in the narrative than a one-dimensional notion of Fall might indicate—and of course it is mind-boggling to ponder the consequences had Milton adjudicated differently.

The awareness of Milton's struggle with the narrative prepares the way for the rereading of this narrative from a very different perspective by Paul Ricoeur.[22] Ricoeur begins with the question, echoing Milton, "What does the serpent signify?" He proposes that the serpent can be understood as "the psychological projection of desire," so that the story invites reflection on the passion of human desire that drives the story.[23] Such a view of the narrative will leave intact the classic interpretation of "the Fall."

Ricoeur, however, goes further, to observe that the serpent is not only "a part of ourselves" but is "also outside." Thus, "every individual finds evil *already there; nobody begins it absolutely.*" From this awareness, Ricoeur speaks of "the radical externality of evil" of which "man is both author and servant."[24] And from this, says Ricoeur, comes later "the great dualisms" which eventuate in the satanic theme. Ricoeur concludes:

> [M]an is not the absolute evil one, but the evil one of second rank, the evil one through seduction; he is not *the* Evil One, the Wicked One, substantively, so to speak, but evil, wicked adjectivally; he makes himself wicked by a sort of counter-participation, counter-imitation, by consenting.[25]

This rather subtle point, which seems to build from Milton's use of "seduced," is important to us for two reasons. First, as "author and servant" of evil, the human person is understood not only as perpetrator but also as victim[26] of the power of sin—responsible, but not in full. Second, the fact that evil is already there means that others, and ultimately God, have "instigated" the production of sin. Now this matter of "author and servant," perpetrator and victim, is not easy to adjudicate, as it is not clear and obvious for Milton. Indeed, Ricoeur does not blink from recognizing the density of the issue, which at its very end implicates God. One cannot ever, in such a reading, exonerate the human agent.

This reading does, however, make clear that in looking seriously at evil and "the power of sin," one cannot proceed in a simplistic moralistic fashion, to generate yet more guilt for human persons. Human persons are from the outset enmeshed in a failure of covetousness, desire, deception, and violence that is already there in the very fabric of creation—or with Steinbeck, sin lying in wait, ready to spring.[27] Therefore the verdict of unmitigated "guilt" so easily given in the classical theological tradition is a misconstrual of the human situation as given in this primal narrative. A true reading of this tale requires a recognition of complexity that softens guilt, allows for a modicum of helplessness in the face of seduction, and dares the notion of some failure already present in creation. Aside from esoteric theological reflections, such a recognition of the cruciality of the serpent may make a practical difference, both in the easement of self-loathing and in the too-ready propensity to blame that so besets our conscience-ridden society.

This subtle strategy of ancient Israel in Genesis 2–3 concerning sin recognizes that something has already happened, has always already happened, before we act. This "already happened" illuminates the wretchedness we so habitually choose for ourselves. But it also provides a measure of solace, through the acknowledgment of the larger truth of our theological context. It draws the creation of the serpent, God's most subtle creature and subject, into the crisis. And this prepares us for our next topic.

IV

A third literary-theological strategy which de-absolutizes and perhaps undermines the absolutizing, oversimplified ethical claim of "sin–punishment" and "deeds–consequences" is expressed in the psalms of complaint. This genre of prayer is a dominant one in the spirituality of the Psalter, and yet it ill fits with the classical traditions of theology that focus on sin and guilt.

The psalm of complaint is the voice of the wounded and weak who cry out in need and pain. This cry is a characteristic element in Israel's piety, reflected, as we have seen, in Exodus 2:23-25. The cry initiates the exodus narrative and mobilizes YHWH to YHWH's liberating work on behalf of Israel. In the life and faith of ancient Israel, the wounded and weak did not characteristically submit in silence to their suffering, as though their wound and weakness denied them voice. On the contrary, such circumstance appears to have evoked a vigorous voice of protest, which, in its utterance, is a voice of hope that believes that the present circumstance is not only untenable but can and must and will be changed.[28]

Claus Westermann has observed that there are regularly three parties in
the prayer of complaint, even as we have suggested in the exodus narrative.[29]
The speaker, God, and the enemy all play a prominent role in these poems.[30]
There may indeed be a touch of paranoia about these psalms, for the speaker
regularly feels put upon by "an enemy." The identification of the enemy is
not obvious, and the identification is not important for our analysis.[31] The
enemy may indeed be another (rich? wicked? exploitative?) Israelite. Or it
may be an external enemy. Or it may be a suprahuman enemy of some cosmic significance. None of that is specified. What is evident is that the
speaker finds himself/herself in a situation of risk, danger, and threat and
has no alternative but to cry out, in an attempt to mobilize God to help.

In an important study of these psalms, Fredrik Lindström has shown
that while these psalms reflect great trouble and need, to the point of des-
peration, there is almost never mention of sin or guilt.[32] That is, the speaker
does not entertain the thought that the situation of trouble is to be understood as punishment for sin and gives no hint of any notion of having
sinned. Rather, the situation of trouble happens because "an enemy" is on
the move, an enemy too powerful for the speaker to resist. And so appeal
is made to YHWH, who is known to be strong enough to resist the enemy
and so to save the speaker.

We may see all of these elements in Psalm 7, which we take as representative of the genre. The speaker refers to the threat in a variety of ways:
"my pursuers" (v. 1), "my foes" (v. 4), "the enemy" (v. 5), "my enemies" (v. 6),
"the wicked" (v. 9), "they" (vv. 14-16). The speaker appeals to God to intervene: "save, deliver" (v. 1), "rise up, lift yourself up, awake" (v. 6), "establish"
(v. 9). The speaker, moreover, is clearly innocent:

> O Lord my God, if I have done this,
> if there is wrong in my hands,
> if I have repaid my ally with harm
> or plundered my foe without cause,
> then let the enemy pursue and overtake me,
> trample my life to the ground,
> and lay my soul in dust.
> the Lord judges the peoples;
> judge me, O Lord, according to my righteousness
> and according to the integrity that is in me. (Ps. 7:3-5, 8)

In the theological self-understanding sponsored by the schemes of "sin–
punishment" and "deeds–consequences," we might expect the speaker to

admit fault and to seek forgiveness from God. But such a note is completely alien to this prayer and, as Lindström has shown, to this entire genre of prayer. This speaker is not a perpetrator, suffering just deserts, but a victim being innocently abused.

The Israelite who lives in and through such a prayer as this lives in a dangerous world. The dangers may be of sickness, or they may be political or military in character. Lindström goes further to suggest a more fundamental dualism in the world, in which the power of Negation, Death, and Nihilism takes many forms, but is untamed and is on the loose.[33] In the face of such cosmic negation, the speaker is helpless. Thus, Lindström identifies a sweeping cosmic dualism, with a power opposed to Yhwh, who is the source of suffering and trouble. In the face of such a threat, only Yhwh is an adequate force to withstand the threat. The power of Death advances as it does not because it is more powerful than Yhwh but because Yhwh is mistakenly and inexcusably neglectful, inattentive, or absent.

Thus, the psalm, the voice of the victim under assault, seeks to get God's attention, to mobilize God to intervene against this ominous threat. When God is actively mobilized, Death is sure to be defeated. Given such a way of understanding reality, this three-part drama suggests that Sin is a power that takes the forms of death, chaos, illness, disorder, and oppression. Sin is not an act taken by the speaker that evokes the power of Nihil, as though an act per se would evoke all the powers of Nihilism. No, rather the power of Nihil is always on the alert to find a place where the power of God is inattentive. When God is absent or inattentive and Nihil advances, the speaker is the hapless victim of such an opening taken by the power of Nihil. The lament psalms insist on the legitimate claims of the wounded and are remote from any simplistic moral reductionism that blames the victim. The speaker has a perfect right to expect God to act in saving ways and seeks in shrill, demanding speech to move God to act. For if God can be summoned to act, the victim will be freed from the threat of the perpetrator.

V

The ways in which the Old Testament moves against simplistic and absolutizing ethical schemes inevitably culminate in the great poem of Job, which gathers together many of the themes we have already considered. The poem of Job, as Westermann has shown, is the extreme articulation of lament in ancient Israel, in which the weak and wounded find voice against their suffering. The astonishing appearance of the satan in Job 1–2 seems to be an extreme development of the serpent motif.[34] And Gustavo Gutiérrez's reflection on Job suggests that the themes of injustice and oppression, so central in the exodus narrative, are again operative here.[35]

The poem of Job features the sufferer Job. The satan's name means "adversary." He is an adversary of the "sin–punishment" scheme. And insofar as God is a function of that system, he is an adversary of God and will take God to court. Job, the sufferer, protests what appears to him to be his senseless, unjustified suffering. He is willing to suffer, if his suffering is a consequence of his sin, for then it makes moral sense. But he is not told what his sin might be, and never in the poem is there a hint that Job has sinned.

Job's counterpart in the drama are the "three friends," who are advocates of the ancient moral schemes to which we have referred. They may be variously understood as proponents of Deuteronomic theology (see Deut. 30:15-20) or of the domesticated sapiential system of the book of Proverbs (see Prov. 8:32-36). Either way, the friends represent the conviction that the world is one of moral coherence and symmetry, and whoever is a victim of suffering, as Job is, is surely a perpetrator of a sin adequate for the punishment inflicted.

The defense of the ethical system on the part of the friends is quite theoretical and untroubled by Job's actual suffering. Their counsel strikes one as condescending and unfeeling:

> Think now, who that was innocent ever perished?
> Or where were the upright cut off? (4:7)
> As for me, I would seek God,
> and to God I would commit my cause. (5:8)
> How happy is the one whom God reproves;
> therefore do not despise the discipline of the Almighty. (5:17)
> If you will seek God
> and make supplication to the Almighty,
> if you are pure and upright,
> surely then he will rouse himself for you
> and restore to you your rightful place. (8:5-6)

The friends believe in and advocate a morally reliable world. The practical consequence of their view is that Job must indeed be guilty of a sin commensurate with his "punishment."

For his part, the sufferer who finds voice for his hurt is not resistant to the theory of the friends. Indeed, Job shares their view. He also believes that suffering is morally situated. But he has no data to relate the theory to his life, and eventually he begins to doubt and then to reject the theory. He can be sarcastic to his friends (12:2; 16:1-5), but his most savage utterances are an assault upon God, who is absent and silent, and in the end unfair:

> If it is a contest of strength, he is the strong one!
> If it is a matter of justice, who can summon him?
> Though I am innocent, my own mouth would condemn me;
> though I am blameless, he would prove me perverse.
> I am blameless; I do not know myself;
> I loathe my life.
> It is all one; therefore I say,
> He destroys both the blameless and the wicked. (9:19-22)

Job's conclusion is that God is morally indifferent and unreliable and that therefore the entire theory of a moral order to reality, advocated by his friends, is absurd. Job refuses to admit, without evidence, that he is a sinner justly suffering. Job breaks the comfortable, reassuring linkage of "deeds–consequences." His great climactic utterance in 31:35-37 is almost Promethean in its defiance and self-assertion:

> Oh, that I had one to hear me!
> (Here is my signature! Let the Almighty answer me!)
> Oh, that I had the indictment
> written by my adversary!
> Surely I would carry it on my shoulder;
> I would bind it on me like a crown;
> I would give him an account of all my steps;
> Like a prince I would approach him.

This is, so far as he or we or anyone knows, an innocent man whose suffering makes no sense and will not be contained in either Deuteronomic or sapiential explanations.

The poem will not leave us there. God must answer. God's answer, however, completely disregards the point of Job's rage, and the domesticated remedies of Job's friends. God's response in the whirlwind is a poem of praise to God's power (Job 38–41). Well, of course. God's power has never been in question (see 9:19). Job can sing a marvelous hymn of praise to God's enormous power (9:4-12) that matches the exuberant doxology of Eliphaz (5:9-16). But all of that misses the point of the dispute that Job has initiated—unless of course the speech of YHWH resolves the dispute! The poem of Job seems to abandon the idea of moral coherence, which means that Job and his friends, and all the readers of the poem, are left in a world where the category of "sin" is largely dismissed, or in any case moved away from the center of the theological discussion. Thus, the poem of Job advances beyond what we have found elsewhere in the Old Testament. In the account of Pharaoh in the exodus narrative, the serpent in the creation narrative, and the "enemies" in the psalms of complaint, "sin" has to some extent been assigned to someone other than the sufferer. In these cases, the sufferer is the victim of someone else's affront. Here, however, there is no other agent, for not even God is so located, even though Job entertains the notion. Rather, the categories of sin and guilt simply evaporate in the face of God's own statement. Job may be a victim, but he is not noticeably a victim of wrongdoing, but only the victim of power that is morally unbridled.

The resolution of the poem of Job, after such a daring foray, is perhaps a bit anemic. We mention two parts of the conclusion. First, Job's "concession speech" is in 42:6. But the statement of Job is notoriously problematic, perhaps made deliberately so by the artist. One cannot determine if Job's final words constitute genuine repentance and submission, or if they are a mocking way of conceding God's power without conceding anything of God's right. In any case, they are his final words.[36]

In response, in the prose conclusion, Job receives this verdict from YHWH:

> . . . my servant Job shall pray for you, for I will accept his prayer not to deal with you according to your folly, for you have not spoken of me what is right, as my servant Job has done. (42:8)

Job, not his friends, has his theological discourse approved by God. Indeed, Job's friends are rebuked by God for engaging in theological "folly." Are the friends rebuked for holding to a moral scheme that God here rejects? It would seem so. In any case, Job is celebrated, seemingly for having pressed his own case against God, for having refused to accept his victimization as morally legitimate and for having fought through to a new kind of freedom in the face of God. This conclusion removes the faith of Israel as far away as it can be, from the tight moral schemes of the primary ethical systems of the Old Testament.

VI

The four strategies of de-absolutizing and undermining that I have reviewed constitute a formidable challenge to the common propensity to reduce the Old Testament to a system of "sin and punishment." After this review, we may refer to one other facet of Old Testament faith that must be mentioned with reference to our subject, but which must not be mentioned too soon. It is this. The God of the Old Testament is

> merciful and gracious,
> slow to anger and abounding in steadfast love.
> He will not always accuse,
> Nor will he keep his anger forever.
> He does not deal with us according to our sins,
> nor repay us according to our iniquities.
> For as the heavens are high above the earth,
> so great is his steadfast love toward those who fear him.
> as far as the east is from the west,
> so far he removes our transgressions from us.
> As father has compassion for his children,
> so the Lord has compassion for those who fear him.
> For he knows how we were made;
> He remembers that we are dust. (Ps. 103:8-14)

The God of the Old Testament is gracious and capable of forgiveness. Therefore, the vicious cycles of sin, insofar as they are acts of rebellion that generate yet more acts of rebellion, can indeed be broken.

This facet of the character of God in the Old Testament is not so well recognized, especially given Christian stereotypes and caricatures of the Old Testament. Nonetheless, Israel has known, since the time of Moses, that the God of Sinai, the one who gives commands and prescribes sanctions, is a God "merciful and gracious" (Exod. 34:6). This marking of God, however, was not plain on the face of it, nor easily and readily given in the midst of harsh sanctions.

Like everything theological in the Old Testament, like everything pertaining to this God, this marking of God had to be contested and struggled for. The context for this disclosure of God in Exodus 34:6 is fought through in the aftermath of Exodus 32, the narrative of the golden calf, and Aaron's savage disregard of YHWH. YHWH in great anger is prepared to consume Aaron and his ilk (Exod. 32:10), for YHWH responds in anger when YHWH's own prerogatives are violated. In the end, there was indeed a great plague upon disobedient Israel (Exod. 32:35). In this narrative, we are in the world of retribution, of "sin and punishment," and God will not be mocked.

But there is more to the story. Moses intercedes to YHWH on behalf of Israel (Exod. 32:11-13). Moses asks God to "turn" and to "change your mind." And YHWH does! It is as though in this crisis, YHWH must fight through to a new way of being toward Israel. Thus, in the midst of enormous anger, at the behest of Moses, YHWH finally asserts YHWH's own self:

> The Lord, the Lord,
> a God merciful and gracious,
> slow to anger,
> and abounding in steadfast love and faithfulness,
> keeping steadfast love for the thousandth generation,
> forgiving iniquity and transgression and sin. (Exod. 34:6-7a)

It is in the very character of YHWH to forgive.

There is still available to God, to be sure, a destructive alternative:

> yet by means clearing the guilty,
> but visiting the iniquity of the parents
> upon the children
> and the children's children,
> to the third and the fourth generation. (Exod. 34:7b)

Which way the future of Israel turns out, in a crisis situation, depends on Moses—and on Moses' daring intervention (Exod. 34:8-9). Only in response to the intervention of Moses, comes God's resolve to begin again with Israel (Exod. 34:10).

We should not miss in this passage the remarkable turn in YHWH's character. What I prefer to accent, however, is the role of Moses. It is Moses, the quintessential person of God, who must risk God's holiness and summon God to a better way, even though God does not easily turn away from wounding affront.[37] Moses, at great risk to himself, summons God to God's best self. And God, in that moment of Mosaic urging, is able and willing to move to a new beginning. Vicious cycles are broken, because of daring human intervention on the part of those who are perpetrators/victims of destructive behavior.

Now it may be, that after the more daring renderings of the exodus narrative, the creation story, the lament psalms, and the poem of Job, a focus on the compassion of God concedes too much to more conventional notions of sin and punishment. The compassion of God, however, is the ultimate de-absolutizing of the "sin–punishment," "deeds–consequences" structures of Israel's faith. The assertion that God does not "keep his anger forever" means that these tight moral calculations are not of ultimate seriousness in the faith of ancient Israel. They are of interest, but only of penultimate interest, and may therefore not be treated in schemes of social interaction as of ultimate importance.

There is no doubt that, theologically, sin is important. Indeed, in terms of social relations, a system of sanctions is an inevitable requirement for the maintenance of social viability. But such modes of discipline are of quite limited interest to this God. To subsume too much of life in such systems is to misconstrue both the character of God and the reality of lived human life. God is not a function of moral sanctions. Well beyond such sanctions, God is the powerful one who resists the power of Nihil. This God is the one who in quite daily ways "knows how we are made," and this knowledge tends to evoke in God a kind of parental compassion.

This larger sphere of God's goodness is an invitation for a new way with God:

> If you, O Lord, should mark iniquities,
> Lord, who could stand?
> But there is forgiveness with you,
> so that you may be revered. (Ps. 130:3-4)

It is also a warning against our excessive valuing of "sin–punishment," "deeds–consequences." Thus, Jonah the prophet, for example, knows well that there is much of God beyond a tight system of sanctions. That "beyond" of God greatly upsets Jonah. In the narrative of Jonah, the people of Nineveh had repented, and so had not been punished, as Jonah had hoped. Jonah, in a spasm of righteous indignation, assaults God for being gracious:

> Is not this what I said while I was still in my own country? That is why I fled to Tarshish at the beginning; for I knew that you are a gracious God and merciful, slow to anger, and abounding in steadfast love, and ready to relent from punishing. (Jonah 4:2)[38]

There is much of God beyond social control. And in a world such as ours, marked by barbarianism and brutality, driven by fear and by self-loathing, we do well to host that of God that refuses to be held in our explanatory codes. In response to the behavior of Nineveh, Jonah was very angry. But God was not!

8

Life or Death: De-Privileged Communication

It strikes me that the most important fact about preaching in the contemporary U.S. church is that proclamation of the gospel is no longer a privileged claim. That is, it can no longer assume or appeal to a broadly based consensus that dominates our culture. By that I do not refer to the fact of pluralism, which is unarguable, nor to the loss of institutional clout for the church, nor to the erosion of the social authority of the pastor, though all of these realities surely are important.

Rather I refer to the recognition we must face that construal of the world *without reference to God* is intellectually credible and socially acceptable as it never has been before in Euro-American culture. I suppose one can say that such assumed atheism (no god) or embraced idolatry (distorted god) is the final victory of Enlightenment consciousness.[1] But that victory has come about, so it seems to me, rather unintentionally and issues in vulgar, unexamined forms.

I

The upshot of that changed intellectual, social climate is that preaching has to start "farther back," because nothing is conceded by the listening assembly at the outset. This is obviously true for people who have long since given up on gospel claims of the church, either because these claims are rightly understood as too costly and too disruptive of a self-focused life. But more important, it appears to me that in some large measure, "nothing is conceded" even in the baptismal community, for even baptized people (including perhaps you, dear reader, and me as writer) have learned to construe the real practice of our lives without reference to the claims of God. Thus, the beginning is not in *assent,* but at the most, in open *wonderment* and perhaps, down deep, in hidden, resentful *resistance.*

In such a social environment, it is evident that a different mode of preaching and different expectations on the part of the preacher may be important. The de-privileging of the claims of the sermon repositions the sermon (and the preacher) in terms of communication. My suggestion, growing out of my recent study of Old Testament theology, is that the genre of *testimony* (as bid for assent), rather than *proclamation* (on an assumption of universal consensus), is how ancient Israel proceeded to claim truth in a like situation.[2] It is how we might, I suggest, rethink the genre of the sermon.

I understand that the term "testimony" in staid Calvinist ears, for example, calls to mind emotive, primitive religious talk among certain Baptists that is not well informed or well disciplined. In ancient usage, however, "testimony" refers not to religious emoting but rather to a courtroom exercise in which the "truth of the matter" is deeply contested and different witnesses are called upon to give accounts of "the truth of the matter" that turn out to be profoundly contradictory. The trials of O. J. Simpson and Timothy McVeigh make available to us a social environment of *contested truth with competing bids for assent.*

With the loss of Christian consensus and theological hegemony, "the truth of the matter" is greatly contested, the truth about the reality and character of God and the consequent reality and character of the world. There was a time of consensus in the West when the preacher could speak from high philosophical and moral ground simply to reiterate "what we all believe." Now, however, the preacher offers a construal of reality that sits alongside other construals of God and world reality, each of which has its adherents and its points of credibility.[3]

The *dethroning of Christian privilege* and the need for the risk of testimony are perhaps illuminated by citing three examples of testimony as *bids for assent:*

1. Elie Wiesel has spent his life in determination that the barbaric reality of the Jewish Holocaust shall not be forgotten. He has observed that the truth of the Holocaust is deeply disputed and that there are those who insist it never happened. More than that, he has observed that the truth of the Holocaust depends completely on the witnesses, people who are not sophisticated but who are credible through the character of their testimony, through their capacity to tell credibly how it was with them.[4]

2. A great deal of attention has been given to the practice of "stories of woundedness" among those who are ill and who require medical attention. "Scientific medicine," rather like "consensus theological truth," has had no need of stories, because it operated out of the "truth of medicine," which was established "from above," as was theological truth. Without denying the important claims of scientific medicine, more recent observers have noticed that suffering people need to tell the story of suffering, so to engage others in a relatedness of suffering whereby healing may happen as a relational phenomenon. Indeed Arthur Frank has offered a chapter entitled "testimony," giving evidence of the ways a sufferer must construe reality "from below," that is, out of pain.[5]

3. The other day at noon I was in a bank-teller line observing to the woman next to me how most bank tellers took long lunch breaks just when I wanted one to be available. That comment triggered in the woman behind me, whom I did not know, the opportunity for her to tell me her story of being cheated by a fast-food place out of fifty dollars of low-pay wages, and to report that she never got a lunch break. She then told me that she planned to bring a suit against the company for having cheated her. She said, "I will probably lose, but I will have been heard." She told me that message three times in four minutes. She was giving "testimony," and she would give more of it in court, stating her bid for truth. It was, moreover, urgent that she be heard, even if the fast-food company would be dominant in court, as she herself anticipated. She will have been heard with her version of truth!

Notice that, in all three cases, testimony comes as a truth "from below" in the face of a "stronger truth" that is hegemonic: (a) Jewish *survivors* amid scientific analysis of what happened; (b) *sufferers* amid medical science; and (c) the *"cheated woman"* in the face of a powerful fast-food chain. Each of these witnesses makes a bid for a version of the truth.

Such testimony is characteristically:[6]

1. *Fragile.* It depends upon the nerve of the teller.

2. *Local.* It makes no sweeping, universal claim, but appeals to what is concretely known.

3. *Persuasive.* The rhetorical casting aims at winning the jury.

4. *Contested.* It dares utterance in the presence of other claims that may be more powerful and more credible.

5. *Fragmented.* It is only a bit of a narrative that brings with it a whole theory of reality that is implied but left unexpressed.

Such claims for truth are not loud, arrogant, or sweeping. They are modest but insistent and sometimes compelling. The connection of *testimony-trial-truth-jury* means that truth is not available ahead of time, before the utterance. It is available only after, through the utterance, when the jury reaches its verdict. So it is with the sermon, when the sermon is de-positioned from the judge's bench to the witness box.

II

It has occurred to me that the Old Testament is essentially de-privileged testimony that construes the world alternatively.[7] It is de-privileged because it is the evidence offered by a community that is early *nomads or peasants* and that is late a community of *exiles*. Either way, as peasants or as exiles, Israel lives a great distance from the great hegemonic seats of power and the great centers of intellectual-theological certitude. Israel always comes into the great courtroom of public opinion and disrupts the court, in order to tell a tale of reality that does not mesh with the emerging consensus that more powerful people have put together.

At the center of this odd account of reality is this Character YHWH, whom Pharaoh does not know (Exod. 5:2) and whom the winners in the world by and large ignore. It is this strange God—so this testimony asserts—who comes among barren women to give births (Gen. 21:1-7), who comes into slave camps to set free (Exod. 15:20-21), who sends bread from heaven into wilderness contexts of hunger (Exod. 16:13-18), who governs the rise and fall of great powers (1 Sam. 2:6-8), who places widows, orphans, and illegal aliens at the center of the economic-political debate (Deut. 24:17-22; Isa. 1:17).

Israel on occasion will tell of this Holy Fidelity that is textured with impatient violence *to outsiders,* inviting others to join in doxology to this odd Character:

Praise the Lord, all you nations,
Extol him, all you peoples! (Ps. 117:1; cf. Ps. 67:3-5)

It is an odd *hutzpah*-filled invitation to ask nations and peoples to join to sing of this alternative Reality on the basis of *local* experience:

For great is his steadfast love toward us,
and the faithfulness of the lord endures forever. (Ps. 117:2)

More characteristically Israel tells this peculiar version of reality to *its own children,* intending that this offbeat testimony at the center of this community will persist as a viable social force into the next generation:

> When in the future your child asks you, "What does this mean?" you shall answer, "By strength of hand the Lord brought us out of Egypt from the house of slavery. When Pharaoh stubbornly refused to let us go, the Lord killed all the firstborn in the land of Egypt, from human firstborn to the firstborn of animals. Therefore I sacrifice to the Lord every male that first opens the womb, but every firstborn of my sons I redeem." It shall serve as a sign on your hand and as an emblem on your forehead that by strength of hand the Lord brought us out of Egypt. (Exod. 13:14-16)

Most regularly, however, this *testimony of alternative truth* is offered to members of the community by members of the community. The purpose of such incessant testimony is to nurture and sustain each other in odd vision, because without such nurture and sustenance, it is for sure that members of the community will fall out of this truth into other, more attractive, more palatable, less costly truth.

III

The clearest evidence for this process of testimony, I take it, is the poetry of Second Isaiah (chapters 40–55). This poetry, it is commonly agreed, is uttered to Jewish exiles who have been deported to Babylon and who must practice their faith and their countertruth in a world of Babylonian hegemony. It is unmistakable that Babylon was not only a political-military superpower; it was also an advanced, sophisticated, winsome culture with its own theological rationale and its own moral justifications. Over time, the powerful attractiveness of Babylon must have been deeply compelling to many Jews.

Into this context of *seduction and resistance* comes the preacher-poet, Second Isaiah. I cite only one pair of verses that evidence the contested, demanding situation of Jewish faith in the empire:

> Do not fear, or be afraid;
> have I not told you from of old and declared it?
> You are my witnesses!

Is there any god besides me?
There is no other rock; I know not one. (Isa. 44:8)

In this brief assurance and summons offered by YHWH, there are three identifiable components:

1. Israel—Jews in exile—are summoned and identified as *witnesses for
YHWH*. Witnesses do not come to court neutrally. They are "friendly" or
"hostile," summoned either by the prosecution or by the defense. Israel is
summoned and authorized to come to the court of public opinion in order
to line out to the court the YHWH-version of reality and to bid for assent
to this truth.

2. The *witness is instructed*. A good attorney briefs the witness; so YHWH
instructs Israel as witness to assert in court that "YHWH is the only one,"
that YHWH is a rock without any competitors.[8]

3. Most astonishingly, YHWH *assures the witness* Israel, "Do not fear, do
not be afraid." The situation is not unlike a fragile person who goes to an
attorney in the secret of the night with evidence that will blow the case
open. But that evidence is dangerous and the witness will be at risk. In order
not to lose the testimony (and consequently the case) because of fearfulness, the attorney assures the witness that "it will be all right." In Babylon,
it was hazardous to the health of Israel to witness to YHWH and so to contradict the massive Babylonian claim to legitimacy and absoluteness. No
wonder the witness must be reassured, "Do not fear."

Jews exist, so says this poetry, to make the case in the empire for a different truth, a different presentation of reality, a different basis for humanness in the world. The case to be made in court by Israel is, of course, not
uncontested. So the text goes on to say,

> All who make idols are nothing, and the things they delight in do not
> profit; their witnesses neither see nor know. And so they will be put
> to shame. (Isa. 44:9)

The empire also has its gods. And those gods also have witnesses. And those
witnesses come into court as well, to make their polished, sophisticated case
before the court. One would expect, of course, that these witnesses would
offer compelling testimony for the empire, because they have all of the best
evidence, the slickest lawyers, the best research, the most compelling style.
Except, says the text, they are *thou*; they are embodiments of chaos, agents
of disorder who are blind and deaf. They are hopeless witnesses advocating
a hopeless truth.

And so the issue is joined in court. The poetry does not pay much attention to the evidence brought by Babylonian witnesses, treating it all as a weak joke (44:9-20). Rather, all the energy goes to the testimony to be given by Israel, for a countertruth about a counter-God with a counterethic in the world.

1. This testimony by Israel offers a past that is saturated with *life-giving miracles,* not a past filled with self-sufficiency achievement. So the poet appeals to Abraham and Sarah, a test case in Israel's memory, for the ways in which this God could take this hopeless old couple and create a vibrant community:

> Look to the rock from which you were hewn,
> and to the quarry from which you were dug.
> Look to Abraham your father
> and to Sarah who bore you;
> for he was but one when I called him.
> but I blessed him and made him many. (Isa. 51:1-2; see Heb. 11:11-12)

From that testimony derives a claim that we live in a world of life-giving miracles, not to be matched or stopped by the empire.

2. This testimony from Israel offers a future that is marked by *circumstance-defying promises* completely freed from the present tense, which is too sober. So it is promised:

> For the mountains may depart and the hills be removed,
> but my steadfast love shall not depart from you,
> and my covenant of peace shall not be removed,
> says the Lord, who has compassion on you.
> O afflicted one, storm-tossed, and not comforted,
> I am about to set your stones in antimony,
> and lay your foundations with sapphires.
> I will make your pinnacles of rubies,
> your gates of jewels,
> and all your wall of precious stones.
> All your children shall be taught by the Lord,
> and great shall be the prosperity of your children.
> In righteousness you shall be established;
> you shall be far from oppression, for you shall not fear;
> and from terror, for it shall not come near you. (Isa. 54:10-14)

For you shall go out in joy,
and be led back in peace ...
Instead of the thorn shall come up the cypress;
instead of the brier shall come up the myrtle. (Isa. 55:12-13)

From this testimony emerges a future of complete *shalom* that is free of violence, brutality, competitiveness, and scarcity, a new governance that displaces that of the empire.

  3. This testimony offers *a present tense filled with neighbors* to whom we are bound in fidelity, in obligation, and in mutual caring. Everywhere on the lips of this witness is the term "justice," which entails inclusiveness for all those whom the empire finds objectionable and unproductive:

I have put my spirit upon him;
he will bring forth *justice* to the nations.
he will not cry or lift up his voice,
or make it heard in the street;
a bruised reed he will not break,
and a dimly burning wick he will not quench;
he will faithfully bring forth *justice*.
he will not grow faint or be crushed
until he has established *justice* in the earth;
and the coastlands wait for his Torah. (Isa. 42:1-4)

Thus appeal is made:

- *a past* of life-giving miracles;
- *a future* of circumstance-defying promise;
- *a present* of neighbors in fidelity.

This testimony matters. It matters to stay in this truth. It matters to practice this version of life. And of course the imperial thought-police, present in every preaching situation, recognize that it matters. It matters because the members of this odd community will not give in to the blandishments of the empire, and so will remain an emancipated, unintimidated counter-culture in the empire. It matters beyond that, because even the agents of the empire occasionally recognize the credible character of this talk that will eventually subvert and collapse the empire.[9]

  The preaching office is an office of an alternative truth that makes its bid for assent. It does so, moreover, in the face of the empire that wants to stop talk of *miracles, promises, and neighbors* because such talk runs against the grain of imperial, ruthless self-sufficiency. And thus soon or late—as every preacher knows—agents of the status quo will move in to halt the countertruth. They may be friendly or hard, open or covert. But they will try. Against such a risk, the sender says, "fear not."

IV

It is my hunch that, give or take a little, every preaching context and every preaching occasion is something like that. The preaching of the gospel is not the voice of the dominant empire, but offers a truthfulness that may be confrontational or subtle, but eventually conflicts with imperial truth. I have no doubt that it is emancipatory for the preacher to recognize our actual preaching context, which, in the past Christian West, is unprecedented. We are de-privileged, but thereby free, because we need no longer carry water for the empire as was a given in a previous power arrangement.

This sense of being de-privileged struck me powerfully the other day. I read in the *New York Times* a report on the violent military-social revolution in Sierra Leone.[10] The *Times* carried a picture of a soldier holding back a protesting crowd. The crowd of young people in that disadvantaged situation faced the power of status quo soldiers. They were waiting eagerly and impatiently for food, and one of the young lads was there with a Nike cap.

And then I thought, Nike, with its U.S. heroes of Tiger and Michael and its complementary Asian sweatshops, has become a universal symbol for greed and individual exploitativeness. (I do not single out Nike or Tiger or Michael, except as they embody in the most effective way the dominant truth of privatized success offered to the young.) It is astounding, in my judgment, that the Nike "Swoosh" has become a universal symbol for success and well-being even without any verbalization. It is a symbol worn by unthinking, affluent suburbanites. It is a symbol worn by poor people in third-world economies who can for a moment entertain a fantasy. It is a symbol worn by the baptized so narcotized that we do not notice the irony.

In the world of Nike, moreover, the cross is a lonesome symbol of costly self-giving for the neighbor. (The cross on the wane perhaps has a companion in waning of the Hammer and Sickle of Marxian thought, which cannot withstand Nike, and the Crescent of Islam, which cannot withstand Nike.)

And so the preacher must stand up and tell the truth in an environment where Nike seems a given and where many "Jewish exiles" submit to Babylonian truth without any awareness what such submission costs for our baptism. When the contradiction between the symbols and between sworn accounts of reality are exposed, imperial agents will be quick to move. In the world of "swoosh," preaching the crucified One is a dangerous business, profoundly de-privileged.

It is de-privileged communication; of that there can be no doubt. But such preaching is, I have no doubt, life or death—because what this gospel asserts matters to our common future.

- It matters if *life-giving miracles* are scuttled for the sake of can-do achievements.

- It matters if *circumstance-defying promises* are silenced for the sake of winning at all costs.

- It matters if *bonded neighbors* are excommunicated in a passion for private *shalom*.

It matters because the makers of phoney cultural icons are *tôhû*, agents of chaos, manufacturers of disorder that brings nothing but abusive trouble among brothers and sisters (Isa. 44:9). It matters! The preacher and the sermon are life-or-death and deeply de-privileged. In the face of that danger with such a freighted alternative truth, the poet says, "Do not fear."

9

Preaching to Exiles

I have elsewhere proposed that the Old Testament experience of and reflection on exile is a helpful *metaphor* for understanding our current faith situation in the U.S. church, and a *model* for pondering new forms of ecclesiology.[1] (Jack Stotts in parallel fashion has suggested that the "period of the Judges" might be a more useful metaphor.[2] Stott's suggestion has considerable merit, but because we are speaking of metaphors, these suggestions are not mutually exclusive.) The usefulness of a metaphor for rereading our own context is that it is not claimed to be a none-on-one match to "reality," as though the metaphor of "exile" actually *describes* our situation. Rather, a metaphor proceeds by having only an odd, playful, and ill-fitting match to its reality, the purpose of which is to illuminate and evoke dimensions of reality that will otherwise go unnoticed and therefore unexperienced.[3]

I

Utilization of the metaphor of "exile" for the situation of the church in the U.S. is not easy or obvious, and for some not compelling. I suggest that the metaphor is more difficult in the South, where establishment Christianity may still be perceived as "alive and well." For those who perceive it so, what follows likely will not be useful or persuasive. My conviction, however, is that even amid such a positive perception of old religious-cultural realities, there is indeed a growing uneasiness about the sustenance of old patterns of faith and life. That uneasiness may be signaled by anxiety about "church growth," and about increasingly problematic denominational budgets.[4]

I wish, however, to tilt the metaphor of exile in a very different direction, one occupied not with issues of institutional well-being or quantitative measure but with the experienced anxiety of "deported" people. That is, my concern is not institutional but pastoral. The exiled Jews of the Old Testament were of course geographically displaced. More than that, however, the exiles experienced a loss of the structured, reliable world that gave them meaning and coherence, and they found themselves in a context where their most treasured and trusted symbols of faith were mocked, trivialized, or dismissed.[5] That is, exile is not primarily geographical, but it is social, moral, and cultural.[6]

Now I believe that this sense of (a) *loss of a structured, reliable "world"*[7] *where* (b) *treasured symbols of meaning are mocked and dismissed,* is a pertinent point of contact between those ancient texts and our situation. On the one hand, I suggest an *evangelical dimension* to exile in our social context. That is, serious, reflective Christians find themselves increasingly at odds with the dominant values of consumer capitalism and its supportive military patriotism; there is no easy or obvious way to hold together core faith claims and the social realities around us. Reflective Christians are increasingly "resident aliens" (even if one does not accept all of the ethical, ecclesiological extrapolations of Stanley Hauerwas and William H. Willimon).[8] And if it be insisted that church members are still in places of social power and influence, I suggest that such Christians only need to act and speak out of any serious conviction concerning the public claims of the gospel, and it becomes promptly evident that we are outsiders to the flow of power. I propose that pastors and parishioners together may usefully take into account this changed social reality of the marginalization of faith, a marginalization perhaps felt most strongly by young people.[9]

On the other hand, I suggest a *cultural dimension* to exile that is more "American" than Christian, but no less germane to the pastoral task. The "homeland" in which all of us have grown up has been defined and dominated by white, male, Western assumptions that were, at the same time, imposed and also willingly embraced. Exile comes as those values and modes of authority are being effectively and progressively diminished. That diminishment is a source of deep displacement for many, even though for others who are not male and white, it is a moment of emancipation. The deepness of the displacement is indicated, I imagine, by the reactive assault on so-called political correctness, by ugly humor and by demonizing new modes of power.[10] For all these quite visible resistances to the new, however, we are now required to live in a new situation that for many feels like less than "home." In such a context, folk need pastoral help in relinquishing a "home" that is gone and in entering a new "dangerous" place that we sense as deeply alien.

I suggest that the "exile" (as metaphor) is a rich resource for fresh discernment, even though a *Christian exile* in a secular culture, and a *cultural exile* with the loss of conventional hegemony are very different. In fact, the two "exiles" (evangelical and "American") arise from the fact that establishment Christianity and establishment culture have been in a close and no longer sustainable alliance. This quite concrete double focus on "exile" is a practical manifestation of what Martin Buber has called "an epoch of homelessness," brought on by the intellectual revolution around the figures of Locke, Hobbes, and Descartes, wherein old certitudes have been lost.[11] My interest is not in a long-term philosophical question but in the quite specific experience of the present church. I believe that this deep sense of displacement touches us all—liberal and conservative—in personal and public ways. For that reason, the preacher must take into account the place where the faithful church must now live.

II

I propose that in our preaching and more general practice of ministry, we ponder the interface of our *circumstance of exile* (to the extent that this is an appropriate metaphor) and *scriptural resources* that grew from and address the faith crisis of exile. (Note well that this suggested interface entails refocusing our attention, energy, and self-perception. In times when the church could assume its own "establishment," it may have been proper to use prophetic texts to address "kings." But a new circumstance suggests a very different posture for preaching and pastoral authority, now as an exile addressing exiles, in which displacement, failed hopes, anger, wistful sadness, and helplessness permeate our sense of self, sense of community, and sense of future.)

The most remarkable observation one can make about this interface of *exilic circumstance* and *scriptural resources* is this: exile did not lead Jews in the Old Testament to abandon faith or to settle for abdicating despair, nor to retreat to privatistic religion. On the contrary, exile evoked the most brilliant literature and the most daring theological articulation in the Old Testament. There is indeed something characteristically and deeply Jewish about such a buoyant response to trouble, a response that in Christian parlance can only be termed "evangelical," that is, grounded in a sense and sureness of *news* about God that circumstance cannot undermine or negate. That "news" which generates buoyant theological imagination in ancient Israel is too "hard-core" that it is prerational and does not submit to the "data" of historical circumstance. I suggest this is a time for us when preachers are "liberated" to assert that hard-core, prerational buoyance in a church too much in the grip of the defeatist sensibility of our evident cultural collapse.

For many preachers, this will require considerations of text (i.e., families of texts) that were not studied in seminary. They were not studied in seminary precisely because "exile" seemed remote from us, something at the most that belonged to "late Judaism."[12] As a guide into these "new" texts, I suggest three useful resources: (a) Peter Ackroyd, *Exile and Restoration*, the classic English text on the subject, providing the "meat and potatoes" of historical criticism; (b) Ralph W. Klein, *Israel in Exile*, a more accessible book, that exhibits theological, pastoral sensitivity; and (c) Daniel L. Smith, *The Religion of the Landless*, a daring sociohistorical study that is most suggestive for seeing into the visceral elements of the circumstance, literature, and faith of the ancient exiles.[13]

III

While the subject of faith is exceedingly rich, here I suggest six interfaces of the *circumstance of exile* and *scriptural resources*:[14]

1. Exiles must grieve their loss and express their resentful sadness about what was and now is not and will never again be. In our culture, we must be honest about the waning of our "great days" of world domination (before the rise of the Japanese economy), and all of the awkward economic complications that we experience in quite personal and immediate ways. In the church, we may be honest about the loss of our "great days" when our churches and their pastors, and even our denominations, were forces for reckoning as they are not now. I suggest that congregations must be, in intentional ways, *communities of honest sadness,* naming the losses. We might be Jews on "the Ninth of Av," when every year Jews celebrate and grieve the destruction of Jerusalem in 587 B.C.E., a destruction that persists for Jews in paradigmatic ways.[15] This community of sadness has as its work the countering of the "culture of denial" which continues to imagine that it is as it was, even when our experience tells otherwise.

The obvious place for scriptural resources for such work is in the book of Lamentations, the text used by Jews for that holy day of grieving on the Ninth of Av. Because the text is "canon," it intends to be used for many sadnesses of a communal kind, well beyond the concrete loss of Jerusalem. In the book of Lamentations, I suggest three motifs among many that warrant attention: (a) The collection of poems begins with a sustained and terrible negativity: "no resting place" (1:3), "no pasture" (1:6), "no one to help" (1:7), "none to comfort" (1:9, 16, 17, 21; 2:13), "no rest" (2:18). The poem is candid and preoccupied about loss. (b) The poetic collection ends with a pathos-filled statement (which may be a dependent clause as in the NRSV, or a question as in the RSV). In either case, the final statement is preceded in v. 20 by a haunting question to which Israel does not know the answer, a question about being "forgotten" and "abandoned" by God. (c) In 3:18-23, we witness the characteristically poignant Jewish negotiation between sadness and hope. Verse 18 asserts that hope is gone. In v. 21, hope reappears, because in vv. 22-23, Israel voices its three great terms of buoyancy, "steadfast love, mercy, faithfulness." These words do not here triumph, but they hover in the very midst of Israel's sadness and refuse to be pushed out of the artistic discernment of the Jews. Because the sadness is fully voiced, one can see the community begin to move in its buoyancy, but not too soon. This practice of *buoyancy through sadness* is one many pastors know about in situations of "bereavement." We have, however, not seen that the category of "bereavement" operates communally as well, concerning the loss of our "great days," as a superpower with an economy to match, or as a church that now tends to be a "has-been."

The sadness of Jews in exile can of course grow much more shrill. It is then not a far move from lament to rage, classically expressed in Psalm 137. The psalm is of course an embarrassment to us, because of its "lethal" ending. And yet every pastor knows about folk with exactly such rage, and for exactly the same reasons. We seethe, as did they, over our unfair losses that leave us displaced and orphaned. With such texts, the church need not engage in pious cover-up or false assurance. This psalm in its rage is an act of "catching up" with new reality. If Zion's songs are to be sung, it will be a long, long way from all old "Zions." The Psalmist is beginning to engage that tough but undeniable reality.

2. The utterance of the terms "forgotten, forsaken" in Lamentations 5:20 (on which see the same verbs and same sentiment in Isa. 49:14), suggests that the exiles are like "a motherless child," that is, an abandoned, vulnerable orphan. Exile is an act of being orphaned, and many folk now sense themselves in that status. There is no sure home, no old family place, no recognizable family food. I suggest the theme of *rootlessness*, as though we do not belong anywhere. The enormous popularity of Alex Haley's *Roots* came about, I suggest, not because of fascination with or guilt about slavery, but because of resonance with the need to recover connection and genealogy.

(On a less dramatic plane, it is astonishing how many people look to Salt Lake City, in order to have the Mormons find their ancestors.)

Exiles need to take with them old habits, old customs, old memories, old photographs. The scriptural resources for such uprooted folk, I suggest, are the genealogies, which have seemed to us boring and therefore have been skipped over.[16] We have skipped over them, I imagine, either because we thought those old names were not intrinsically interesting, or because we thought they referenced some family other than our own. The recovery of these genealogies could indeed give an index of the mothers and fathers who have risked before us, who have hoped before us, and who continue even now to believe in us and hope for us. The genealogies might be useful in the recovery of baptism, because in that act, we join a new family. And we are like any new in-law at a first family reunion, when we meet all the weird uncles and solicitous aunts who seem like an undifferentiated mass, until they are linked with lots of stories.[17] After the stories are known, then the list becomes meaningful, and is simply shorthand that makes and keeps the stories available. Two easy access points for such genealogy are (a) the Matthean genealogy, which includes some of our most scandalous mothers (Matt. 1:1-17); and (b) the recital in Hebrews 11 of all our family "by faith."

The texts serve to overcome the isolation of the orphan and our sense of "motherless" existence, by giving us the names of mothers and fathers, and by situating us in a "communion of saints" who are the living dead who continue to watch over us. I suggest that if the genealogical indices are well handled, they become a way to recover old narratives that contextualize our present faith. When well done, moreover, local congregations can extend the list, not only of members of their own congregation but of folk known publicly, beyond the congregation, who have risked for and shaped faith. It is inevitable that with this evocation of gratitude to those on the list, we enter our names on the same list with a sense of accountability and begin to understand what it might mean to have our own names written in "the book of life."[18]

3. The most obvious reality and greatest threat to exiles is the *power of despair.* On the one hand, everything for which we have worked is irretrievably lost. On the other hand, we are helpless in this circumstance and are fated here forever. In ancient Israel, this despair of a theological kind is rooted in two "failures of faith." On the one hand, Israel doubts *God's fidelity,* that is, God's capacity to care and remember (cf. Lam. 5:20, quoted in Isa. 49:14). On the other hand, Israel doubts *God's power* to save, even if God

remembers (cf. Isa. 50:2; 59:1). On both counts, Israel has concluded that in its exile, it is without a God who makes any difference, and it is therefore hopelessly in the grip of the perpetrators of exile.

The scriptural resource against this despair is voiced especially in Isaiah 40–55. This is a text well known to us, if for no other reason, than that Handel has made it available to us. Very often, however, critical study of this text has been focused on distracting questions such as "Who is the Suffering Servant?" Leaders of exilic communities in despair, as I suspect some of us are, would do better to focus on the primary intent of the poetry, namely, that God's powerful resolve is to transform the debilitating reality of exile. Of the rich resources in this poetry, we may identify especially four motifs voiced as hope against despair:

(a) It is this poetry that transforms the word "gospel" (*bśr*, "to bring good news") into a theological term. In 40:9 and 52:7, the "good news" is that YHWH has triumphed over the power of exile, that is, over Babylonian gods (cf. 46:1-4) and over Babylonian royal power (47:1-11). As a result, Israel's self-definition need not be derived from that harsh, seemingly permanent regime.

(b) It is Second Isaiah's words that explode the faith of Israel into creation faith (cf. 40:12-17; 42:5; 44:24). Now the scope of God's saving power is not a "nickel-and-dime" operation in Israel, but the whole of global reality is viewed as a resource whereby God's transformative action is mobilized on behalf of this little, needy community. In this poetry, creation is not an end in itself but an instrument of rescue. Israel is urged to "think big" and to "sing big" about the forces of life at work on its behalf.

(c) Speeches of judgment show God, as construed by this poet, engaged in a heavy-handed dispute with Babylonian gods, in order to delegitimate their claims and to establish the proper claims of Yahwistic faith (41:21-29; 44:6-7; 45:20-21). The purpose of such rhetorical action is to give Israel "spine," to enable Israel not to give up its covenantal identity for the sake of its ostensive masters. That is, Israel is invited to *hutzpah* in holding to its own peculiar identity.

(d) This defiant speech against the other, phoney gods is matched by an affirmative tenderness expressed in salvation oracles (41:13, 14-16; 43:1-5). Rolf Rendtorff and Rainer Albertz have noticed that "creation language" is used in salvation oracles not to refer to "the creation of the world" but for the creation of Israel, who is God's treasured creature.[19] As is often recognized, Isaiah 43:1-5 articulates something like baptismal phrasing: "I have called you by name, you are mine." That baptismal language, however, is cast in creation speech forms.

This combination of defiance and tenderness indicates that Israel's seem-ingly helpless present is teeming with liberating intentionality. Israel is expected, in this poetry, to cease its mesmerized commitment to the rulers of this age (here Babylon) who thrive on the despair of Israel, and to receive through this poetry the freedom of imagination to act "as" a people headed "home."[20] In our contemporary circumstance of ministry, I suggest that despair is our defining pathology, which robs the church of missional energy and of stewardship generosity. The poet who uttered these words has dared to voice an originary option against all the visible evidence. But then, faith is precisely and characteristically "the assurance of things hoped for, the conviction of things not seen" (Heb. 11:1). As long as the exiles hope for nothing and are convinced of nothing unseen, it is guaranteed that they will stay in thrall to Babylon. The poet refuses such a pitiful, shameful aban-donment of identity.

4. Exile is an experience of *profaned absence.* That is, the "absence of God" is not only a personal, emotional sense but a public, institutional awareness that "the glory has departed." In ancient Israel this sense had to do with the destruction of the temple, the departure of God from Jerusalem (cf. Ezek. 9–10) so that God "had no place," and the abusive handling of temple vessels, so that the very "vehicles for God" were treated like a tradeable commodity.[21]

In our time, it is clear that what have long been treasured symbols are treated lightly or with contempt. (I suspect that this is what is entailed in the great passion generated by "flag burning" and "bra burning," and such acts of defiance against "sacred order.") Very many people have concluded with chagrin that "nothing is sacred anymore." With the absence of God, larger "meanings" become impossible. And because God is absent, we become increasingly selfish and brutalizing, because without God, "every-thing is possible." (No doubt popular, "right-wing" religion trades effectively on this sense of loss.)

Unfortunately, critical scholarship (and especially Protestant usage) has neglected the texts that pertain to the "crisis of presence," which are found especially in the "Priestly (P) texts" of the Pentateuch.[22] With our deep-seated Protestant resistance to any sacramentalism that sounds automatic and/or routine, the P texts have been treated by us with a rather consistent lack of interest, if not disdain.

It is important for us, in our exilic situation, to renotice that these texts constitute a major pastoral response to the exilic crisis of absence. I suggested that these texts might be useful resources for ministry, if we understand them as a recovery of sacrament as a way to "host the holy" in a context of profane absence. That is, the priests had no inclination, or found it impossible, to affirm that God was everywhere loose in the exile of Babylon. Indeed, a case could be made in priestly perception, that God would refuse to be available in such a miserable context as Babylon. Where then might God be? The answer is, in the sacramental life of Israel, so that God becomes a counterpresence to Babylonian profanation. The reason for coming to "the holy place" is to come into "the presence" that is everywhere else precluded in this exile, which is under hostile management.

I suggest three aspects of this recovery of the sacramental (plus a footnote): (a) Central to the sacramental life of Israel was *circumcision* (see Gen. 17). To be sure, that powerful cultic act is profoundly patriarchal. In the exile, however, it becomes a rich and larger metaphor for faith (see Deut. 10:16; 30:6; Jer. 4:4). Moreover, the "marking" of circumcision is transposed in Christian practice into baptism, which, like circumcision, is a mark of distinctiveness. It distinguishes its subjects from the definitions of the empire, even if the Babylonians cannot see it. (b) *Sabbath* emerges as a primal act of faith in exile. I understand the Sabbath to be a quiet but uncompromising refusal to be defined by the production system of Babylon, so that life is regularly and with discipline enacted as a trusted gift and not as a frantic achievement. (c) Most important, the *tabernacle* is an imaginative effort to form a special place where God's holiness can be properly hosted and therefore counted upon (Exod. 25–31; 35–40, cf. Ezek. 40–48 on an exilic concern for cultic presence). I am not convinced that this text of Exodus 25–31; 35–40 describes any concrete, practiced reality in exilic Israel. It may be nothing more than a textual fantasy. Nonetheless, it is a fantasy about presence, about the willingness of the exodus God to sojourn amid this displaced people of the wilderness. While God is thus willing to occupy and visit a disestablished people, the presence of God is not casual or haphazard. It requires discipline and care that are almost punctilious.

It is thoroughly biblical to attend to modes of presence that are visible (material, physical), so that the whole of presence is not verbal (or sermonic). I understand the reasons why conventional Protestantism has avoided such modes of thought and practice. Such a resistance was necessary in order to break the terrible and destructive power of the old sacramentalism in the sixteenth century. It is the case, however, that our present "exilic" crisis is not marked by a threat of "popish sacramentalism," as in the sixteenth century. Our threat rather is a technological emptiness that is filled by the liturgies of consumerism and commodification. And the issue in our own context is whether holy presence can be received, imagined, and practiced in ways that counteract that powerful, debilitating ideology. It is clear that the letter to the Hebrews (chapters 7–10) does not flinch from thinking christologically in terms of tabernacle presence. I suspect that for exiles, a verbal presence by itself is too thin, which is why the Priestly materials came to dominate the canon. It is also why Reformed faith in the magisterial tradition may want to make ecumenical moves to reengage the very sacramentalism it scuttled. Exiles who live in a profaned context have a deep need to "touch and handle" things unseen.

5. Exile is an experience of *moral incongruity*. That is, the displacement and destructiveness of exile make one aware that the terrible fate of displacement is more massive than can be explained in terms of moral symmetry. The classic biblical response to exile is that exile is punishment from God for the violation of Torah. Such a guilt-focused interpretation does indeed keep the world morally coherent and reliable. But at enormous cost! The cost of protecting God's moral reliability is to take the blame for very large disorders. This sense of "blame," in my judgment, exacts too high a cost for moral symmetry, and so produces the practical problem of theodicy, the awareness that this "evil" cannot be explained by or contained in our "fault." Something else besides our "fault" is loose and at work in the destabilizing of our world.[23]

In the Old Testament, the problem of theodicy—that is, the thought that God is implicated in a morally incoherent world—surfaces in the book of Job. While the book of Job cannot be securely tied to the context of exile, most scholars believe it belongs there, and many believe it is a direct and intentional response to the oversimplification of retribution theology.[24]

Mutatis mutandis, the problem of theodicy belongs appropriately to our own exilic circumstance. If exile be understood as "the failure of the established church," it is difficult to think that this failure is "our fault," for the forces of secularism are larger than us, and it does not much good to blame somebody. If exile be understood as "the failure of the white, male, Western hegemony," it is difficult to take the blame as a white male, even if one is generically implicated. The book of Job is able to entertain in any exile, including ours, that something more is at work than fault, so that our circumstance of exile is not easily reduced to moral symmetry.

I think that the honest surfacing of this issue of theodicy, in Joban terms, would be a liberating act among us. It is an act that fully acknowledges moral asymmetry, that does not reduce reality to "scorekeeping," that refuses to accept all the blame, and that dares to entertain the unsettled thought of God's failure. In the poem of Job, both the terrible indictment of God (9:13-24) and the confident self-affirmation of Job (chapters 29–31) prepare the way for the whirlwind, which blows away all moral issues (38:1—42:6). In the extremity of exile, I believe it would be an important pastoral gain to have the whirlwind obliterate and blow away many of our all-consuming moral questions. In the poem of Job, the questions of failure, fault, blame, and guilt simply evaporate. We are invited to a larger vista of mystery that contains wild and threatening dimensions of faith. The poem extricates Israel from the barrenness of moral explanation and justification and thinks instead of dangerous trust and affirmation in a context where we cannot see our way through. The world of Job is filled with wondrous crocodiles (41:1-34) and hippopotamus (40:15-24) along with cunning evil, deep, unanswered questions, and vigorous doxology.

It is also a world where, through the dismay, gifts are given and life inexplicably goes on (42:7-17). If Job be misunderstood as an intellectual enterprise, it may cut the nerve of faith. But if it be taken as a pastoral opportunity to explode petty, narcissistic categories for a larger field of mystery, it might indeed enable exiles to embrace their self-concern, and then to move past it to larger, more dangerous dimension of living in an unresolvable and inexplicable world where God's mystery overrides all our moral programs.

6. The danger in exile is to become so preoccupied with self that one cannot get outside one's self to rethink, reimagine, and redescribe larger reality. Self-preoccupation seldom yields energy, courage, or freedom. In ancient Israel, one of the strategies for coping shrewdly and responsibly beyond self were the narratives of defiance and cunning that enjoined exiles not to confront their harsh overlords directly but to negotiate knowingly between faith and the pressures of "reality."[25]

If we can get past difficult critical problems, we may take some such narratives as models and invitations for living freely, dangerously, and tenaciously in a world where faith does not have its own way. Smith shows how these narratives perform a crucial strategic function and includes in his analysis the tales of Daniel, Joseph, and Esther. We may comment briefly on these resources: (a) The story of Joseph concerns the capacity of an Israelite to cooperate fully with the established regime (perhaps too fully), but to maintain at the same time an edge of discernment that permits him to look out for his folk. He does not fully adopt the "reality" defined by his overlords. (b) The tale of Esther shows a courageous Jew willing and able to outflank established power, to gain not only honor for herself but well-being for her people. (c) The story of Daniel shows a young man pressed into the civil service of the empire, able to exercise authority in the empire precisely because he maintained a sense of self rooted quite outside the empire.

This practice of narrative admits of no easy "Christ against culture" model, but recognizes the requirement of an endlessly cunning, risky process of negotiation. Such negotiations may seem to purists to be too accommodationist. And to accommodationists, they may seem excessively scrupulous. If, however, assimilation into the dominant culture is a major threat for exiles, the lead characters of these narratives do not forget who they are, with whom they belong, nor the God whom they serve. I imagine many baptized exiles must live such a life of endless negotiation. These narratives might name and clarify the process, and tilt self-perception toward membership in the faithful community. The stunning characters in these narratives are indeed "bilingual," knowing the speech of the empire and being willing to use it, but never forgetting the cadences of their "mother tongue."

IV

It is clear that "exile" is a rich and supple metaphor. As the biblical writers turned the metaphor of exile in various and imaginative directions, so may we. Note well, I have made no argument about the one-to-one match between metaphor and reality. I have proposed only that this metaphor mediates our experience to us in fresh ways, and gives access to scriptural resources in equally fresh ways.

There are two by-products in the utilization of a countermetaphor that I will mention. On the one hand, pondering this metaphor helps us think again about a rich variety of metaphors in Scripture that can function as a kaleidoscope, to let us see our life and faith in various dimensions, aspects, angles, and contexts. Such an exercise may move us past a single, frozen metaphor that we take as a permanent given. On the other hand, the availability of a countermetaphor that opens us to a plurality of metaphors helps us notice that our usual, "taken-for-granted" world is also a metaphorical construct, even if an unrecognized or unacknowledged one. That is, postmodern awareness helps us to consider that there is no "given reality" behind our several constructs, but even our presumed given reality is itself a rhetorical construct, whether of the cold war, or consumer capitalism, or the "free world," or the male hegemony, or whatever.[26] An awareness of this reality about "world" and about "self" opens the way to liminality, which permits transformation of all those "givens."[27]

1. In the argument I have made, there are important interpretive issues to be considered by the preacher. I suggest that the Bible be understood as a set of models (paradigms) of reality made up of images situated in and contextualized by narratives.[28] These narrative renderings of reality in the Bible (as elsewhere) are not factual reportage, but are inevitably artistic constructs that stand a distance from any "fact" and are filtered through interest of a political kind. I think it a major gain to see that the Bible in its several models is an artistic, rhetorical proposal of reality that seeks to persuade (convert) to an alternative sense of God, world, neighbor, and self.

2. As there are interpretive implications to the argument I have made, so there are also crucial ecclesial implications in construing life through the metaphor of exile. This literary, rhetorical focus invites the baptismal community to construe its place in the world differently and, I imagine, faithfully.[29] The engagement with this metaphor may deliver pastors and people from magisterial notions of being (or needing to be) chaplains for the establishment and guardians of stable public forms of life.

I understand the liberty given through this metaphor quite practically and concretely. As the preacher stands up to preach among the exiles, the primal task (given this metaphor) concerns the narration and nurture of a counteridentity, the enactment of the power of hope in a season of despair, and the assertion of a deep definitional freedom from the pathologies, coercions, and seductions that govern our society. The preacher is not called upon to do all the parts of public policy and public morality, but to give spine, resolve, courage, energy, and freedom that belong to a counteridentity.

As the congregation listens and participates in this odd construal of reality, the metaphor might also make a decisive difference in the listening. The working woman or man knows that "it is a jungle out there," and that one without a resilient, resistant identity can indeed be eaten alive. The teenager off to school is in the rat race of success and popularity, leave alone competence and adequacy. And now every man, woman, and child is invited to a zone of freedom which the dominant culture cannot erode. That zone of freedom is grounded in what the baptized know:

- that our sense of *loss and sadness* is serious and honorable, and one need not prop up or engage in denial;

- that our *rootedness* enables us to belong, so that we are not swept away by every wind of doctrine, every market seduction, or every economic coercion, knowing who we are;

- that the promises of the Creator surge in our life and in our world, so that the *manipulatable despair* of the hopeless, which turns folk into commodity consumers, is not the live edge of our existence;

- that there is a *holy, awesome presence* that persists against the emptied profanation of promiscuous economic and lustful sexuality, that true *desire* is for the presence that overrides all of our trivialized desires that are now robbed of authority;

- that the world is *not morally coherent,* but there is a deep incongruity in which we live, that we need neither to resolve, explain, or deny. A raw, ragged openness is linked to the awesome reality of God's holiness;

- that we are always about to be domesticated, we have these *narrative models of resistance, defiance, and negotiation* which remind us that there is more to life than conformist obedience or shameful accommodation. We know the names of those who have faced with freedom the trouble that is caused by faith.

3. There is nothing in this faith model of "sectarian withdrawal" of the kind of which Hauerwas and Willimon are often accused.[30] The baptized do indeed each day find themselves finally in the presence of those who preside over the exile, that is, in the presence of "Babylonians." They are unavoidable, even in this model, or especially in this model. This baptismal identity is not designed for a ghetto existence. It is rather intended for full participation in the life of the dominant culture, albeit with a sense of subversiveness that gives unnerving freedom.

Jeremiah knew about the dangers of withdrawal from dominant culture. For that reason, in his letter to the exiles, the prophet encourages the exiles with amazing, endlessly problematic words.[31]

> But seek the welfare (*shalom*) of the city where I have sent you into exile, and pray to the Lord on its behalf, for in its welfare (*shalom*) you will find your welfare (*shalom*). (Jer. 29:7)

There is no "separate peace" for exiles, no private deals with God, no permitted withdrawal from affairs of the empire. The only *shalom* these troubled Jews would know is the *shalom* wrought for Babylon. The letter implies that the exiled community of Jews can indeed impact Babylon with the *shalom* through its active concern and prayer, but only as the community knows that it is not Babylon. The distance from Babylon makes possible an impacting nearness to Babylon.

4. Finally, but not too soon, the preacher's theme for exiles is homecoming. The home promised to the exiles, however, is not any nostalgic return to yesteryear, for that home is irreversibly gone. Rather, the home for which the exiles yearn and toward which they hope is the "kingdom of God," an arena in which God's good intention is decisive. The New Testament struggles to speak concretely about that realm and can do so only indirectly and by allusion, for that realm lies beyond all our known categories.

It is no stretch to link *homecoming* to *gospel* to *kingdom*. The linkage is already made in Isaiah 40–55 and in Ezekiel 37:1-14. It is telling that Karl Barth speaks of the "obedience of the Son of God" under the rubric of "The Way of the Son of God into a Far Country."[32] The textual allusion is of course to the Prodigal Son, though Barth's accent is on the "emptying and humiliation" of Jesus, as in Philippians 2:5-11.[33] Conversely, in speaking of the exaltation of Jesus, Barth writes of "the Homecoming of the Son of Man."[34] An important critique may be made of Barth's usage, for it reflects his characteristic transcendentalism, whereby the course of human existence is by definition exile. It is my intention to suggest that the metaphor of exile–homecoming, which Barth handles christologically and which Buber handles philosophically, be understood among us ecclesiologically with reference to the concrete realities of economics, politics, and social relations.

Consider, then, what it means to be exiles awaiting and hoping for homecoming to the kingdom of God! In the Bible, the image of "kingdom of God" is stitched together by narratives of miracle and wonder, whereby God does concrete acts of transformation that the world judges to be impossible. The "kingdom" is a time and place and context in which God's "impossibilities" for life, joy, and wholeness are all made possible and available.[35] In the meantime, the waiting, hoping exiles are fixed upon these impossibilities. In so doing, the exiles refuse the world's verdict on the impossibilities, and, as a result, they pay less heed and allegiance to the world's wearisome possibilities. The alternative to this subversive entry into the world is to accept the world's possibilities as the only chance for the future. Such a decision rejects the miracles of God and so enters endlessly into the seductive land of exile. Failing the countervision of the gospel, we will no doubt "labor for that which does not satisfy" (Isa. 55:2).

10

Preaching a Sub-Version

There was a time, perhaps 250 years ago, when the Christian preacher could count on the shared premises of the listening community, reflective of a large theological consensus. There was a time, a very long time ago, when the *assumption of God* completely dominated Western imagination, and the Holy Catholic Church uttered roughly the shared consensus of all parties. That shared consensus was rough and perhaps not very healthy, but at least the preacher could work from it.

In that ancient world—moving to the modern—the consensus, deep and broad, made it all but impossible to be an atheist. Not only was the thought of atheism intellectually not available, but emotionally and culturally there was no receptive context for such a notion. Indeed, Michael Buckley has traced the intellectual developments of the seventeenth and eighteenth centuries that made atheism a credible intellectual alternative for the first time, and then an emotionally and culturally bearable interpretive posture.[1] As time has gone on, through the nineteenth century, we have had to make a series of adjustments and settlements, seemingly unending adjustments and settlements, always at the expense of theism and in concession to atheism. Those concessions have been required primarily because of the emergency of a thinking autonomy in the world, rooted in Descartes and expressed belatedly in Robert Bellah's report on "Sheilaism."[2] By the time of the twentieth century, the settlement largely has been that God is still a cherished affirmation in private matters ("family values"), but the public realm is mostly atheistic, without God, so that "might makes right." Appeal is characteristically made to legitimation other than God, appeal to a public God having become increasingly difficult and embarrassing.

And now, so it seems to me, by the time of the twenty-first century, the intellectual-emotional-cultural situation of the seventeenth century, for

147

complex reasons, has been completely reversed. Atheism is now a credible, perhaps a consensus option for what is serious in life, and the articulation of life-with-God has become a risky intellectual outpost, perhaps as difficult and as odd and as embarrassing as was atheism in the seventeenth century. It seems to me not so important to review all of the complex reasons for that inversion—reasons that include the rise of scientific thinking, the emergence of Enlightenment autonomy, and the shift into high-gear technology as the way to better our life—high-gear technology that begins in research and development and that ends, inevitably I believe, in militarism. It is more important to recognize our fairly recently changed intellectual-emotional-theological situation in which we do our preaching and, for that matter, in which we do what we can of our own trusting and believing.

A Freeing and Primitive Act

In the seventeenth century, it was hard, courageous work to imagine—consequently to reimagine—the world *without* God. And now, as we move into the twenty-first century, in the face of Enlightenment autonomy issuing in autonomous power and autonomous knowledge, it is hard, courageous work to imagine—consequently to reimagine—the world *with* God.

Of course, I am speaking with evangelical particularity. I have used the terms "atheism" and "theism" for purposes of symmetry. But I do not in fact mean "theism," for theism of sorts is alive and well in our postmodern world. Indeed, the polls show that, in its indeterminate forms, almost everybody believes in God. But I mean the peculiar trinitarian claims for God concerning the one we confess in the history of Israel and in the narrative of Jesus. Theism of certain kinds is still culturally credible, but we are speaking of none other than the creator of heaven and earth whose quintessential intention showed up, we confess, in the absence of Friday.

And so I pursue a single point: In a culture that has learned well how to imagine—how to make sense of—the world without reference to the God of the Bible, it is the preacher's primary responsibility to invite and empower and equip the community to reimagine the world as though YHWH were a key and decisive player. The task is as up-stream as was seventeenth-century atheism. This is an uncommonly difficult intellectual task, almost sure to be misunderstood. Its difficulty is compounded, moreover, by its inescapable economic by-product, because the God of the Bible is endlessly restless with socioeconomic power arrangements that the world takes as normal. If you are like me, you keep hoping Sunday by Sunday, as we do our hard intellectual work, that folks will not immediately notice the inescapable economic implications that come with it.

I recently gave some lectures at Baldwin-Wallace College. The lectures were endowed by a very generous family that is concerned that religion should be prominent in the life of that school. Two sons of the original donor, enterprising gracious businessmen, attended the lecture in which I offered a biblical critique of capitalism. The task was not easy. It turned out all right, however, because all that was noticed by the appreciative donors was that I had quoted lots of Bible. The rest was happily lost on them. I understand the moment of preaching, in the designated place of preaching, to be a *freeing and primitive act* that flies in the face of all our accepted certitudes, conservative and liberal.

The Old, Elusive Text

I speak as an Old Testament teacher, though I think it is not significantly different in the New Testament. The preacher has some considerable resources for this dangerous, problematic task of reimagining the world with YHWH as its key player. There is the deep faith of the present community that matters more than I think we usually credit. There is the long history of the church, written in creeds and manifestos and architecture, and set deep in the lives of saints who in their dangerous innocences made this primitive faith claim unavoidable.

But mainly, in the midst of these evidences and testimonies, what the preacher has is this old text, so remote, so difficult, so misleading, so problematic, so unintimidated. It is the enduring sound of a thousand unclear witnesses offering a cacophony of truthfulness, the script for our own dangerous, primitive reimagining.

Of all that could be said of this script, my initial point is a simple but crucial one. It is in *Hebrew,* not Latin. I do not say that to suggest that one cannot read it without knowledge of Hebrew grammar, though such knowledge is a good idea and a real advantage. I say it rather to make the point that this text, in its very utterance, in its ways of putting things, is completely unfamiliar to us.[3] The utterance of the primitive God of Scripture is an utterance that is in an unfamiliar mode. Let me say what I mean.

Hebrew, even for those who know it much better than I do, is endlessly imprecise and unclear. It lacks the connecting words; it denotes rather than connotes; it points and opens and suggests, but it does not conclude or define. That means it is a wondrous vehicle for what is suggested but hidden, what is filled with imprecision and inference and innuendo, a vehicle for contradiction, hyperbole, incongruity, disputation. Now the reason this may be important is that in a society of technological control and precision, we are seduced into thinking that if we know the codes, we can pin all meaning down, get all mysteries right and have our own way, without surprise, without deception, without amazement, without gift, without miracle, without address, without absence, without anything that signals mystery or risk. In such a society as that, the church and its preachers practice another mode of speech, so that the *way we imagine* is congruent with *who it is that we imagine.*[4]

Long before our contemporary technology, the church tried the same trick with Latin; one does not need to know much Latin to know that it is regular, precise, and symmetrical. It goes from one margin of the page to the other; it admits of only controllable cadences. For some of us who left the Latin liturgy in the sixteenth century, our alternative strategy has been *historical criticism,* another "Latin-like" attempt to control and reduce and tame and understand and limit and manipulate.

But testimony to the God of Israel known in Jesus is not "Latin-like," and it is not historical criticism-like. It is more like depth psychology, for Freud was, in his larger discernments, thoroughly Jewish.[5] Freud understood that in dreams, in the unconscious, in the hiddenness of utterance, there are *endless zones of contradiction* that we keep negotiating—occasionally with Freudian slips—and there are *endless layers of interpretation,* no one of which can ever be more than provisional. And the reason depth psychology is marked as "depth" is that one can always push deeper into another layer of hiddenness and there find yet another disclosure of significance.

Preachers have on their hands a Subject who is not obvious and a mode of speech that is endlessly open and demanding ... that makes preaching deeply demanding in a congregation schooled in one-dimensional, technological certitude. The offer of such technological certitude, however, not only misreads the text and the God of the text; it seriously distorts and misrepresents the true human scene, as every pastor knows, for the human scene is one of endless zones of contradiction and endless layers of interpretation, no one of which can ever be more than provisional. I suggest, for that reason, that faithful speech about God is sure to be faithful speech about the complexity of being human, and this in a society determined to oversimplify. I summarize the problematic of the Bible about God in this way:

1. The God of the Bible is endlessly *irascible*—capable of coming and going, judging and forgiving, speaking and remaining silent—in ways that make the next time endlessly uncertain. I do not want to overstate the case. But it is this quality that pushes the Psalmists to the extremity of their imagination, and it is this quality that evokes in the prophets daring images and affrontive metaphors, because no easy language will ever get this God said right.

2. The testimony we have concerning this God is *endlessly elusive*. Sometimes there is a direct offer of God, but more often there is fantasy, sideways figures, odd articulations, some of which are covered over by church cliché, some of which are lost in the caution of translators.

3. The *irascible* character of God and the *elusive* rhetoric of the text mean that the outcome of textual testimony is deeply *polyvalent*, that is, it speaks with many voices and is profoundly open to rich variation in rendering.

Preachers stand up to make utterance about this odd, problematic God in a society that is flattened in atheism, and they have on their hands a quality of the *irascible*, the *elusive*, and the *polyvalent*. Almost none of this, moreover, is available to or recognized among most of our listeners. Because it is too unsettling and difficult, we tend to fall back on more familiar ground of safe practices, blessed ideologies, scholastic closures, or liberal crusades. Don't we all!

But the God of Israel, belatedly bodied in Jesus of Nazareth, is our Subject. Such utterance is unsettling, open, freeing, demanding. Such utterance in our time, as in all the times of our mothers and fathers, generates possibilities—public and personal—that are not otherwise possible, not otherwise doable or thinkable. When this God is uttered, the closed world of atheism is shattered; those who hear dream dreams and see visions, sense power and receive courage, take up energy for newness where none seemed offered. It is a lot to expect from an utterance, taken off from an old non-Latin Subject. But it is what our mothers and fathers have long counted on. It is, moreover, more or less what people hope for, even in our great fear that it might come to pass.

Preaching as Sub-Version

My thesis is that preaching is a *sub-version*. The play that I intend is obvious. Preaching is never dominant version, never has been. It is always a sub-version: always a version, a rendering of reality that lives under the dominant version. We may adopt a strategy of making our "under-version" sound closely like the dominant version, or an alternative strategy of showing our "under-version" to be in deep tension with the dominant version.

The *dominant version* of reality each of us would mark differently, but we likely would not disagree much on its nature. Perhaps the logo of the dominant version is a *swoosh*, à la Nike, a "life is for winners" motto of a private, individualized kind for those who can make it in the market or in the sports arena, who live well, are self-indulgent, but who never get involved in anything outside of their own success. The Nike version of reality, deeply rooted in Western Enlightenment consumerism and in U.S. democratic capitalism, has an old history. In the Old Testament, it appears as coercive Babylonian imperial expectations looking back to Egyptian brick quotas. In the New Testament, it is the endless requirements of Jewish punctiliousness or the demand of Roman emperor worship; it is Luther's "works," and in our day perhaps it is "the end of welfare as we know it," the pressure to get kids into the right preschools for the sake of working someday for Intel. It is an act of dominant imagination that screens out all "neighbors," neighbors who can be screened out if the God of all Neighborliness can be refashioned into a God who celebrates the virtues of private achievement. It is dominant, so dominant, that it is taken as a given, so dominant that it sustains both liberal and conservative ideology, so dominant that even we who critique it are deeply committed to it, so dominant it isn't worth criticizing—too costly.

And then we preachers are summoned to get up and utter a *sub-version* of reality, an alternative version of reality that says another way of life in the world is not only possible, but peculiarly mandated and peculiarly valid. It is a *sub-version* because we must fly low, stay under the radar, and hope not to be detected too soon; sub-version, because it does indeed intend to *subvert* the dominant version and to empower a community of *sub-versives* who are determined to practice their lives according to a different way of imaging.

I understand, then, that preaching is a peculiar, freighted, risky act each time we do it:

- entrusted with an irascible, elusive, polyvalent Subject;
- flying low under the dominant version with a *subversive* offer of *another version* to be embraced by *subversives*.

I focus this strange act precisely on one pivot point that is fairly obvious as illustrative. The *dominant version* of reality among us is a narrative of *vio-*

lence. This can run all the way from sexual abuse and racial abuse to the strategy of wholesale imprisonment of "deviants" to military macho that passes for policy. It eventuates in road rage and in endless TV violence piped into our homes for our watching pleasure. I suspect that underlying all of these modes of violence is the *economic violence* embedded in free-market ideology that denies an obligation of openness to the neighbor who is in truth a deep inconvenience and a drain upon resources.

If we take that as dominant version, then the preacher is to sub-vert by an act of sustained imagination that is an antidote to a culture of violence and this in the name of God whose own history is marked on numerous occasions by acts of violence.[6] I suggest an easy identification of three dimensions of violence and three antidotal responses:

1. The taproot of violence is *material deprivation,* fostered by a myth of scarcity, the driving power of market ideology. The counter to material deprivation is a practice of sharing that is rooted in and appeals to *an affirmation of abundance.* That affirmation of abundance, rooted in the generosity of God, is deeply subversive to the deep social myth of scarcity.[7] The preacher has available the memories of that time in the wilderness when bread inexplicably came down from heaven, and "nobody had too little and nobody had too much" (Exod. 16:17-18). And we have that memory of Jesus with compassion on the crowd; he took, he blessed, he broke, he gave . . . he fed five thousand with twelve baskets of bread left over (Mark 6:30-44), and then two chapters later he did it all over again, he took, he blessed, he broke, he gave—four thousand and seven baskets (Mark 8:1-9). And then he said to his bewildered disciples: "You don't get it, do you?" (Mark 8:21). When the gospel is trusted, loaves abound!—and violence from common deprivation becomes obsolete.

2. The taproot of violence is a *breakdown of connections,* the severing of elemental social relationships so that folk are driven into isolation and then made desperate and frantic. I commend a book by Fox Butterfield, *All God's Children,* a five-generation family history that begins in the legendary violence of South Carolina in slavery and culminates in black urban crime in New York city, driven by black urban rage.[8] The focus is on the fifth generation—Willie—who is now in a New York prison, the most violent criminal ever held in that state system.

The argument of the book is that the failure to sustain a human, familial communal social fabric, a failure rooted in the intrinsic violence of slavery, makes the strategy of violence inevitable. Of course it is easy to spot violence among poor blacks. But it is the same violence (is it not?) working by and among the white urban elites who know nothing but self-indulgence at the expense of the neighbor, and so the entire social fabric is reduced to a violent context to see who can have the most and who can have first and who can have best, called "opportunity" by free-market violence, wanting to escape regulation, called by Nike, "It's not about playing well, it's about winning."

I understand none of this to be a proper theme for preaching—except that since the violence of Pharaoh against the slaves, the God of Sinai has offered an alternative and an antidote to violence, an offer of covenant, a vision, a structure, and a practice that bind the "haves" and the "have-nots" into one shared community, so that we are indeed members of one another. We live in a world of kinship, where when one suffers all suffer and when one rejoices all rejoice together. It is indeed covenantal community that is the only available alternative to the dissociation that fosters and legitimates and thrives on violence from below and violence from above.

3. The taproot of violence is surely *silence*, of being vetoed and nullified and canceled so that we have no say in the future of the community or of our own lives. How odd, in the midst of a technological revolution offering broad communication that serious input into our common future is increasingly limited and monopolized, so that we cynically conclude that our say does not matter anyway. The silenced are increasingly like a driven, helpless, desperate two-year-old who, having no say will enact a tantrum; and so the tantrums build in Northern Ireland and among the Palestinians and in our own abandoned cities. Or, to take it more intimately: We can count on it, every time a neighbor gets a machine gun and kills seventeen neighbors, the next day the comment is sure to be, "I don't know, he lived alone, kept to himself, and never talked to anybody." And we collude in the silence, the abused protecting the abuser until the killing comes.

We of all people have the textual resources authorizing and legitimating and modeling *speech that breaks the silence* of violence and the violence of silence. At the very outset of our story, it says of our victimized mothers and fathers in Egypt, "they groaned and cried out," and God heard and God saw and God knew and God remembered and God came down to save (Exod. 2:23-25). But unlike our high Calvinist notions of sovereignty, the break comes *from below* in the daring speech of the silenced. Out of that comes this richness of complaint psalms and lament psalms and psalms of rage and hate and resentment, the voice from below refusing the silence, speaking truth amid power, speaking truth to holiness and evoking newness.[9] It is all there in the preacher's script. Except that the colluding church and we colluding preachers and our colluding hymnal committees cover the Psalms, enhance the silence, and foster in our naïve ways more violence.

The antidotes to violence in the text of the preacher—the text of the church—are small and incidental and local, as the work of the preacher always is:

1. The *offer of bread* amid the material deprivation is told in little ways:

> When David [fled for his life] ... Barzillai the Gileadite from Roge-lim brought beds, basins, and earth vessels, wheat, barley, meal, parched grain, beans, lentils, honey and curds, sheep, and cheeses for David and the people with him to eat, for they said, "The troops are hungry and weary, and thirsty in the wilderness." (2 Sam. 17:27-29)

The gesture of Barzillai may have been calculated politics and military strategy. In the midst of that, though, the preacher can show that the narrative of public life depends on the concrete offer of bread that resists deprivation. What strikes me about the text is the quintessential human act of being sure that bread is passed to those who need bread, an act that anticipates by centuries the mandate:

> Is not this the feast that I choose. . . .
> Is it not to share your bread with the hungry,
> and to bring the homeless poor into your house? (Isa. 58:6-7)

The violence dissipates where natural linkages are made.

2. The affirmation of *covenantal solidarity* amid social dissociation is rooted in the practice of God's own life:

> For the Lord your God is God of gods and Lord of lords, the great God, mighty, awesome, who is not partial and takes no bribe, who executes justice for the orphan and the widow, who loves the stranger, providing them food and clothing. You shall love the stranger for you were strangers in the land of Egypt. (Deut. 10:17-19)

Imagine YHWH, the strongest one in the community, running a food pantry and collecting clothing for widows and orphans, physical gestures of solidarity that concretely and intensely bind the God of all creation to the undocumented workers and welfare recipients. In the end, Moses says, "You do it too."

3. The *legitimation of speech* in a context of enforced silence is given us even in the story of Jesus:

> Bartimaeus, a blind beggar, was sitting by the roadside. When we heard that it was Jesus of Nazareth, he began to shout and say, "Jesus,

Son of David, have mercy on me!" Many sternly ordered him to be quiet, but he cried out even more loudly, "Son of David, have mercy on me!" Jesus stood still and said, "Call him to me." (Mark 10:46-49)

Jesus did not initiate the action. Bartimaeus pushed his way in. He pushed his way in by loud insistence while "many" shushed him. Perhaps "many" includes some disciples who were interested in a nice meeting. Health came to this blind man by abrasive insistence and disruption. Had he been finally shushed, moreover, at best there would be no healing, at worst perhaps he would have begun throwing angry stones at Jesus and his bunch, because he would have been refused access.

Now my point is not to focus on violence per se. I do so only because violence saturates the dominant textual versions of our social reality. That dominant version (a) thinks *bread must be guarded*, and not shared; (b) thinks it is *each against all*, with no ground for community; and (c) thinks *silence can authenticate the status quo*. Our best strategies for the maintenance of advantage carry with them the very seeds of upheaval and disruption. The preacher has the script and the burden and the chance of a sub-version of social reality, whereby bread and covenantal speech offer a humanity against violence. It strikes me afresh that the preacher's sub-version of reality is not given in large ideological slogans, but in small, dense, particular texts:

- a gesture by Barzillai with a detail down to beans and lintels;
- a clothing drive for widows and orphans operated by the Lord of the Exodus;
- Bartimaeus the beggar who crowds into the doctor's office to demand and receive healing.

These local, cherished memories seed our reimagination of reality outside the killing fields that the dominant version takes as normative.

Exile, Oddity, Utterance

My theme is *alternative,* sub-version to version, the sermon as a moment of alternative imagination, the preacher exposed as point-man, point-woman, to make up out of nothing more than our memory and our hope and our faith, a radical option to the normalcy of deathliness. It occurs to me that the *scandal of particularity* so prominent in the election of Israel and so decisive in the incarnation of Jesus is pervasive in biblical faith, always so particular, always so peculiar, always so at odds. It occurs to me that the *Jewish imagination* of the Old Testament is so peculiar and so particular because Jews are always the odd men and women out, always at odds, always at risk, always in the presence of an empire with its insistent version of reality, always telling the boys and girls that we are different, different because we have been in the demanding presence of the Holy One, and now we must keep redeciding for a life propelled by that Presence. The Jews, over time, devised signals of oddity—Sabbath, kosher, circumcision.[10]

In parallel fashion, for like reasons, the baptismal imagination of the New Testament is so peculiar and so particular because Christians are always odd men and women come together in odd communities and congregations, always at odds, always at risk, always in the presence of large cultural empires that want to dissolve our oddity for reason of state, always telling the girls and boys we are different because we have been with Jesus. We are forever reimagining and retelling and reliving our lives through the scandal of Friday and the rumor of Sunday. We, like Jews, devise signals of oddity, the notice of new life, the bread of brokenness, the wine of blessedness, and the neighbor—always the neighbor—who is for us a signal of the love of God.

The maintenance of oddity—that creates freedom for life, energy for caring, and joy through the day—is the first task of the preacher. It spins off into public policy and proposes reordered public life. But the first task is the maintenance of oddity for the people in the room in the sound of the preacher's voice. When an Old Testament teacher thinks about the maintenance of oddity, the inevitable beginning place is Second Isaiah, not only for what is said, but for what we imagine the context to be.

I believe that in "the Christian West" the baptized community is now in something like *exile,* a place I characterize as hostile or indifferent to our primal faith claims.[11] So it is as in Babylon when the Jewish prism of life was regarded as an imperial problem, or at least an inconvenience. And so it is in consumer-oriented capitalism in the West, where the church is a cultural problem or at least an inconvenience. That is what the Babylonians thought, and the evidence is that many of the Jews agreed. Many of the Jews found it too expensive or troublesome to maintain odd identity, because you could not get good jobs and you could not get your kids into good schools. Consequently, giving up oddity is a small price to pay for well-being offered by the empire.

Then there arises this daring *hutzpah*-filled poet who seeks to resist the sellout of Jewishness and to foster and evoke and enhance the oddity. It is his urging, in utterance after utterance, that odd Yahwistic identity is valid and viable, because Yʜwʜ, the key player in this odd identity, is back in play in the empire. The power and persuasiveness of the dominant Babylonian version of reality had all but eliminated Yʜwʜ, and nobody thought Yʜwʜ was a factor any more. Yʜwʜ becomes an available factor in the life of the community only through the daring utterance of the poet. The poet anticipates the overthrow of Babylon and its dominant version of reality through Cyrus the Persian. Cyrus is an agent—so says the poet—of Yʜwʜ, the real governor of world history.

The story line is given through a variety of rhetorical ventures, of which I will comment on four. This poet is a daring preacher, and I want you to see simply that given faith and given imagination, one can do almost anything rhetorically.

1. *Isaiah 41:21-29.* The poet imagines and creates before the imagination of the listening community of not-quite-convinced Jews, a law court. That law court exists only on the lips of the poet; but the scene is vivid enough to last through eight verses, enough for twenty minutes if you talk slowly. Yʜwʜ, the creator of heaven and earth, holds court. The question before the court is, *Who is a true God?* The court summons the gods of Babylon for questioning. Those gods did not expect to be summoned by a Jewish court; but they are. They had been in charge so long they did not anticipate that they had to give a detailed account of themselves and so justify their claims.

In the court, the poet has Yʜwʜ speak, in order to taunt the Babylonians. I suppose some Jews were fed up with Babylonian arrogance and would have liked to taunt, but did not dare. And now the poet does it in the protected place of Jewish utterance. The gods of the empire are asked:

Tell us what happened . . . silence;
tell us what is to happen . . . silence;
tell us what is to come hereafter . . . silence;
do good . . . silence;
do harm . . . silence;
frighten us . . . silence.

These gods cannot say "boo."

Verdict: You are nothing!
           Your work is nothing!
           Your worshipers are nothing!

Then YHWH takes the stand; and YHWH can talk! YHWH has authority and energy and vitality. Unlike the silence of the empire, this irascible YHWH can give evidence for YHWH's claim:

I stirred up Cyrus;
I first declared it;
I gave Jerusalem a herald of good tidings;
no one helped;
no one consoled;
no one answered.

Verdict: I am the real thing; they are empty wind.

The rhetoric is and is intended to be subversive. It addressed the imagination of Jews. It asserts that the military-industrial authority of Babylon cannot keep its promises, cannot make you happy, cannot make you safe. YHWH is unlike all of this . . . particular, peculiar, scandalous, odd, resilient, reliable. Go YHWH!

The result is modest, as with most sermons. The Jews leave the place of utterance. There is a chance now that they will stay Jews, with freedom for action, with energy for caring, with resolve to stay odd. What is given in the liturgical moment, of course, is not known by the Babylonian authorities. No doubt many in that meeting where they heard the daring poetry were ambivalent: why Jewish, why odd, why circumcised, why baptized? The evidence *out there* seems to be against the claims made *in here* for YHWH, but the poet makes the claims anyway. The images offered haunt and haunt and will haunt again, and will not quit.

2. Isaiah 41:8-13. In the same chapter, the God who speaks abrasively in the courtroom to expose the pitiful gods of the empire here speaks pastorally in the family. Here there are no Babylonians, only bewildered Jews, treasured people of YHWH who thought they had been abandoned. The God of the exiles speaks:

You Israel, my servant,
Jacob whom I have chosen,
offspring of Abraham, my friend,
you whom I took from the end of the earth.
I called from its farthest corners,
saying to you, "You are my servant,
I have chosen you, I have not cast you off."

The chosen in exile had almost forgotten and had almost been forgotten. It had been a long time since they had been called by their intimate names of faith, because in Babylon they were nothing more than imperial statistics.

And now speaks the God who remembers. This God names their names, their family names, the names of most intimate identity, and in so doing mobilizes the precious stories of promise in Genesis, situating these exiles among Jacob and Abraham, who are friend, chosen, gathered. The poem is like the television show *Cheers* . . . where everybody knows your name! Imagine, exiles have not been called by their baptismal names for a long time. For many exiles in this technological rat race, the church is the only place in town where everybody knows your name.

This God continues to speak, the most personal utterance we all crave, the one we first hear from mother; now speaks the mothering God to the motherless exiles: "Fear Not. . . . Do not be afraid. . . . I am with you. . . . I am right here." Do not be afraid; I am your God. I am here in Babylon. I am here in exile. I am God here in the empire. You are not alone. Stay with me. This is an intimate word of assurance. It is an intimate word on the lips of the creator of heaven and earth, the one who authorizes oddity, the one who speaks the words the empire would most like to stop, because people mothered beyond fear are not so easily managed or administered or intimated.

> I will strengthen you;
> I will help you;
> I will uphold you with my right hand
> . . . those who war against you will be nothing at all,
> for I, the Lord God, hold your right hand;
> It is I who say to you,
> "do not fear . . . I will help you."

This is only an utterance. It is only poetry. And then the Jews must leave their special place of poetry and imagination, some cynical, some bewildered, some touched, some sensing the strangeness . . . tingling, held, affirmed, empowered, not so downcast, not so bought off, not so compromised. And the Babylonians haven't a clue! They do not know about the strangeness that opens for newness through utterance. But it has been spoken. And here and there it has been heard.

3. *Isaiah 52:7-10.* The defeat of the Babylonians goes on in an imaged *courtroom.* The "fear not" of YHWH is uttered in circles of *familial intimacy.* These two daring rhetorical strategies prepare the ground for *gospel,* the

news uttered among exiles. It is this poet among our people who makes the word "gospel" into a core theological term:

> How beautiful upon the mountains
> are the feet of the messenger
> who announces *shalom*,
> who brings good news,
> who announces salvation,
> who says to Zion . . . "Your God reigns."

The word is "gospel." The good news as gospel is that YHWH as God has just now regained governance.

The outcome is that Babylon has been defeated; the Babylonian gods are weak; they are nothing to fear, nothing to lose, nothing to pay, nothing to joy. The news is that the dominant vision of reality has been defeated. The odd sub-version of reality now has a chance. The sentinels lift up their voices, for they had been waiting and watching for a long time. The ruins of Jerusalem sing. The despairing dance. The desolate are in wonder. Because the odd God of this odd people in this odd version of reality has come to power.

It is gospel . . . but only a poetic moment among exiles. It is news, but not yet public. It is only liturgy, only utterance, only imagination. The same sort of liturgical utterance in imagination is offered when Jesus of Nazareth came to say, "repent . . . the kingdom of God is at hand" (Mark 1:15). He just said it, and some believed and began a new trajectory of existence. Everything begins in the utterance.

4. *Isaiah 52:10-11.* So, says the poet, on the basis of the news, "depart, depart." Leave Babylon. Leave the dominant version of reality. Leave the place of fear and anxiety. Leave and head home to Jewishness, to obedience, to joy, to freedom. The gospel is an alternative to the dominant version of reality that is always reductive, endlessly robbing us of our humanity. The way is clear for a seriously different way of life. The poem offers a future that can be taken up as we are able.

Departure

But of course this *gospel of departure* in the poetry of Second Isaiah is only a retelling of the primal narrative of the exodus. The exodus narrative is not historical reportage. It is rather stylized liturgy in order that "you may tell your children in time to come." What you shall tell your children is:

- "we groaned and cried out" (Exod. 2:23-25), going public in our protest against the dominant narrative version of reality that incessantly said, "Make more bricks";

- the technological program of research and development in ancient Egypt matched YHWH's first two miracles (plagues). But we knew we had reached the outer limit of Egyptian technological capacity and the far reach of Egyptian power to make life possible, when with the third event of this contest it is concluded, "the Egyptians could not" (Exod. 8:18);

- we danced the dance of new life at the edge of the waters, on the day Miriam and the other women took their tambourines and danced by the waters of liberation (Exod. 15:21-22);

- we watched while YHWH "made sport" of Pharaoh, while YHWH undid the power of Pharaoh (Exod. 10:1-2), and we noticed an opening for alternative existence outside the control of Pharaoh.

So we will tell our sons and daughters—and all those who will listen—that life under the demanding quotas and insistences of the empire is not the only way to have life. So we left; we walked through the waters of chaos, we reached dry land on the other side, we received the bread of miracle; and we arrived finally at Sinai where we bound our life to the life of God and the life of the neighbor. We will tell our children about the darkness of Passover, so that they may know another life is possible in the world. The children will be astonished when they realize that the second book of our sacred canon is named "Departure." The dominant version of reality is undermined and subverted by the conviction that staying is not our own option. The liturgy is always authorizing an alternative humanity, and sometimes we go; sometimes we linger in wistful reluctance, wishing we had chosen, lacking courage—sometimes choosing the fleshpots that enslave but knowing that in the end our belly is not our god (see Phil. 3:10).

Jesus the Subversive

But, of course, in Christian reading, the *gospel of departure* writ large in the exodus narrative and sung buoyantly in the lyrics of Second Isaiah is but a long-term anticipation of the odd story of Jesus. As the story goes, Jesus came to those paralyzed by the overpunctilious requirements of some forms of Judaism that had been diverted from the claims of God and neighbor, and by the comprehensive ideology of the Roman government, which wanted to eliminate the God of the Jews from its horizon. As the story goes, Jesus came among those frozen in narratives of anxiety and alienation, of slavery and fear; he authorized a departure into the new world of God's governance. He appeared abruptly, and he said,

> Repent—turn—change—switch,
> For the new governance is at hand.

And then he acted it out: summoning, forgiving, instructing, cleansing, healing, empowering, feeding. The new governance given in the very person of Jesus brings all of life—public and personal, human and nonhuman—into a regime of wholeness. He came with a mandate to do for the world what the creator had intended from the outset. He found it all there in the scroll that authorized him:

> The spirit of the Lord is upon me,
> because he has anointed me
> to bring good news to the poor.
> He has sent me to proclaim
> release to the captives
> and recovery of sight to the blind,
> to let the oppressed go free,
> to proclaim the year of the Lord's favor. (Isa. 61:1; cf. Luke 4:18-19)

Those who were settled deep in the dominant version of reality tried to kill him. They recognized immediately that their big version of reality is here subverted.

He subverted by his mercy, miracles they had declared impossible. He subversioned by his emancipator teaching that was not quite clear (parabolic) but that was marked by quixotic irony, as though mocking the way it had been for a long time. He seemed to authorize and invite a rethinking of reality, and eventually a reliving of reality. Those who had been with him were restored to their sanity and began to live in ways that the world could not bear. His subversion sounded familiar cadences, but it was never quite the same. As a result, John—bold, unintimidated, direct John—bewildered and genuinely uncertain, sent word from prison: "Are you for real?"

Ever cagey as an evangelical subversive must always be, Jesus refused a direct answer. How could he answer such a big question in such a restrictive context, since the creeds had not been formulated that would provide him with a firm *homoousia* identity? So he answers John from the data at hand:

> Go tell John—the blind see, the lame walk, lepers are cleaned, the deaf hear, the dead are raised, the poor have their debts canceled. (Luke 7:22)

Go tell John: new life swirls around me. Go tell John that where I am present, impossible things happen. Go tell John that people are switching over to my narrative because they are worn out by blindness and want to see, they are tired of deadness and want to live. Go tell John a new world is being birthed among those who no longer accept dominant notions of the possible.

That sub-version of course constitutes a threat to the way things are. It is a threat that must be stopped by action of the state or whatever action is available to us, violent if necessary. But go tell John, the stoppage of new life and triumph of the dominant version lasted only thirty-six hours and no more. Because by Sunday new life was turned loose beyond the frightened, confined ways of the conventional. That new power has stayed loose, sometimes retarded, sometimes domesticated, but ever loose in the world, breaking bonds, shattering closures in order to:

> bring down the powerful from their thrones
> and lifting up the lowly,
> filling the empty with good things
> and sending the rich away empty. (Luke 1:52-53)

This odd community has continued to reflect upon, to practice, and to invite others into this account of reality. Most of the data on which we count and to which we cling is local and specific. There have been among us, however, those eloquent lyricists capable of larger articulation. One among us has gone very large indeed, to assert:

> He is the image of the invisible God, the firstborn of all creation; for in him all things in heaven and on earth were created, visible and invisible, whether thrones or dominions or rulers or powers—all things have been created through him and for him. He himself is before all things, and in him all things hold together. (Col. 1:15-16)

The claim is stupendous. But what we have found, generation after generation, is that we could not cease to make claims, even as we could not cease to ponder and engage in new practices, always dangerous, always at the cusp of new life.

Another World

I say things already long known. We keep saying them to each other, because if they are left unsaid, the old powers of death creep back in and take over. We say them to each other, because we depend on the fresh utterance to give fresh edge of possibility to our lives. We say these things to each other, because the utterances mediate the Easter option . . . without utterance, no such option.

The sense of this utterance, in which we are participants, we preachers, is that an alternative world is possible. The old world is not a given; it is a fraud. Another world is possible—*in our imagination:* We listen and imagine differently. In our liberation, we entertain different realities not yet given in hardware, so far only in very-soft-ware, carried only by narrative and song and poem and oracle, said before being embodied, but said and we listen. As we listen, we push out to the possibility and are held by it like a visioning child with a dream.

Another world is possible—*in our practice.* We are only a few, but we are some. We can do little, but something. As we stay with the cadences of our defining utterance, we begin to enact another world. Foolishly, we enact obedience to a daring claim, obedience to a possibility; we specialize in cold water and shared bread, in welcome speech, hospitality, sharing, giving, compassion, caring—in small ways—and in setting the world fresh.

Another world is possible—we imagine—*in public policy,* for we do not doubt that the small deed—here and there—ripples into reallocated funds, redirected vision, reassigned power, which issue in caring health, in mercy as policy, in peace that overrides war, in hope that overcomes poverty. This is often not possible, because of the stubbornness of Caesar and the intransigence of corporate wealth. But we have enough public access because we are no longer contained in old tired refusals.

We listen and we answer.
If we are Black enough, we may say "Amen" and "my, my";
if we are Episcopal, we may say "ummmm";
if we are frozen Calvinists, we may not answer,
but only ponder and then act.

In all our several ways of answering, we calculate the possibilities and move to the sub-version . . . sometimes as tough as nails. We refuse dominant versions of reality, seeing the flow of newness and acknowledging the chance.

We are indeed a *sub-people* . . . sub-versive, sub-verted, sub-verting, sub-rosa, sub-tle. We are on the ground, underneath official versions. Our sub-ness is rooted

- in our pain, because you cannot fool pain;
- in our hope, because hope comes without our permission.

But after our pain and after our hope, the rootage of our *sub* is in God's holiness, a holiness we have seen and trusted, whose name we know, a holiness untamed, thick, abrasive . . . newness unashamed.

A final text, Acts 3:11-16: Peter and John had just authorized a lame man to walk. They said to him, we are told, "In the name of Jesus of Nazareth, stand up and walk. . . ." Then, "Jumping up, he stood and began to walk, and he entered the temple with them, walking and leaping and praising God." It was not supposed to happen. But it did.

> The people were astonished. But Peter answered simply: Why do you stare at us, as though our power or our piety made him walk? It is not us, but faith in his name. To this we are witnesses.

And witnesses and witnesses and witnesses. Not more than that, but surely not less than that.

11

Truth-Telling as Subversive Obedience

The ninth commandment—"You shall not bear false witness against your neighbor"—has not been an accent point in biblical ethics or an emphasis in Mosaic-covenantal faith. Moreover, the commandment is easily reduced to a kind of banal moralism, as though "lying" is a bad thing and should be avoided, a notion that is as thin as one can make the commandment. We here reconsider this commandment both as an exploration in interpretive method, and to see how this commandment may be a primal carrier of a Mosaic-covenantal vision of reality that is oddly pertinent to our moment of social crisis.[1]

I

It is important at the outset to recognize that the commandment, expressed in absolute terms, is part of the Decalogue given at "the holy mountain." As such it constitutes a part of the most elemental insistence of the Sinai covenant.[2] More than that, it voices an important dimension of the Mosaic vision of social reality and social possibility.

The commandment brings into stark juxtaposition two terms that assure its covenantal intent: "neighbor—false." The prohibition is not simply against "false witnesses," but it is a false witness against *your neighbor,* that is, a fellow member of the covenant community. The horizon of the prohibition is the well-being of the neighbor and the enhancement of the neighborhood. More broadly the prohibition concerning practices and conditions that make a neighborhood viable and genuinely human.

The antithetical term here is "false" (*sqr*). In the second version of the Decalogue, the term is *šāw'*, but the intention is not different (Deut. 5:20). The term "false" concerns utterance that distorts or misrepresents or skews. Viable community, according to Mosaic vision, depends on accurate, reliable utterance. The process of community is profoundly vulnerable to distorted speech, which inevitably skews social relations and social structures.

The commandment, however, is even more particular. It alludes to the precise setting in which false utterance is possible, seductive, and dangerous. "You shall not answer with false testimony." The verb "answer" and the noun "witness" indicate that we are concerned with solemn utterance under oath in a judicial context. In short, the commandment seeks to assure a reliable, independent judiciary) The Ten Commandments, as a whole, seek to bring every facet of social life under the aegis of YHWH and into the context of covenant. This ninth commandment concerns the court system and insists that evidence given in court must be honest and reliable and uncontaminated by interest. It is astonishing that in its most elemental summary, Yahwistic ethics insists on a reliable, independent judiciary as one of the pillars of viable human life.[3]

It is clear that the notion of a court that gives reliable utterance is a continuing concern of the tradition of Moses. In Exodus 18:13-23, offered as a Mosaic innovation, Moses is instructed to find reliable judicial officers:

> You should also look for able men among all the people, men who fear God, are trustworthy, and hate dishonest gain. (v. 21)[4]

And in speaking of judges subsequently,

> You must not distort justice; you must not show partiality; and you must not accept bribes, for a bribe blinds the eyes of the wise and subverts the cause of those who are in the right. Justice, and only justice, you shall pursue. (Deut. 16:19-20)

The courts are seen to be crucial, because in social disputes that relate to political, economic matters, it is the capacity and responsibility of the court to *determine, limit, and shape reality.* And therefore if power and interest can intrude upon truth—by way of influence, manipulation, or bribe—then truth has no chance. It is reduced to power, and the powerless are then easily and predictably exploited.

Recent public events make altogether evident that a reliable, independent judiciary is indispensable to a viable society. In the United States, it was the courts that were finally able to insist on a constitutional vision of human and civil rights when all other aspects of the public process had failed. In old colonial powers and in the dictatorships of "banana republics," it is often only the judiciary that prevents legitimated exploitation and brutality. Indeed, even as I write this, it is a "truth commission" with something like quasi-judicial powers at work in South Africa that has a chance to put to rest the long nightmare of brutality in that society. This commandment insists, in a direct and unadorned way, that "social truth" inheres in neighborly transactions and is not open to the easy impact of raw power which denies human reality. The commandment guarantees that *reality* is not an innocent product of *power*. The future of humanity is not open to endless "reconstruction" by those who have the capacity to do so, but must adhere to what is "on the ground."

II

The commandment is likely articulated in a simple, face-to-face agrarian society. It is a simple requirement that neighbors not distort shared social reality. But as is characteristic in biblical traditions, this simple agrarian provision is transformed into a larger social concern by the imaginative power of the prophets. The requirement of truth-telling is matured by the prophets, first by enlarging its scope to include royal reality with its penchant for distorted public policy and, second, by turning a "rule of evidence" into a Yahwistic claim. Examples of this larger maneuver include Nathan's word to David concerning the violation of Uriah (2 Sam. 12:7-12) and Elijah's word against Jezebel, who had manipulated truth by royal power (1 Kgs. 21:19-24). In both cases, it is important that it is the issue of truth that is at stake in the prophetic confrontation. Both David and Jezebel have borne false witness, David against Uriah, Jezebel against Naboth. Such distorting actions cannot stand, even if performed by the royal house.

In the prophetic period, powerful royal interests were skillful at the management of symbols and the control of information (disformation) so that scenarios of "virtual" reality could be constructed completely remote from lived reality. The tradition of Jeremiah is preoccupied with *falseness* whereby managed reality yields a phoney sense of life and well-being.[5] The poet counters such control:

From the least to the greatest of them,
everyone is greedy for unjust gain;
and from prophet to priest,

everyone deals falsely.
They have treated the wound of my people carelessly,
saying "Peace, peace,"
when there is no peace. (Jer. 6:14; cf. 8:11)

Now the concern is not one citizen deceiving another, as it might have been in a neighborly, agrarian society. Now it is the great organs of news and information in society being managed to serve distorted public ends, calculated to deceive on a grand scale.

Working the same rhetoric, the prophet Ezekiel holds religious leadership peculiarly guilty for such programmatic distortion:

> In truth they [the prophets] have misled my people, saying "peace" when there is no peace. . . . When the people build a wall, their prophets smear whitewash on it. (Ezek. 13:10)

These recognized voices of established reality deliberately misrepresent the true state of the economy and of foreign policy. Society has broken down and is not working and they legitimate the dysfunction and give false assurance. The voices of accepted legitimacy present a fake reality, with failed face disguised as workable fantasy. The prophetic traditions accepted as canonical are agreed that such fantasy will bring devastation upon a deceived community.[6]

We have here made a large leap from face-to-face neighborliness into the royal engine room of public distortion. With this leap, I may suggest three facets of "false witness" that invite to killing distortions. These distortions in our contemporary world echo those against whom the great prophets railed:

1. *Euphemism.* The use of euphemism consists in describing a reality by labeling it in terms that completely disguise and misrepresent. Long ago Isaiah had noted the capacity to deceive by giving things false names:

> Ah, you who call evil good
> and good evil,
> who put darkness for light,
> and light for darkness.
> who put bitter for sweet,
> and sweet for bitter. (Isa. 5:20)[7]

Those who control the media have vast opportunity for such sustained intentional distortion. Robert Lifton has chronicled the way in which the perpetration of the Jewish Shoah cast these deathly operations in "toxic euphemisms," so that the entire process of the death camps could be presented as a practice of medicine.[8]

In our own time, moreover, Noam Chomsky has characterized the ways in which the public apparatus is endlessly submissive to deliberate misnomer.[9] The deceiving work of euphemism—which is a public pattern of false witness against neighbor—is especially effective in two areas of our common life. First, the entire military industry and the so-called defense program of the world's last superpower are regularly disguised by euphemism, for the simple reason that a massive killing enterprise to protect inequity in the world dare not be called by its right name. This is evident in giving peaceable names for missiles capable of massive destruction. Second, in like manner, the rapacious free-market economy delights in euphemism, in order to cover over the human pain and cost of extraordinary and unconscionable profits. Thus, as Chomsky notes, unemployment becomes "downsizing," "jobs" has now become a four letter word for "profit," and greed operates under the name of "opportunity."

2. The capacity for misrepresentation is especially poignant in television *advertising*,[10] which posits a never-never land born in the happy ways of the "product." In that land there is never pain, never hurt, never fear, never poverty, never any negation that is not overcome by "the product." One would not ever know from such ads that the gap between rich and poor grows like a cancer in our society. The ads present a "virtual reality" enormously attractive but remote from where the world must be lived.

3. Closely related to advertising, is the incredible world of *propaganda*, which offers a vested interest as a totality of truth, which generates false certitudes and false loyalties that belie the reality of human life.[11]

The church in its accommodating timidity has characteristically wanted to keep the commandments of Sinai safely in modest zones of moralizing. It is unmistakable, however, that *euphemism, advertising,* and *propaganda* all serve to bear false witness against neighbor. And since dominant "word-making" and "world-making" are always in the hands of those who control technology, these pseudo-versions of reality are regularly the work of the strong against the weak, the haves against the have-nots, the consequence of which is to make invisible and unavailable the truth of life in the world.

III

The rhetoric of the courtroom operates where "truth" is unsettled, in dispute, and still to be determined. The ancient agrarian prohibition against false witness seeks to stop social distortions that make life brutal, exploitative, and unbearable. Against these propensities, the prophets urge that the deathly truth of the world must be told, a truth that characteristically lives and works at the expense of the weak.

Along with *the truth of the world* in its failure, however, this commandment concerns *telling the truth about God.* This may seem so obvious as not to warrant comment. Except that "God" is completely enmeshed in social-political-economic realities.[12] In order to maintain social advantage, it is often necessary to tell the truth about God in false ways, because the "really real," that is, the gospel truth about God, is revolutionary, subversive, and disruptive.

In Second Isaiah, we may see how this simple agrarian prohibition is now turned into a theological agenda whereby YHWH is "the Neighbor" about whom the truth must be told. Israel must bear true witness to this Neighbor in the midst of exile. Some exiled Jews, apparently, had come to terms with Babylonian realities, accepted the legitimacy of Babylonian gods, and engaged in Babylonian modes of life. That is, the claims of God had to be conformed—by false witnesses—to power realities. The prophet critiques "the witnesses," who submit to "idols" that can neither see nor hear nor do anything (Isa. 44:9). These false gods to whom false witness is given generate false lived reality.

The poet seeks to counter that entire cache of falseness by a summons to truth telling. Israel is to tell the truth about YHWH, to be YHWH's true witnesses:

Do not fear, or be afraid;
have I not told you from of old and declared it?
You are my witnesses!
Is there any god besides me?
There is no other rock; I know not one. (Isa. 44:8)

In the preceding chapter, YHWH asserts to the exiled Jews: "You are my witnesses" (43:10). And the testimony to be given concerns YHWH's capacity to initiate an alternative in the world, to work a newness in society, to emancipate Israel, and to overcome the military-industrial power and hubris of Babylon. When true witness is given to this awesome Neighbor, it is about rescue, liberation, and transformation:

> I, I am the Lord,
> and besides me there is no savior.
> I declared and saved and proclaimed,
> when there was no strange god among you
> and you are my witnesses,
> says the Lord.
> I am God, and also henceforth I am he;
> there is no one who can
> deliver from my hand;
> I work and who can hinder it? . . .
> Thus says the Lord,
> who makes a way in the sea,
> a path in the mighty waters,
> who brings out chariot and horse,
> army and warrior, . . .
> I am doing a new thing;
> now it springs forth,
> do you not perceive it? (Isa. 43:11-19)

The truth about YHWH is that YHWH is about to disrupt and make a newness. If Israel tells falsehood about YHWH, then YHWH will be weak, passive, and impotent, yet another adornment of the status quo. This truth or falsehood about this holy, magisterial Neighbor is not a cognitive matter of having the right "idea." It is rather a practical, concrete matter of voicing the authority, energy, and legitimacy of living a liberated life and thereby going home. False or true witness concerns the actual future of life in the world. Those who are "kept" and domesticated by Babylon may lie about YHWH. Those prepared for YHWH's alternative future, however, tell the truth, which causes the dismantling of the powers of alienation and death, powers that thrive only on falsehood.

IV

When this ancient agrarian prohibition is made larger and more public by the prophets, and then is carried into the New Testament, the requirement of *telling the truth about God* devolves into *telling the truth about Jesus.* The Fourth Gospel, like Second Isaiah, is cast in juridical rhetoric, in order to make an argument and stage a dispute about the true character of Jesus. In this regard, Israel is not to bear false witness against its neighbor, and the church is not to bear false witness against Jesus.[13]

In the Fourth Gospel, John the Baptizer is the forerunner of Jesus to whom witness is first of all made:

> You yourselves are my witnesses, that I said, "I am not the Messiah." (John 3:28)

The same rhetoric is employed by Jesus:

> If I testify about myself, my testimony is not true. There is another who testifies on my behalf and I know that his testimony to me is true. You sent messengers to John and he testified to the truth. . . . But I have a testimony greater than John's. The works that the Father has given me to complete, the very works I am doing, testify on my behalf that the father has sent me. And the father who sent me has himself testified on my behalf. (John 5:31-37)

The Fourth Gospel is presented as a dispute about the truth of Jesus. The assertion and vindication of that truth concern the character of Jesus, his relation to his Father, and his crucifixion and resurrection.

The Fourth Gospel apparently culminates in the "trial of Jesus," or better, "the trial of Pilate."[14] Before the Roman governor, Jesus asserts:

> For this I was born and for this I came into the world, to testify to the truth. (John 18:37)

And Pilate hauntingly responds:

> What is truth? (v. 38)

What indeed! The gospel narrative is notoriously enigmatic. But surely it makes a claim, certainly in its own idiom, that in Jesus of Nazareth the things of the world are settled on God's terms. That is the truth before which the Roman governor stands in dismay.

The world—the recalcitrant world presided over by the Roman governor—cannot bear the truth of Jesus, for that truth moves beyond our capacity to control and our power to understand. And so the world "gives false witness" about Jesus. In doing so, it gives false representation about the world. Just as exilic Jews preferred not to tell the truth about Yнwн because it is a truth too subversive, so many of us in the church choose to bear false witness about Jesus, because the managed, reassuring truth of the empire is more compelling. The truth evidenced in Jesus is not an idea, not a concept, not a formulation, not a fact. It is rather a way of being in the world in suffering and hope, so radical and so raw that we can scarcely entertain it.

V

Telling *the truth about God*, telling *the truth about Jesus*, and telling *the truth about the world* are intimately connected to each other. They are intimately connected in the Sinai covenant whereby God asserts a powerful relation to the world: "It is all mine" (Exod. 19:5-6). They are even more visibly linked in the life of Jesus, wherein the purposes of God take fleshly form. Conversely, it is inescapably the case that lying about God, lying about Jesus, and lying about the world are inextricably related to each other.

- We have learned to lie well.[15]
- We imagine that God is not the bestirrer of radical newness.
- We conclude that the suffering of Jesus is not our redemptive vocation.
- We assert that the world—and our economy—is all fine, fine on its own terms with imperial gods and a pliable Jesus.
- We, even with our resolved faith, tend to live inside that reassuring ideology that can recognize nothing deathly and that can receive nothing new.

The world of the Bible consists in a dispute about evidence. The baptized community is "in the dock," summoned to tell the truth and not to bear false witness. The preacher, moreover, is regularly and visibly put on exhibit, to tell the church's truth to the world and to tell God's truth to the church. Very often the world refuses to hear, and of course the church is regularly recalcitrant in receiving testimony. And even the preacher, on occasion, cringes from what must be said, so much are we ourselves accommodated to "the lie."

We can admit all of that. And yet! And yet preaching goes on, folks gather, waiting fearfully but also hopefully for another witness that tells the whole truth. And so, good preacher, we may acknowledge the pressure and the way we flinch. But there is also the enduring possibility: Truth in dispute, and our feeble utterance to be sure that our Neighbor is rightly offered and discerned.

The truth now to be told concerns our failed society:

> Political power is now firmly in the hands of the money power in a symbiotic relationship that feeds inequity and injustice. Wealth is derived from power. And power in America is exercised almost exclusively by the wealthy.[16]

The prophets know this and cannot call it "peace." But there is more. The gods of death have pushed hard on Friday. But faithful testimony requires a Sunday "bulletin" that expresses our amazement against the Friday forces of our life.

I am no romantic. I know this explosiveness of Easter, which exposes all "prior" truths as false witnesses, cannot be said in many churches. The wonder is that it is available to us. It is a truth we not only fear but also crave. Happily some in the church besides us preachers already know. Truth-telling is not easy work. But it is freeing. And it is the only defense the neighborhood has, both our *lower case neighbors* and our *Capital Neighbor.* And we are invited to take no bribes!

Notes

Introduction: At Risk with the Text

1. Karl Barth, "The Word of God and the Task of Ministry," in his *The Word of God & the Word of Man* (New York: Harper & Brothers, 1957), 186.

2. Here my focus is on the word preached; but of course the church is rightly evoked by both Word and Sacrament. It is for good reason that the word rightly preached and the sacraments rightly administered have been taken as the true marks of the church. In contemporary formulation that is not by itself adequate, but it surely is the proper starting place for rethinking the church.

3. See Daniel Smith-Christopher, *A Biblical Theology of Exile*, Overtures to Biblical Theology (Minneapolis: Fortress Press, 2002).

4. See Walter Brueggemann, *Cadences of Home: Preaching among Exiles* (Louisville: Westminster John Knox, 1997).

5. Frederick Buechner has explored the matter of homesickness and loss of home in a compelling way (*The Longing for Home: Recollections and Reflections* [San Francisco: Harper, 1996], 7-28). In his novels a sense of "place" is primary to his ongoing narrative.

6. See Gerhard von Rad, *Theology of the Old Testament* (San Francisco: Harper & Row, 1965), 2:188–277.

7. The same misconstrual of YHWH is evident in the mocking speeches on the lips of the Assyrians in Isaiah 36–37; the category mistake voiced there is that YHWH is taken to be like the other defeated gods who could not withstand the empire, powerless like them. The intent of the narrative account of the rescue of Jerusalem is precisely to refute that category mistake.

8. On the term "gospel" in Second Isaiah, see Walter Brueggemann, *Biblical Perspectives on Evangelism: Living in a Three-Storied Universe* (Nashville: Abingdon, 1993), 14–47.

9. On the exodus theme in Second Isaiah, see Bernhard W. Anderson, "Exodus Typology in Second Isaiah," in *Israel's Prophetic Heritage: Essays in Honor of James Muilenburg*, edited by Bernhard W. Anderson and Walter Harrelson (New York: Harper & Brothers, 1962), 177–95; idem, "Exodus and Covenant in Second

Isaiah and Prophetic Tradition," in *Magnalia Dei, The Mighty Acts of God: Essays on the Bible and Archaeology in Memory of G. Ernest Wright*, edited by Frank Moore Cross et al. (Garden City, N.Y.: Doubleday, 1976), 339–60.

10. The definitive article on prophetic call is Norman Habel, "The Form and Significance of the Call Narratives," Zeitschrift für die alttestamentliche Wissenschaft 77 (1965), 297–323.

11. The classic and overused discussion of call in ecclesial perspective is by H. Richard Niebuhr, *The Purpose of the Church and Its Ministry: Reflections on the Aims of Theological Education* (New York: Harper & Brothers, 1956), 63-66.

12. On the divine council, see Patrick D. Miller, *Genesis 1-11: Studies in Structure & Theme*, Journal for the Study of the Old Testament Supplement 8 (Sheffield: University of Sheffield, 1978), 9–26.

13. The classic confrontation is between Jeremiah and Hananiah in Jeremiah 28; more broadly see James L. Crenshaw, *Prophetic Conflict: Its Effect Upon Israelite Religion*, Beihefte zur Zeitschrift für die alttestamentliche Wissenschaft 124 (Berlin: de Gruyter, 1971).

14. See Christopher R. Seitz, "The Divine Council: Temporal Transition and New Prophecy in the Book of Isaiah," *Journal of Biblical Literature* 109 (1990): 229–47.

15. On the formula, see W. Eugene March, "Prophecy," in *Old Testament Form Criticism*, edited by John H. Hayes (San Antonio: Trinity University Press, 1974), 143–57.

16. On the resilience of the text and its refusal to be easily dismissed, see Jeremiah 36; the king is unable to eradicate the scroll!

17. It was an appreciation of the personal voice within the text that caused James Muilenburg ("Form Criticism and Beyond," *Journal of Biblical Literature* 88 [1969]: 1–18) to make his daring move beyond form criticism, a move that has opened up subsequent textual work in unparalleled ways.

18. The linkage between the narratives of 2 Kings 22 and Jeremiah 36 is a measure of the connection between the traditions. See W. Thiel, *Die deuteronomistische Redaktion von Jeremia 1-25*, Wissenschaftliche Monographien zum Alten und Neuen Testament 41 (Neukirchen-Vluyn: Neukirchener, 1972); idem, *Die Deuteronomistische Redaktion von Jeremia 26-45*, Wissenschaftliche Monographien zum Alten und Neuen Testament 52 (Neukirchen-Vluyn: Neukirchener, 1981). Unfortunately the usual approach, represented by Thiel, treats the relationship as one of editorial transactions rather than a living circle of tradition in which the prophet is situated. On the latter perspective, see Robert R. Wilson, *Prophecy and Society in Ancient Israel* (Philadelphia: Fortress Press, 1980), 135–252.

19. See Michael Fishbane, *Biblical Interpretation in Ancient Israel* (Oxford: Clarendon, 1985), 307–12.

20. William L. Moran, "End of Holy War and the Anti-Exodus," *Biblica* 44 (1963): 333–42.

21. The classic study of this relationship is by Walter Baumgartner, *Jeremiah's Poems of Lament*, Historic Texts and Interpreters in Biblical Scholarship 7 (Sheffield: Almond, 1987).

22. It is because Jeremiah's utterance collided with the ideological force of the Jerusalem establishment that he was brought to trial and nearly executed as an enemy of the state (Jer. 26).

23. In his splendid book *The Collapse of History: Reconstructing Old Testament Theology*, Overtures to Biblical Theology (Minneapolis: Fortress Press, 1994), Leo G. Perdue takes Jeremiah as a representative case for all that is under way in Old Testament scholarship. In parallel fashion, I suggest that Jeremiah is a representative case for what proclamation may characteristically mean in a world of biblical proportion.

24. John McClure shrewdly notices the hazards in counter-description that may only evoke resistance and reinforcement in dominant description ("From Resistance to Jubilee: Prophetic Preaching and the Testimony of Love," in *Colloquium: Music, Worship, Arts*, vol. 2 [New Haven: Yale Institute of Sacred Music, 2005], 79–85).

25. Karl Barth, "The Strange New World within the Bible," in his *The Word of God & the Word of Man*, 28–50.

26. The classic example of such choice in the Old Testament is in Joshua 24:14-15, though the matter of such decision is everywhere in Deuteronomic and prophetic speech; on Joshua 24, see Brueggemann, *Biblical Perspectives on Evangelism*, 48–70.

27. On exceptionalism in U.S. ideology and its destructive implications, see Gary Dorrien, "Consolidating the Empire: Neoconservatism and the Politics of American Domination," *Political Theology* 6:4 (2005) 409–28.

28. I use the term "evangelical" to refer to all those, liberal and conservative, who intend that the truth of the gospel should define their lives. When the term "evangelical" is used in a more popular—though hardly correct—way, there is good news about movement among conservative Christians. See Matthew J. O. Scott, "American Evangelicals' Copernican Revolution on Foreign Policy," *Review of Faith & International Affairs* 3 (Winter 2005–6): 41–44.

1. Preaching as Reimagination

1. See Richard Rorty, *Philosophy and the Mirror of Nature* (Princeton, N.J.: Princeton University Press, 1979), 335 passim.

2. I am aware that the term "handmaiden" is beset by a history of sexism. I use it intentionally and in recognition of what it implies for historical criticism.

3. On the presuppositional, intellectual, and ideological revolution wrought in the rise of criticism, see Paul Hazard, *The European Mind, 1680–1715* (New York: World, 1963); and Susan Bordo, *The Flight to Objectivity: Essays on Cartesianism and Culture* (Albany: SUNY Press, 1987).

4. On what I call "the emerging criticism," see Steven L. McKenzie and Stephen R. Haynes, eds., *To Each Its Own Meaning: An Introduction to Biblical Criticisms and Their Applications* (Louisville: Westminster John Knox, 1993).

5. It is conventional to view most worshiping congregations as profoundly homogeneous, and that is no doubt true. But within such homogeneous communities, it

is increasingly the case that there are wide-ranging convictions and opinions, so wide-ranging that it is often difficult to identify any basis of consensus. Such heterogeneity is very different from a kind of diversity rooted in a shared core of perspective.

6. See David Lochhead, *The Dialogical Imperative: A Christian Reflection on Interfaith Encounter* (Maryknoll: Orbis, 1988); and especially David Tracy, *Plurality and Ambiguity: Hermeneutics, Religion, Hope* (San Francisco: Harper & Row, 1987).

7. Alasdair MacIntyre has observed that even in such a formidable situation as the Gifford Lectures, a chanted epistemological climate now permits the lecturer only to make a proposal but not to announce a conclusion to be received by the audience (*Three Rival Versions of Moral Enquiry: Encyclopaedia, Genealogy, and Tradition* [Notre Dame, Ind.: University of Notre Dame Press, 1990]).

8. See the famous distinction made by Krister Stendahl, "Biblical Theology, Contemporary," *The Interpreter's Dictionary of the Bible,* edited by Keith Crim (Nashville: Abingdon, 1962), 1:418–32; and the critical response of Ben Ollenburger, "What Krister Stendahl 'Meant'—A Normative Critique of 'Descriptive Theology,'" *Horizons in Biblical Theology* 8 (June 1986): 61–98.

9. See especially Susan A. Handelman, *The Slayers of Moses: The Emergence of Rabbinic Interpretation in Modern Literary Theory* (Albany: SUNY Press, 1982).

10. Handelman, *Slayers of Moses,* 21, 34 passim. See also Moshe Idel, "Infinities of Torah in Kabbalah," in *Midrash and Literature,* edited by Geoffrey H. Hartman and Sanford Budick (New Haven: Yale University Press, 1986), 141–57; and, more generally, the entire volume.

11. See Handelman, *Slayers of Moses,* 141–52 passim.

12. Paul Ricoeur, "From the Hermeneutics of Texts to the Hermeneutics of Action," in *From Text to Action* (Evanston, Ill.: Northwestern University Press, 1991), 105–222. See also Richard Harvey Brown, *Society as Text: Essays on Rhetoric, Reason, and Reality* (Chicago: University of Chicago Press, 1987).

13. Ricoeur, *From Text to Action,* 121.

14. On the classic, see David Tracy, *The Analogical Imagination: Christian Theology and the Culture of Pluralism* (New York: Crossroad, 1981).

15. See Paul Ricoeur, "Biblical Hermeneutics," *Semeia* 4 (1975): 127 passim. In a very different frame of reference, see also the notion of construal and reconstrual in David H. Kelsey, *The Uses of Scripture in Recent Theology* (Philadelphia: Fortress Press, 1975).

16. Philip Rieff, *The Triumph of the Therapeutic: Uses of Faith after Freud* (New York: Harper & Row, 1966). More generally on the Enlightenment, see Bordo, *Flight to Objectivity;* and Stephen Toulmin, *Cosmopolis: The Hidden Agenda of Modernity* (New York: Free, 1990). In *Texts under Negotiation: The Bible and Postmodern Imagination* (Minneapolis: Fortress Press, 1993), chapter 1, I have tried to assess the significance of the changes in Enlightenment consciousness for biblical interpretation.

17. In addition to Hazard, *European Mind,* see Klaus Scholder, *The Birth of Modern Critical Theology: Origins and Problems of Biblical Criticism in the Seventeenth Century* (Philadelphia: Trinity International, 1990).

18. Bordo suggests that the loss of "mother church" required finding another certitude that could nurture like a mother (*Flight to Objectivity*).

19. On the emergence of the individual self in the Cartesian program, see Charles Taylor, *Sources of the Self: The Making of the Modern Identity* (Cambridge, Mass.: Harvard University Press, 1989).

20. For a positive alternative to such individualism, see Paul R. Sponheim, *Faith and the Other: A Relational Theology* (Minneapolis: Fortress Press, 1993).

21. See Milton L. Myers, *The Soul of Modern Economic Man: Ideas of Self-Interest, Thomas Hobbes to Adam Smith* (Chicago: University of Chicago Press, 1983), on the "text" of Hobbes behind the work of Adam Smith.

22. See Neil Postman, *Entertaining Ourselves to Death: Public Discourse in the Age of Show Business* (New York: Penguin, 1986); and idem, *Technopoly: The Surrender of Culture to Technology* (New York: Random House, 1993).

23. See Godfrey Hodgson, *The Colonel: The Life and Wars of Henry Stimson, 1867–1950* (New York: Alfred A. Knopf, 1990).

24. See Walter Isaacson and Evan Thomas, *Wise Men: Six Friends and the World They Made* (New York: Touchstone, 1988). Of the "Wise Men," Kai Bird writes: "As men possessing a measure of *gravitas*, McCloy and other Establishment figures always claimed they could rise above the private interests they represented and discern the larger public good. Ultimately, this claim is not sustainable" (*The Chairman, John J. McCloy: The Making of the American Establishment* [New York: Simon & Schuster, 1992], 664).

25. In *Darwin* (New York: Warner, 1991), Adrian Desmond and James Moore make a compelling case that social Darwinism was not remote from the awareness of Darwin himself. He knew where he was located socially as he did his research.

26. See the discussion of David McLellan, *The Thought of Karl Marx: An Introduction* (London: Macmillan, 1971), 41–51.

27. Concerning the role of "social theatre" in the establishment and maintenance of social relations, see E. P. Thompson, *Customs in Common* (New York: New, 1991), 86–87 passim.

28. See Leon Festinger, *A Theory of Cognitive Dissonance* (Stanford: Stanford University Press, 1962).

29. Victor Turner, *The Ritual Process: Structure and Anti-Structure* (Ithaca, N.Y.: Cornell University Press, 1969). For an exposition and critique of Turner's work, see Bobby C. Alexander, *Victor Turner Revisited: Ritual as Social Change*, American Academy of Religion Academy Series 74 (Atlanta: Scholars, 1991).

30. The basic study of this coherence is Robert Bellah, "Civil Religion in America," *Daedalus* 96 (Winter 1967): 1–21. See his larger discussion in *The Broken Covenant: American Civil Religion in Time of Trial* (New York: Crossroad, 1975). Part of the power of Martin Luther King, Jr., was that he was still able to appeal to this coherence.

31. In *Texts under Negotiation*, I have suggested that the work of Scripture interpretation is to fund counterimagination (pp. 2–25).

32. Wallace Stevens, "A High-Toned Old Christian Woman," in *The Collected Poems of Wallace Stevens* (New York: Vintage, 1954), 59.

33. Garrett Green, *Imagining God: Theology and the Religious Imagination* (San Francisco: Harper & Row, 1989), 73, 140 passim.

34. David J. Bryant helpfully explored what it means to "take as" (*Faith and the Play of Imagination: On the Role of Imagination in Religion* [Macon, Ga.: Mercer University Press, 1989], 155).

35. On the "myth of the given," in addition to Thomas Kuhn, *The Structure of Scientific Revolutions* (Chicago: University of Chicago Press, 1962), see also the important work of Mary Hesse and Michael Arbib, *The Construction of Reality* (Cambridge: Cambridge University Press, 1986).

36. The claim of David R. Blumenthal, *Facing the Abusing God: A Theology of Protest* (Louisville: Westminster John Knox, 1993), 47–54 passim, that we live "*seriatim,*" has much to commend it. But it is likely an overstatement for anyone.

37. See Brevard S. Childs's most recent statement in *Biblical Theology of the Old and New Testaments: Theological Reflection on the Christian Bible* (Minneapolis: Fortress Press, 1992), 70–94 passim.

38. Toulmin has nicely argued positively for a retreat from universal assertion (*Cosmopolis,* 186–201).

39. See, for example, Gabriel Josipovici, *The Book of God: A Response to the Bible* (New Haven: Yale University Press, 1988), 75–89, and his treatment of the Joseph narrative.

40. John R. Donahue, *The Gospel in Parable: Metaphor, Narrative, and Theology in the Synoptic Gospels* (Philadelphia: Fortress Press, 1988) provides a rich study of the parables and fully understands the parabolic character of gospel truth. He observes the cruciality of such speech when living in a "desert of the imagination" (p. 212).

41. Sandra M. Schneiders, *The Revelatory Text: Interpreting the New Testament as Sacred Scripture* (San Francisco: Harper, 1991), 102–8.

42. Jacob Neusner, *The Enchantments of Judaism: Rites of Transformation from Birth through Death* (New York: Basic, 1987), 214: "We are Jews through the power of our imagination."

43. On the history of imagination, see Green, *Imagining God,* chapter 1; Richard Kearney, *The Wake of Imagination: Toward a Postmodern Culture* (Minneapolis: University of Minnesota Press, 1988); and idem, *Poetics of Imagining: From Husserl to Lyotard* (San Francisco: Harper, 1991).

44. Kearney (*Poetics of Imagining,* 88–111) provides a useful entry to Bachelard. It is from Kearney that I have taken my lead here. Of the work of Bachelard, see *The Poetics of Space* (Boston: Beacon, 1969); and *On Poetic Imagination,* edited by Colette Gandin (New York: Bobbs Merrill, 1971).

45. Kearney, *Poetics of Imagining,* 95.

46. John E. Thiel, *Imagination and Authority: Theological Authorship in the Modern Tradition* (Minneapolis: Fortress Press, 1991).

47. The statement is programmatic for Ricoeur. See, for example, Paul Ricoeur, *The Conflict of Interpretations* (Evanston: Northwestern University Press, 1974), 288.

48. On imagination as the originary point of possibility, see Paul Ricoeur, *The Philosophy of Paul Ricoeur,* edited by Charles E. Reagan and David Stewart (Boston: Beacon, 1978), 231–38.

49. Brueggemann, *Texts under Negotiation*, 64–70.

50. Hans Urs von Balthasar, *Theo-Drama: Theological Dramatic Theory*, vol. 1, *Prolegomena* (San Francisco: Ignatius, 1988); vol. 2, *Dramatis Personae: Man in God* (San Francisco: Ignatius, 1990); Frances Young, *Virtuoso: The Bible and Interpretation* (Cleveland: Pilgrim, 1993).

51. G. Ernest Wright, *God Who Acts: Biblical Theology as Recital*, Studies in Biblical Theology 8 (London: SCM, 1952); G. Ernest Wright and Reginald H. Fuller, *The Book of the Acts of God: Christian Scholarship Interprets the Bible* (Garden City, N.Y.: Doubleday, 1957); and C. H. Dodd, *The Apostolic Preaching and Its Developments* (New York: Harper & Brothers, n.d.).

52. See, for example, Owen C. Thomas, ed., *God's Activity in the World: The Contemporary Problem*, AAR Studies in Religion 31 (Chico, Calif.: Scholars, 1983); James B. Wiggins, ed., *Religion as Story* (New York: University Press of America, 1975); and Stanley Hauerwas and L. Gregory Jones, eds., *Why Narrative? Readings in Narrative Theology* (Grand Rapids: Eerdmans, 1989).

53. On dramatic rendering as it pertains to theological discourse, see Dale Patrick, *The Rendering of God in the Old Testament* (Philadelphia: Fortress Press, 1981).

54. Hayden White, "The Politics of Historical Interpretation: Discipline and De-Sublimation," in *The Politics of Interpretation*, edited by W. J. T. Mitchell (Chicago: University of Chicago Press, 1983), 119–43; idem, *The Content of the Form: Narrative Discourse and Historical Representation* (Baltimore: Johns Hopkins University Press, 1987); and idem, *Metahistory: The Historical Imagination in Nineteenth Century Europe* (Baltimore: Johns Hopkins University Press, 1973).

55. Alasdair MacIntyre, *Whose Justice? Which Rationality?* (Notre Dame, Ind.: University of Notre Dame Press, 1988).

56. Amos Wilder, "Story and Story-World," *Interpretation* 37 (1983): 353–64. See my summary on "world-making" in Brueggemann, *Israel's Praise: Doxology against Idolatry and Ideology* (Philadelphia: Fortress Press, 1988), 1–28, 157–60.

57. Brevard S. Childs, "Psalm Titles and Midrashic Exegesis," *Journal of Semitic Studies* 16 (1971): 137–50.

58. On the cruciality of rhetoric, see the suggestive distinction between "rhetorical man" and "serious man" made by Richard A. Lanham, *The Motives of Eloquence: Literary Rhetoric in the Renaissance* (New Haven: Yale University Press, 1976), 1–35. And see the comments on Lanham's distinction by Stanley Fish, "Rhetoric," in *Critical Terms for Literary Study*, edited by Frank Lentricchia and Thomas McLaughlin (Chicago: University of Chicago Press, 1990), 206–9. Such arguments suggest that the privilege long assigned to Plato and Aristotle against the Sophists may be usefully reexamined.

59. See, for example, Num. 11:4-6; 14:1-4; Exod. 16:3.

60. Brueggemann, *Texts under Negotiation*, 21–25.

61. Walter Brueggemann, *Biblical Perspectives on Evangelism: Living in a Three-Storied Universe* (Nashville: Abingdon, 1993).

62. Peter L. Berger and Thomas Luckmann, *The Social Construction of reality: A Treatise in the Sociology of Knowledge* (Garden City, N.Y.: Doubleday, 1967), 156–57.

63. For a standard summary of critical judgments about Deuteronomy, see Patrick D. Miller, *Deuteronomy* (Louisville: John Knox, 1990), 2–17.

64. See Thompson, *Customs in Common.*

65. See Walter Brueggemann, "As the Text 'Makes Sense': Keep the Methods as Lean and Uncomplicated as Possible," *Christian Ministry* 14 (November 1983): 7–10.

2. The Preacher, the Text, and the People

1. On avoidance in interpretation at a practical level, see Richard L. Rohrbaugh, *The Biblical Interpreter: An Agrarian Bible in an Industrial Age* (Philadelphia: Fortress Press, 1978).

2. Murray Bowen, *Family Therapy in Clinical Practice* (New York: J. Aronson, 1978); Edwin H. Friedman, *Generation to Generation: Family Process in Church and Synagogue* (New York: Guilford, 1985).

3. On interpretive distance, see especially Paul Ricoeur, "The Hermeneutical Function of Distanciation," in *Paul Ricoeur: Hermeneutics and the Human Sciences*, edited by John B. Thompson (Cambridge: Cambridge University Press, 1981), 131–44.

4. I do not want to go as far as Walter Wink, *The Bible in Human Transformation: Toward a New Paradigm for Biblical Study* (Philadelphia: Fortress Press, 1973) in his initial broadside; but his statement is congruent with my sense that historical criticism has denied the text its voice.

5. Walter Brueggemann, "The 'Uncared For' Now Cared For Jer. 30:12-17: A Methodological Consideration," *Journal of Biblical Literature* 104 (1985): 419–28.

6. The process of texts breaking out from under the dominant consensus is what is happening in much recent liberation exegesis and especially feminism. The clearest examples are those of Phyllis Trible, *Texts of Terror: Literary-Feminist Readings of Biblical Narratives,* Overtures to Biblical Theology (Philadelphia: Fortress Press, 1984).

7. Wayne C. Booth, *The Rhetoric of Fiction* (Chicago: Chicago University Press, 1983). See also Wolfgang Iser, *The Implied Reader: Patterns of Communication in Prose Fiction* (Baltimore: Johns Hopkins University Press, 1978).

8. As I understand it, this is the intent of Brevard S. Childs, *Introduction to the Old Testament as Scripture* (Philadelphia: Fortress Press, 1979). In order for the text to have its own voice, it cannot be dependent on its locus of historical origin. Whereas Childs speaks directly about "canon," David Tracy, *The Analogical Imagination: Christian Theology and the Culture of Pluralism* (New York: Crossroad, 1981) speaks of "classic." I understand Tracy to be speaking of a canonical text, but to do so on foundationalist and not confessional grounds.

9. See Milton L. Myers, *The Soul of Modern Economic Man: Ideas of Self-Interest, Thomas Hobbes to Adam Smith* (Chicago: University of Chicago Press, 1983).

10. "Old ecstasies" and "old hurts" live with enormous vitality in a congregation, and the pastor will hear these narrative construals of the past endlessly reiterated.

11. On such hidden texts and invisible loyalties, see Ivan Boszormenyi-Nagy and Geraldine Spark, *Invisible Loyalties: Reciprocity in Intergenerational Family Therapy* (New York: Harper & Row, 1973).

12. The popular psychology of being scripted has been articulated by Eric Berne, *Games People Play: The Psychology of Human Relationships* (New York: Grove, 1964). On the text as a Jewish enterprise, see Jose Faur, "God as a Writer: Omnipresence and the Art of Dissimulation," *Religion and Intellectual Life* 6 (1989): 31–43. On religious script and rewriting the script, see Robert Davidson, *The Courage to Doubt* (London: SCM, 1983), pp. 178–79 passim.

13. On the abandonment of the text in modernity, the classic statement is by Hans W. Frei, *The Eclipse of Biblical Narrative: A Study in Eighteenth and Nineteenth Century Hermeneutics* (New Haven: Yale University Press, 1974).

14. George Steiner ("The Good Books," *The New Yorker* [Jan. 11, 1988], now reprinted in *Religion and Intellectual Life* 6 [1989]: 9–16) has given an eloquent and passionate expression to this problem.

15. Walter J. Ong, *Interfaces of the Word: Studies in the Evolution of Consciousness and Culture* (Ithaca, N.Y.: Cornell University Press, 1977), 53–81. See the utilization of Ong's argument by R. Alan Culpepper, *Anatomy of the Fourth Gospel: A Study in Literary Design* (Philadelphia: Fortress Press, 1983), 205–11.

16. On the matter of letting the text have a say to which we can yield, see George Lindbeck, "Barth and Textuality," *Theology Today* 43 (1986): 361–76.

17. Victor W. Turner, *The Ritual Process: Structure and Anti-Structure* (Chicago: Aldine, 1969), 94–130 passim.

18. Such texts are indeed "classic" in Tracy's sense, but they must be understood as more than classic. Such a category leaves too much to the human assessment of the text, and such a criterion is never adequate for serious faith that relates to its text as revelatory word of God.

19. The use of this phrase by Elisabeth Schüssler Fiorenza, *Bread Not Stone: The Challenge of Feminist Biblical Interpretation* (Boston: Beacon, 1984), is exactly pertinent to the point I am making.

20. Tracy has expressed the way in which classic texts keep yielding new interpretations and keep requiring new interpretive attention (*Analogical Imagination*, 102–3).

21. This point is well voiced by Herbert N. Schneidau, *Sacred Discontent: The Bible and Western Tradition* (Berkeley: University of California Press, 1976).

3. Ancient Utterance and Contemporary Hearing

1. Patrick D. Miller has seen most clearly how the cry of the Psalms connects to the requirements of Torah ("Deuteronomy and Psalms: Evoking a Biblical Conversation," in Miller's *Israelite Religion and Biblical Theology: Collected Essays,* Journal for the Study of the Old Testament Supplement 267 [Sheffield: Sheffield Academic, 2000], 318–36).

2. The normative work on God's pathos is Abraham J. Heschel, *The Prophets,* 2 vols. (New York: Harper & Row, 1962).

3. The data on the scribes have been usefully summarized by Philip R. Davies, *Scribes and Schools: The Canonization of the Hebrew Scriptures*, Library of Ancient Israel (Louisville: Westminster John Knox, 1998).

4. See Walter Brueggemann, *The Prophetic Imagination* (Philadelphia: Fortress Press, 1978; 2nd ed., Minneapolis: Fortress Press, 2002).

5. See Walter Brueggemann, "An Imaginative 'Or,'" in *Testimony to Otherwise: The Witness of Elijah and Elisha* (St. Louis: Chalice, 2001), 5-25.

4. An Imaginative "Or"

1. Jon D. Levenson has explored Jewish antecedents to the Christian foundation of "Father-Son" (*The Death and Resurrection of the Beloved Son: The Transformation of Child Sacrifice in Judaism and Christianity* [New Haven: Yale University Press, 1993]).

2. For a critical summary of Newbigin's accent on ecclesiology, see George R. Hunsberger, *Bearing the Witness of the Spirit: Lesslie Newbigin's Theology of Cultural Pluralism* (Grand Rapids: Eerdmans, 1998).

3. See Walter Brueggemann, "Ecumenism as the Shared Practice of a Peculiar Identity," *Word & World* 18 (Spring 1998): 122–35.

4. See my discussion in Walter Brueggemann, *Cadences of Home: Preaching among Exiles* (Louisville: Westminster John Knox, 1997).

5. The either/or I will exposit is essentially that of the Deuteronomic theology, which speaks with conviction that one choice is good and one is bad (see Deut. 30:15-20). That is to say, the *either/or* of the Deuteronomist is completely without the irony of which Søren Kierkegaard can write:

> Marry, and you will regret it. Do not marry, and you will also regret it. Marry or do not marry, you will regret it either way. Whether you marry or you do not marry, you will regret it either way. Laugh at the stupidities of the world, and you will regret it; weep over them, and you will also regret it. Laugh at the stupidities of the world or weep over them, you will regret it either way. Whether you laugh at the stupidities of the world or you weep over them, you will regret it either way. Trust a girl, and you will regret it. Do not trust her, and you will also regret it. Trust a girl or do not trust her, you will regret it either way. Whether you trust a girl or do not trust her, you will regret it either way. Hang yourself, and you will regret it. Do not hang yourself, and you will also regret it. Hang yourself or do not hang yourself, you will regret it either way. Whether you hang yourself or do not hang yourself, you will regret it either way. This, gentlemen, is the quintessence of all the wisdom of life. (*Either/Or I*, translated by Howard V. Hong and Edna H. Hong [Princeton: Princeton University Press, 1987], 38–39)

6. It is instructive that in both narratives of Abraham (Gen. 15:6) and Moses (Exod. 4:1), the key term is *ʾmen*, "trust." It is "trust" that makes the "or" of YHWH

choosable against the "either" that characteristically seems given and easy to embrace.

7. Of that intentional decision, Jacob Neusner writes, "All of us are Jews through the power of our imagination" (*The Enchantments of Judaism: Rites of Transformation from Birth Through Death* [New York: Basic Books, 1987] 212).

8. Gerhard von Rad, to be sure, takes chapter 24 to be an early credo and Joshua 21:43-45 to be the culmination of the Hexateuch (*The Problem of the Hexateuch and Other Essays* [New York: McGraw-Hill, 1966], 73–74, 96). The placement of chapter 24, however, is important to the argument concerning its significance, even if he regards it as early.

9. See Walter Brueggemann, *Biblical Perspectives on Evangelism: Living in a Three-Storied Universe* (Nashville: Abingdon, 1993), 48–70.

10. Von Rad, *Problem of the Hexateuch,* 6–7.

11. On narratives producing worlds, see Amos Wilder, "Story and Story-World," *Interpretation* 37 (1983): 353–64.

12. The term "far be it from" is an exceedingly strong expression, suggesting the complete inappropriateness of the action, for such an action would profane and render its subject unworthy. See a usage with reference to YHWH's own action in Genesis 18:25.

13. On this negative command, see the parallel in Genesis 35:1-4. Some scholars, following Albrecht Alt, suggest that a ritual performance is here envisioned whereby the foreign gods are dramatically banished from the community.

14. The fundamental rhetorical analysis is that of Claus Westermann, "Sprache und Struktur der Prophetie Deuterojesajas," in *Neudrucke und Berichte aus dem 20. Jahrhundert,* Theologische Bücherei 24, Altes Testament (Munich: Kaiser, 1964), 92–170.

15. See Walter Brueggemann, *Theology of the Old Testament: Testimony, Dispute, Advocacy* (Minneapolis: Fortress Press, 1997), 92–170.

16. It is evident that "testimony" is a way to make a claim from "below," when one lacks the tools and authority to make a more established sort of claim for truth. See my comments on Paul Ricoeur and Elie Wiesel in *Theology of the Old Testament.*

17. See Brueggemann, *Biblical Perspectives on Evangelism,* especially 26–30.

18. The most fundamental analysis is that of Jacques Ellul, *The Technological Society* (New York: Random House, 1967). See more specifically to our point, Jacques Ellul, *The Humiliation of the Word* (Grand Rapids: Eerdmans, 1985).

19. On the integrity of speech and matching speech to life, see Wendell Berry, *Standing by Words: Essays* (San Francisco: North Point, 1983), 24–63.

20. In recent times, Paul Ricoeur has understood most clearly and most consistently that serious religious language must be spoken in "figure," thus his accent on imagination. Speech that is not in "figure" runs the prompt risk of idolatry, of producing what can be controlled. See the several essays in his book nicely entitled *Figuring the Sacred: Religion, Narrative, and Imagination,* edited by Mark I. Wallace (Minneapolis: Fortress Press, 1995).

21. See a summary of this scholarship by Terence E. Fretheim, *Deuteronomic History,* Interpreting Biblical Texts (Nashville: Abingdon, 1983).

22. On this pivotal command, see Jeffries M. Hamilton, *Social Justice and Deuteronomy: The Case of Deuteronomy 15*, Society of Biblical Literature Dissertation Series 136 (Atlanta: Scholars, 1992).

23. See Walter Brueggemann, "Faith with a Price," *The Other Side* 34, no. 4 (July & August 1998): 32–35.

24. The "or" of covenantal power is nicely put in the words of Jesus in Mark 10:42-44.

25. On neighborliness extended to outsiders and the weak insiders, see Luke 4:26-27.

26. See Grace I. Emmerson, *Isaiah 56–66*, Old Testament Guides (Sheffield: Sheffield Academic, 1992); and Elizabeth Achtemeier, *The Community and Message of Isaiah 56–66* (Minneapolis: Augsburg, 1982).

27. The New Testament counterpart to such "foreigners and eunuchs" is perhaps "publicans and sinners," on which see Mark 2:15-17.

28. On neighborly attentiveness as a condition of well-being, see Matthew 25:31-46.

29. Among the most helpful treatments of the parables is John R. Donahue, *The Gospel in Parable: Metaphor, Narrative, and Theology in the Synoptic Gospels* (Philadelphia: Fortress Press, 1988).

30. This is a slightly abbreviated version of my address to the annual meeting of the Academy of Homiletics on December 3, 1998, in Toronto.

5. That the World May Be Redescribed

1. The defining text for sociological method is Norman K. Gottwald, *The Tribes of Yahweh: A Sociology of the Religion of Liberated Israel, 1250–1050 B.C.* (Maryknoll: Orbis Books, 1970). See also Robert R. Wilson, *Sociological Approaches to the Old Testament*, Guides to Biblical Scholarship (Philadelphia: Fortress Press, 1984). Rhetorical criticism as a method was initiated in the field by James Muilenburg. See Phyllis Trible, *Rhetorical Criticism: Context, Method, and the Book of Jonah*, Guides to Biblical Scholarship (Minneapolis: Fortress Press, 1994).

2. The reader will notice that my suggested procedure does not include text criticism. That is because I believe most students are not equipped to do text criticism, but must follow the guidance of commentaries and translators' notes.

3. Consultation of electronic coding of words may be useful, but it will be no substitute for the kinds of informed judgments that the interpreter must make.

4. Following J. Hollander, Richard B. Hays uses the apt term "echo" for the kinds of textual connections that are less than precise or self-evident (*Echoes of Scripture in the Letters of Paul* [New Haven: Yale University Press, 1989]).

5. There is a textual problem here; I follow a conventional emendation.

6. The other side is perhaps voiced by Hananiah in Jeremiah 27–28; see H. Mottu, "Jeremiah vs. Hananiah: Ideology and Truth in Old Testament Prophecy," in *The Bible and Liberation: Political and Social Hermeneutics*, edited by Norman K. Gottwald (Maryknoll: Orbis Books, 1983), 235–51.

7. See, e.g., H. Cazelles, "Zephaniah, Jeremiah, and the Scythians in Palestine," in *A Prophet to the Nations: Essays in Jeremiah Studies,* edited by Leo G. Perdue and Brian W. Kovacs (Winona Lake, Ind.: Eisenbrauns, 1984) 129–49.

6. The Social Nature of the Biblical Text for Preaching

1. On the work of the community in generating the text, see Michel Clévenot, *Materialist Approaches to the Bible* (Maryknoll: Orbis Books, 1985), esp. chapters 12–15. Leonardo Boff has seen the critical implications of this insight of production concerning the ideological control that the interpreting community exercises over the text (*Church, Charism and Power: Liberation Theology and the Institutional Church* [New York: Crossroad, 1985], 110–15).

2. On the freedom exercised and the choices made in such construal, see David H. Kelsey, *The Uses of Scripture in Recent Theology* (Philadelphia: Fortress Press, 1975). On a "canonical construal" of the Old Testament, see Brevard S. Childs, *Old Testament Theology in a Canonical Context* (Philadelphia: Fortress Press, 1986).

3. Michael Fishbane has shown in a compelling way the dynamic relation between traditum and traditio, that is, the tradition and the ongoing traditioning process (*Biblical Interpretation in Ancient Israel* [Oxford: Clarendon, 1985]). It is often the case, clearly, that the tradition becomes the new traditium. See also his more succinct statement of the matter, "Torah and Tradition," in *Tradition and Theology in the Old Testament,* edited by Douglas A. Knight (Philadelphia: Fortress Press, 1977), 275–300. In this later work he comments: "Hereby the danger inherent in the dialectical process between a divine Torah-revelation and a human exegetical Tradition has been disclosed. Tradition has superseded the Torah-teaching and has become an independent authority. Indeed, in this case, Tradition has replaced Torah itself" (294).

4. In the "rendering" of the text, one "renders" God in a new way. On the theme, see Dale Patrick, *The Rendering of God in the Old Testament* (Philadelphia: Fortress Press, 1981).

5. On the methodological possibilities in "reader response," see Wolfgang Iser, *The Act of Reading: A Theory of Aesthetic Response* (Baltimore: Johns Hopkins University Press, 1978), and the collection of essays *The Reader in the Text: Essays on Audience and Interpretation,* edited by Susan R. Sulieman and Inge Crosman (Princeton, N.J.: Princeton University Press, 1980).

6. For brief introductions to this method of study, see Robert R. Wilson, *Sociological Approaches to the Old Testament* (Philadelphia: Fortress Press, 1984), and Norman K. Gottwald, "Sociological Method in the Study of Ancient Israel," in *Encounter with the Text: Form and History in the Hebrew Bible,* edited by Martin J. Buss (Philadelphia: Fortress Press, 1979), 69–81.

7. See Rudolf Bultmann, "Is Exegesis without Presuppositions Possible?" in *Existence and Faith: Shorter Writings of Rudolf Bultmann* (Cleveland: World, 1960), 289–96. Given our current sociological inclination, the formula has come to have different, and perhaps more radical, implications than originally suggested by Bultmann.

8. This is a central argument of Norman K. Gottwald, *The Tribes of Yahweh: A Sociology of the Religion of Liberated Israel 1250–1050 B.C.E.* (Maryknoll: Orbis Books, 1979). See, for example, chapter 13, where he speaks of substructure and superstructure and narratives as "objectifications of the tradition superstructure."

9. This point has been well argued by Elisabeth Schüssler Fiorenza, *Bread Not Stone: The Challenge of Feminist Biblical Interpretation* (Boston: Beacon, 1984). For startling examples of tendentious interpretation, see Robert Ericksen, *Theologians under Hitler: Gerhard Kittel, Paul Althaus, and Emanuel Hirsch* (New Haven: Yale University Press, 1985).

10. Richard L. Rohrbaugh, *The Biblical Interpreter: An Agrarian Bible in an Industrial Age* (Philadelphia: Fortress Press, 1978).

11. On the neutralizing effect of much scholarship, see José Cárdenas Pallares, who has observed the power of "Guild scholarship" to avoid the central interpretive issues. He writes, "Today, Sacred Scripture is studied with the benevolent approval of the pax imperialis; no exegetical activity disturbs the tranquility of the 'empire' for a single moment. What biblical periodical has ever fallen under suspicion of being subversive? Biblical specialists have curiously little to suffer from the Neros and Domitians of our time" (*A Poor Man Called Jesus: Reflections on the Gospel of Mark* [Maryknoll: Orbis Books, 1986], 2).

12. The notion of a hermeneutic of suspicion has been normatively presented by Paul Ricoeur, *Freud and Philosophy: An Essay on Interpretation* (New Haven: Yale University Press, 1970). See the programmatic use made of it by David Tracy, *The Analogical Imagination: Christian Theology and the Culture of Pluralism* (New York: Crossroad, 1981), 346–73 passim.

13. On production and consumption in relation to texts, see Kuno Füssel, "The Materialist Reading of the Bible," in *The Bible and Liberation: Political and Social Hermeneutics,* edited by Norman K. Gottwald (Maryknoll: Orbis Books, 1983), 134–46.

14. The preacher characteristically and by definition uses words in a performative manner. See J. L. Austin, *How to Do Things with Words* (Cambridge, Mass.: Harvard University Press, 1962). On the definitional impossibility of a "neutral pulpit," see Brueggemann, "On Modes of Truth," *Seventh Angel* 12 (March 15, 1984): 17–24.

15. C. Wright Mills exhibits the categories of discernment that have been generated and nurtured by sociology in *The Sociological Imagination* (New York: Oxford University Press, 1959).

16. See Robert A. Nisbet, *The Sociological Tradition* (New York: Basic Books, 1966), for a survey of the characteristic themes of classical sociology.

17. This is, of course, the focus of Marx's critique of religion. It is important that his critique be taken in a specific context and not as a general statement. For a positive sense of Marx's critique of religion, see José Porfirio Miranda, *Marx against the Marxists: The Christian Humanism of Karl Marx* (Maryknoll: Orbis Books, 1980).

18. See Robert N. Bellah, "Biblical Religion and Social Science in the Modern World," *NICM Journal for Jews and Christians in Higher Education* 6 (1982): 8–22.

19. See Alvin Gouldner, *The Coming Crisis of Western Sociology* (New York: Basic Books, 1970).

20. The writings of Marx are complex and not easily accessible. The best access point I know of is the introduction by David McLellan, *The Thought of Karl Marx: An Introduction* (New York: Macmillan, 1971). On alienation in Marx in relation to religious questions, see Arend van Leeuwen, *Critique of Heaven* (New York: Scribner, 1972), *Critique of Earth* (New York: Scribner, 1974); and Nicholas Lash, *A Matter of Hope: A Theologian's Reflections on the Thought of Karl Marx* (Notre Dame, Ind.: University of Notre Dame Press, 1982). See most recently, René Coste, *Marxist Analysis and Christian Faith* (Maryknoll: Orbis Books, 1985).

21. On the emergence of "laws of the marketplace," which are regarded as detached from social pressures and values, see Karl Polanyi, *The Great Transformation* (Boston: Beacon, 1957).

22. Weber's works are scattered, but a useful sourcebook is *From Max Weber: Essays in Sociology*, edited by H. H. Gerth and C. Wright Mills (New York: Oxford University Press, 1946). For an accessible introduction to Weber, see Frank Parkin, *Max Weber* (London: Tavistock, 1982).

23. See Robert N. Bellah et al., *Habits of the Heart: Individualism and Commitment in American Life* (Berkeley: University of California Press, 1985), 44–51.

24. Robert King Merton has well articulated Durkheim's attentiveness to the crisis of normlessness (*Social Theory and Social Structure* [New York: Free, 1957], chapters 4 and 5).

25. Emile Durkheim, *Suicide: A Study in Sociology* (New York: Free, 1951). More generally on Durkheim, see Kenneth Thompson, *Emile Durkheim* (London: Tavistock, 1982).

26. For a more general critical survey of recent sociological thought, see Robert W. Friedrichs, *A Sociology of Sociology* (New York: Free, 1970).

27. See Fishbane, *Biblical Interpretation,* 1 passim.

28. Narrative is essentially this act of recasting and interpreting the memory to meet a new crisis. Unfortunately narrative theology has been frequently presented as a sense of relief at being delivered from Enlightenment modes of historicity, without attention to the dynamic, positive act of reconstitution. On the power and significance of story, see James Barr, "Story and History in Biblical Theology," in his *The Scope and Authority of the Bible* (London: SCM, 1980), 1–17; and Tracy, *Analogical Imagination,* 275–81. On the cruciality of narrative, see Fred B. Craddock, *The Gospels* (Nashville: Abingdon, 1981), 27: "A writer has in the sources available the sayings and the events for a narrative about Jesus Christ. A church has needs to be addressed. The intersection of the two is called a Gospel, a literary work of immense courage and freedom."

29. Gerhard von Rad has shown how these two crises are pivotal for Israel's interpretive action (*Old Testament Theology* [New York: Harper & Row, 1962], 1:36–85).

30. See Hans Walter Wolff, "The Kerygma of the Yahwist," in *The Vitality of Old Testament Traditions*, by Walter Brueggemann and Hans Walter Wolff (Atlanta: John Knox, 1975), 41–66.

31. See more generally Brueggemann and Wolff, *Vitality of Old Testament Traditions.*

32. On the exile as a situation requiring and permitting bold interpretation, see Ralph W. Klein, *Israel in Exile: A Theological Interpretation* (Philadelphia: Fortress Press, 1979).

33. On the canonical process and its significance in the New Testament, see James D. G. Dunn, "Levels of Canonical Authority," *Horizons in Biblical Theology* 4 (1982): 13–60.

34. For a formidable introduction to the issues, see Anthony C. Thiselton, *The Two Horizons: New Testament Hermeneutics and Philosophical Description with Special Reference to Heidegger, Bultmann, Gadamer, and Wittgenstein* (Grand Rapids: Eerdmans, 1980). See also Richard E. Palmer, *Hermeneutics: Interpretation Theory in Schleiermacher, Dilthey, Heidegger, and Gadamer* (Evanston, Ill.: Northwestern University Press, 1969). Unfortunately both Thiselton and Palmer are confined to the tradition of Heidegger. This tradition needs to be carefully critiqued by a political hermeneutic rooted in Marx as suggested by Ernst Bloch and the Frankfurt School. A more balanced view that takes into account the liberation trajectory is offered by David Tracy (*Analogical Imagination,* chapter 5 passim).

35. On the shape of religious problems and possibilities in a postmodern context, see William Beardslee, "Christ in the Post-Modern Age," in *The Post-Modern Condition: A Report on Knowledge,* edited by Jean-Francois Lyotard (Minneapolis: University of Minnesota Press, 1984); and Mark C. Taylor, *Erring: A Postmodern, A-Theology* (Chicago: University of Chicago Press, 1984).

36. Walter Brueggemann, *David's Truth: In Israel's Imagination & Memory* (Philadelphia: Fortress Press, 1985).

37. Peter L. Berger and Thomas Luckmann, *The Social Construction of Reality: A Treatise in the Sociology of Knowledge* (New York: Doubleday, 1966).

38. On constructive work in education, see Jack L. Seymour, Robert T. O'Gorman, Charles R. Foster, *The Church in the Education of the Public* (Nashville: Abingdon, 1984), 134–56. More generally on the constructive work of imagination see Paul W. Pruyser, *The Play of the Imagination: Toward a Psychoanalysis of Culture* (New York: International Universities Press, 1983), chapter 4 passim.

39. Friedrichs shows how the tension of transformation and equilibrium has operated in sociology (*Sociology of Sociology*). Concerning Old Testament study, see Walter Brueggemann, "A Shape for Old Testament Theology, I: Structure Legitimation," *Catholic Biblical Quarterly* 47 (1985): 28–46; "A Shape for Old Testament Theology, II: Embrace of Pain," *CBQ* 47 (1985): 395–415.

40. See Walter Brueggemann, "Trajectories in Old Testament Literature and the Sociology of Ancient Israel," *Journal of Biblical Literature* 98 (1979): 161–85.

41. See Gottwald, *Tribes of Yahweh,* chapter 50, on the interface between his method and the classical traditions of sociology. See my presentation of the paradigm of the two trajectories in tension in *The Prophetic Imagination* (Philadelphia: Fortress Press, 1978).

42. Ferdinand Toennies, *Community and Society* (1887), translated by C. P. Loomis (New York: Harper & Row, 1963).

43. Robert R. Wilson has pursued the same textual paradigm with a typology of central and peripheral prophets. Following Wilson's language, one may say that there are texts that are "central" and those that are "peripheral" (*Prophecy and Society in Ancient Israel* [Philadelphia: Fortress Press, 1980]).

44. The presentation of a religious world of equilibrium to those who crave equilibrium is what Marx referred to by his famous characterization of religion as "the opiate of the people."

45. Fishbane has shown how Second Isaiah is a reinterpretation of Genesis 1 for quite specific purposes in a polemical situation (*Biblical Interpretation,* 322–26).

46. On the text, see Walter Brueggemann, "The Prophet as a Destabilizing Presence," in *The Pastor as Prophet,* edited by Earl E. Shelp and Ronald H. Sunderland (New York: Pilgrim, 1985), 48–77.

7. The Shrill Voice of the Wounded Party

1. It is evident that the commandments in Israel were non-negotiable. It is equally evident that they were, in the interpretive process of Israel, endlessly negotiated. See Walter Brueggemann, *Finally Comes the Poet: Daring Speech for Proclamation* (Minneapolis: Fortress Press, 1989), chapter 4; and *Interpretation and Obedience: From Faithful Reading to Faithful Living* (Minneapolis: Fortress Press, 1991), 145–58.

2. Exodus 20:18-21 appears to be an anticipation or an authorization for the "office" of Moses. See Hans-Joachim Kraus, *Die prophetische Verkündigung des Rechts in Israel* (Zollikon: Evangelischer, 1957); and James Muilenburg, "The Office of the Prophet in Ancient Israel," *The Bible in Modern Scholarship,* edited by J. Philip Hyatt (Nashville: Abingdon, 1965) 74–97.

3. On authority in wisdom teaching generally and in Proverbs in particular, see the essays in Leo. G. Perdue and John G. Gammie (eds), *The Sage in Israel and the Ancient near East* (Winona Lake: Eisenbrauns, 1990).

4. Klaus Koch, "Is There a Doctrine of Retribution in the Old Testament?" in *Theodicy in the Old Testament,* edited by James L. Crenshaw (Philadelphia: Fortress Press, 1983), 57–87.

5. The classic statement is that of Walther Zimmerli, "The Place and Limit of Wisdom in the Framework of the Old Testament Theology," *Scottish Journal of Theology* 17 (1964): 148: "Wisdom thinks resolutely within the framework of a theology of creation." For a fuller exposition of the linkage between creation and wisdom, see Hans Heinrich Schmid, *Gerechtigkeit als Weltordnung: Hintergrund und Geschichte des Alttestamentlichen Gerechtigkeitsbegriffes,* Beiträge zur Historischen Theologie 40 (Tübingen: Mohr Siebeck, 1968).

6. The most likely proposals for the location of wisdom teaching are the family or clan, the school, or the royal court. It now seems evident that there is not sufficient evidence to establish with certainty any of these possible locations; there is enough suggestive evidence for each, so that each remains a live option. For a discussion of the several possible contexts for wisdom instruction and reflection,

which are not mutually exclusive, see the essays by R. N. Whybray, Carole R. Fontaine, and André Lemaire in *The Sage in Israel and the Ancient Near East*, edited by John G. Gammie and Leo G. Perdue (Winona Lake, Ind.: Eisenbrauns, 1990), 133–39, 155–64, 165–81, respectively.

7. It is commonly agreed that it is only in the text of Ben Sirah, dated about 180 B.C.E., that wisdom and Torah claims converge and are explicitly identified with each other.

8. Erhard Gerstenberger, *Wesen und Herkunft des apodiktischen Rechts*, Wissenschaftliche Monographien zum Alten und Neuen Testament 20 (Neukirchen-Vluyn: Neukirchener, 1965).

9. Gerstenberger, *Wesen und Herkunft des apodiktischen Rechts*, 110–17.

10. See my exposition of these matters in "Exodus," in *The New Interpreter's Bible* (Nashville: Abingdon, 1994), vol. 1. See also Brueggemann, "The Exodus Narrative as Israel's Articulation of Faith Development," in *Hope within History* (Atlanta: John Knox, 1987), 7–26.

11. It is important that the material be understood as liturgical, without making historical claims. On the liturgical aspects of the text, see Johannes Pedersen, *Israel: Its Life and Culture III-IV* (Copenhagen: Branner, 1940), 728–37.

12. On Pharaoh and the power of chaos, see Terence E. Fretheim, "The Plagues as Ecological Signs of Historical Disaster," *Journal of Biblical Literature* 110 (1991): 285–96.

13. On the role of the prophet in such "class conflict," Micah may be cited as an exemplary voice. On Micah in this context, see Hans Walter Wolff, "Micah the Moreshite—The Prophet and His Background," in *Israelite Wisdom: Theological and Literary Essays in Honor of Samuel Terrien*, edited by John G. Gammie et al. (Missoula, Mont.: Scholars, 1978), 77–84; and George V. Pixley, "Micah—A Revolutionary," in *The Bible and the Politics of Exegesis: Essays in Honor of Norman K. Gottwald on His Sixty-fifth Birthday*, edited by David Jobling et al. (Cleveland: Pilgrim, 1991), 53–60.

14. Robert R. Wilson, *Prophecy and Society in Ancient Israel* (Philadelphia: Fortress Press, 1980).

15. It should be noted that the use of the term "pardon" and much of the vocabulary of Western theology has picked up on the juridical cast of much of the Old Testament. While the usages of the Old Testament are quite varied, much of Western theology has been reduced to this single model, which has made it enormously heavy-handed in the production of guilt. For a recent, thoughtful exposition in this theological tradition, see Cornelius Plantenga, Jr., "Locked in Sin: The Theology of Corruption," *Christian Century* (December 21–28, 1994): 1218–22.

16. I leave aside the question of whether Augustine and Luther, in their heavy accent on sin and guilt, misread Paul. See Krister Stendahl, "Paul and the Introspective Conscience of the West," in *Paul among Christians and Jews and Other Essays* (Philadelphia: Fortress Press, 1977).

17. Stephen Orgel and Jonathan Goldberg, eds., *John Milton* (New York: Oxford University Press, 1991) 356.

18. Orgel and Goldberg, *Milton*, 356–57.

19. John Milton, *Christian Doctrine*, 382–83, as quoted by Robert Crosman, *Reading Paradise Lost* (Bloomington: Indiana University Press, 1980), 25.

20. Arthur Sewell, *A Study in Milton's Christian Doctrine* (London: Oxford University Press, 1939), 80.

21. Crosman, *Reading Paradise Lost*, 25.

22. Paul Ricoeur, *The Symbolism of Evil* (Boston: Beacon, 1967), 252–60.

23. Ricoeur, *Symbolism of Evil*, 255, 257.

24. Ricoeur, *Symbolism of Evil*, 257–58.

25. Ricoeur, *Symbolism of Evil*, 259.

26. Ricoeur, *Symbolism of Evil*; Ricoeur uses the term "victim."

27. John Steinbeck plays with the imagery of sin "crouching" in threat in *East of Eden* (*Five Novels* [New York: Octopus Books, 1988], 685–91 passim).

28. Erhard Gerstenberger has shown how it is that Israel's complaint and protest are in fact acts of hope (*Der bittende Mensch: Bittritual und Klagelied des Einzelnen im Alten Testament*, Wissenschaftliche Monographien zum Alten und Neuen Testament 51 [Neukirchen-Vluyn: Neukirchener, 1980]).

29. Claus Westermann, "Struktur und Geschichte der Klage im Alten Testament," in *Forschung am alten Testament*, Theologische Bücherei 24 (Munich: Kaiser, 1964), 269–72.

30. On the drama of complaint as having three members, see my discussion of Psalms 9 and 10 in "Psalms 9–10: A Counter to Conventional Social Reality," in *Bible and the Politics of Exegesis*, edited by Jobling et al., 3–15.

31. For a complete review of the problem, see Stephen Croft, *The Identity of the Individual in the Psalms* Journal for the Study of the Old Testament Supplement 44 (Sheffield: Sheffield Academic, 1987).

32. Fredrik Lindström, *Suffering and Sin: Interpretations of Illness in the Individual Complaint Psalms*, Coniectanea Biblica Old Testament 37 (Stockholm: Almqvist & Wiksell, 1994).

33. On the untamed power of Nihil, see Fredrik Lindström, *God and the Origin of Evil: A Contextual Analysis of Alleged Monistic Evidence in the Old Testament*, Coniectanea Biblica 21 (Lund: Gleerup, 1983); Karl Barth, "God and Nothingness," in *Church Dogmatics* III.3 (Edinburgh: T&T Clark, 1960), 289–368; and Jon D. Levenson, *Creation and the Persistence of Evil: The Jewish Drama of Divine Omnipotence* (San Francisco: Harper & Row, 1988).

34. Ricoeur suggests that the serpent in Genesis 3 "represents the first landmark along the road of the Satanic theme which, in the Persian epoch, permitted the inclusion of a near-dualism in the faith of Israel" (*Symbolism of Evil*, 259).

35. Gustavo Gutiérrez, *On Job: God-Talk and the Suffering of the Innocent* (Maryknoll: Orbis Books, 1987).

36. On the interpretive possibilities in Job 42:6, in addition to the commentaries, see Jack Miles, *God: A Biography* (New York: Knopf, 1995), 425–30.

37. A like role is played by Abraham in the encounter of Genesis 18:22-33, though in that narrative the mood does not seem as dangerous and freighted as is the narrative of Exodus 32, in which Moses makes an intercession on behalf of Israel.

38. On the subtlety of this text and especially the response of Jonah, see Phyllis Trible, *Rhetorical Criticism: Context, Method, and the Book of Jonah* (Minneapolis: Fortress Press, 1994), 199–204.

8. Life or Death: De-Priveleged Communication

1. On the production of atheism as a viable alternative in modernism, see Michael J. Buckley, *At the Origins of Modern Atheism* (New Haven: Yale University Press, 1987).

2. I have explicated this theme at length in *Theology of the Old Testament: Testimony, Dispute, Advocacy* (Minneapolis: Fortress Press, 1997).

3. Hayden White comments on the work of a historian and the construction of a historical account:

> It is the fact that they can be recorded otherwise, in an order of narrative, that makes them, at one and the same time, questionable as to their authenticity and susceptible to being considered as tokens of reality. In order to qualify as historical, an event must be susceptible to at least two narrations of its occurrence. Unless at least two versions of the same set of events can be imagined, there is no reason for the historian to take upon himself the authority of giving the true account of what really happened. (*The Content of the Form: Narrative Discourse and Historical Representation* [Baltimore: Johns Hopkins University Press, 1987], 20)

Mutatis mutandis, the same is true for the preacher. The only reason the preaching task is important is that the same data of life can be construed differently, that is, without reference to Yhwh, who is the main character is "our" version. This recognition that the truth of the matter can be given in an alternative, credible version is an important facet of our new preaching situation.

4. This is in general the burden of the writing program of Wiesel. Reference may be made, for example, to *The Trial of God (as It Was Held on February 25, 1649 in Shamgorod): A Play in Three Acts* (New York: Random House, 1978). An assessment of this work concerning testimony by Wiesel is offered by Robert McAfee Brown, *Elie Wiesel: Messenger to All Humanity* (Notre Dame, Ind.: University of Notre Dame Press, 1983), and see Wiesel's own account of his work, Eli Wiesel, *Memoirs: All Rivers Run to the Sea* (New York: Knopf, 1995). The most poignant statement of Wiesel on the theme of "testimony" is, Wiesel, "The Holocaust as Literary Inspiration," in his *Dimensions of the Holocaust: Lectures at Northwestern University* (Evanston: Northwestern University Press, 1977), 9: "If the Greeks invented tragedy, the Romans the epistle, and the Renaissance the sonnet, our generation invented a new literature, that of testimony." Wiesel refers to the requirement of testimony with reference to the holocaust, because the truth of the Holocaust is in dispute and the outcome depends on the witnesses.

5. Arthur W. Frank, *The Wounded Storyteller: Body, Illness, and Ethics* (Chicago: University of Chicago Press, 1995).

6. The same qualities mark the primal stories that the early church told about Jesus, which became the basis for the worship and faith of the early church.

7. I will stick to the Old Testament; but it is clear that the same de-privileged situation operates in the New Testament, as is evident in Paul's testimony before imperial officials in the book of Acts.

8. It is on this basis that scholars characteristically declare that the rise of monotheism in the Old Testament is linked to Second Isaiah. See the evidence summarized by Bernhard Lang, *Monotheism and the Prophetic Minority: An Essay in Biblical History and Sociology*, The Social World of Biblical Antiquity 1 (Sheffield: Almond, 1983) and more recently, *The Triumph of Elohim: From Yahwisms to Judaisms*, edited by Diana Vikander Edelman (Grand Rapids: Eerdmans, 1995). However that may be, it is unmistakable that the establishment of monotheism was no concern of the poet.

9. The "education" of Pharaoh through the processes of the exodus narrative is a case in point. At the outset Pharaoh disclaims any awareness of YHWH (Exod. 5:2). By 8:25, he acknowledges "your God." In 8:28 he again refers to "your god," and asks for prayers. In 10:16 he confesses sin against "your god" and by 12:21 recognizes that blessing is in the power of the God of Moses. The learning curve for Pharaoh is perhaps typical for those who live out of a different, hegemonic narrative.

10. *New York Times*, June 11, 1997.

9. Preaching to Exiles

1. Walter Brueggemann, "Disciplines of Readiness," *Occasional Paper No. 1*, Theology and Worship Unit, Presbyterian Church (U.S.A.) (Louisville, 1989), and "Rethinking Church Models Through Scripture," *Theology Today* 48 (July 1991): 128–38.

2. Jack Stotts, "Beyond Beginnings," *Occasional Paper No. 2*, Theology and Worship Unit, Presbyterian Church (U.S.A.) (Louisville, 1989).

3. On the significance of metaphor for reading the biblical text and for theological reflections, see Phyllis Trible, *God and the Rhetoric of Sexuality*, Overtures to Biblical Theology 2 (Philadelphia: Fortress Press, 1978), 31–59, and Sallie McFague, *Metaphorical Theology: Models of God in Religious Language* (Philadelphia: Fortress Press, 1982), 1–66 passim.

4. In my discussion of the church in relation to pluralism, I have decided not to address what I consider to be the related issue of the faltering of denominations. On that crisis, see Dorothy Bass, "Reflections on the Reports of Decline in Mainstream Protestantism," *Chicago Theological Seminary Register* 79 (1989): 5–15; eadem, "Teaching with Authority? The Changing Place of Mainstream Protestantism in American Culture," *Religious Education* 85 (Spring 1990): 295–310.

5. On the trivializing of such symbols in the life of ancient Israel, see Peter Ackroyd, "The Temple Vessels: A Continuity Theme," in *Studies in the Religion of Ancient Israel*, Vetus Testamentum Supplement 23 (Leiden: Brill, 1972), 166–81.

6. Jacob Neusner has shown how the historical-geographical experience of exile has become a paradigm for Judaism, so that Jews who did not share the actual concrete experience of exile must nonetheless appropriate its paradigmatic power in order to be fully Jewish (*Understanding Seeking Faith: Essays on the Case of Judaism*, Brown Judaic Studies [Atlanta: Scholars, 1986], 137–41). In what follows, I am especially informed by the splendid study of Daniel L. Smith, *The Religion of the Landless: The Social Context of the Babylonian Exile* (Bloomington: Meyer Stone Books, 1989).

7. I use "world" here in the sense of Alfred Schutz, *The Phenomenology of the Social World* (Evanston, Ill.: Northwestern University Press, 1967). A more accessible rendering of the same notion of world is found in Peter L. Berger and Thomas Luckmann, *The Social Construction of Reality: A Treatise in the Sociology of Knowledge* (Garden City, N.Y.: Doubleday, 1966).

8. Stanley Hauerwas and William H. Willimon, *Resident Aliens: A Provocative Christian Assessment of Culture and Ministry for People Who Know That Something Is Wrong* (Nashville: Abingdon, 1989).

9. The long-term threat to the viability of faith is not right-wing religious, ominous and destructive as that is, but secularism. I think it most unfortunate that the church uses as much energy as it does on the former, when the latter is so pervasive and relentless among us.

10. On the theme of "political correctness," see Rosa Ehrenreich, "What Campus Radicals? The P.C. Undergrad Is a Useful Specter," *Harper's Magazine*, December 1991, 57–61; and Louis Menand, "What Are Universities For? The Real Crisis on Campus Is One of Identity," *Harper's Magazine*, December, 1991, 47–56.

11. Martin Buber writes: "in the history of the human spirit, I distinguish between epochs of habitation and epochs of homelessness" (*Between Man and Man* [New York: Macmillan, 1965], 126). Buber understands our own epoch to be one of homelessness. On the same theme, informed by Buber, see Nicholas Lash, "Eclipse of Word and Presence," in his *Easter in Ordinary: Reflections on Human Experience and the Knowledge of God* (Charlottesville: University Press of Virginia, 1988), 199–218.

12. The disregard of "late Judaism" in Christian scholarship and theological education reflects the power of the "Wellhausian hypothesis," in which the postexilic period was regarded as degenerate, inferior, and not worthy of attention. More recent scholarship has to some modest extent broken loose of the grip of that hypothesis in order that the period can be taken with theological seriousness.

13. Peter Ackroyd, *Exile and Restoration: A Study of Hebrew Thought of the Sixth Century B.C.*, Old Testament Library (Philadelphia: Westminster, 1968); Ralph W. Klein, *Israel in Exile: A Theological Interpretation*, Overtures to Biblical Theology (Philadelphia: Fortress Press, 1979); and Daniel L. Smith, *Religion of the Landless*. Smith's study represents a most important advance beyond Ackroyd and Klein in terms of method, as he pays attention to the interaction between the social realities of the exile and its impact on the way in which literature functions.

14. It is evident that I will proceed with something like a "method of correlation" not unlike that proposed by Paul Tillich. I find such an approach practically

useful in establishing a "dynamic analogy" with the text for our own time. The method is a convenience for me and reflects no commitment to a program like that of Tillich, about which I have great reservations.

15. See Delbert R. Hillers, *Lamentation: A New Translation with Introduction and Commentary*, Anchor Bible 7A (Garden City, N.Y.: Doubleday, 1972), xl–xli.

16. For a critical understanding of the function of the genealogies, see Marshall D. Johnson, *The Purpose of the Biblical Genealogies: With Special Reference to the Genealogies of Jesus*, Society for New Testament Studies Monograph Series 8 (London: Cambridge University Press, 1969); and Robert R. Wilson, *Genealogy and History in the Biblical World* (New Haven: Yale University Press, 1977).

17. A wonderful example of such stories and such characters to people imagination are the biographical statements by Russell Baker, *Growing Up* (New York: New American Library-Dutton, 1983); and idem, *The Good Times* (New York: New American Library-Dutton, 1991).

18. See Exod. 32:32f.; Isa. 4:3; 56:5; Dan. 12:1; Rev. 3:5; 13:8; 17:8; 20:12, 15; 21:27.

19. Rolf Rendtorff, "Die theologische Stellung des Schöpfungsglaubens bei Deuterojesaja," *Zeitschrift für Theologie und Kirche* 51 (1954): 3–13; Rainer Albertz, *Weltschöpfung und Menschenschöpfung: Untersucht bei Deuterojesaja, Hiob und in den Psalmen*, Calwer Theologische Monographien 3 (Stuttgart: Calwer, 1974).

20. On "as" as "the copula of imagination," see Garrett Green, *Imagining God: Theology & the Religious Imagination* (San Francisco: Harper & Row, 1989), 73, 140 passim.

21. Ackroyd shows how the temple vessels can be narrated to report a complete and decisive break in historical continuity or, conversely, can be used to enact continuity in the midst of enormous discontinuity ("Temple Vessels").

22. On the general theme and problem of presence, see Samuel Terrien, *The Elusive Presence: Toward a New Biblical Theology*, Religious Perspectives 26 (New York: Harper & Row, 1978). More specifically, on presence as understood in the Priestly tradition, see Robert B. Coote and David Robert Ord, *In the Beginning: Creation and the Priestly History* (Minneapolis: Fortress Press, 1991), especially chapters 9–11.

23. Paul Ricoeur traces the way in which Genesis portrays human persons as both *perpetrators* and *victims* (*The Symbolism of Evil* [Boston: Beacon, 1967], 255–60). Already in that narrative, which is characteristically read as though it concerned only fault, Israel has carefully nuanced the ambiguity in social experience.

24. See Samuel Terrien, "Job as a Sage," in *The Sage in Israel and the Ancient Near East*, edited by John G. Gammie and Leo G. Perdue (Winona Lake, Ind.: Eisenbrauns, 1990), 231–42; and Rainer Albertz, "The Sage Adds Pious Wisdom in the Book of Job: The Friends' Perspective," in ibid., 243–61.

25. Concerning these narratives, I am primarily informed by Smith, *Religion of the Landless*, 153–78.

26. Green has taught me the most concerning the fact that our "givens" are dependent on paradigmatic construals of reality (*Imagining God*, 41–60). On the cruciality of rhetoric for reality, see the suggestive interface of religion and rhetoric

suggested by Wayne C. Booth, "Rhetoric and Religion: Are They Essentially Wedded?" in *Radical Pluralism and Truth: David Tracy and the Hermeneutics of Religion,* edited by Werner G. Jeanrond and Jennifer L. Rike (New York: Crossroad, 1991), 62–80.

27. On the use of the notion of liminality from Victor Turner in the interest of religious transformation, see Urban T. Holmes, "The Priest as Enchanter," in *To Be a Priest: Perspectives on Vocation and Ordination,* edited by Robert E. Terwilliger and Urban T. Holmes (San Francisco: Harper & Row, 1975), 173–81; and Marchita B. Mauck, "The Liminal Space of Ritual and Art," in *The Bent World: Essays on Religion and Culture,* edited by John R. May, Annual Publication of the College Theology Society 1979 (Chico, Calif.: Scholars, 1981), 149–57.

28. See Roy Schafer, *Retelling a Life: Narration and Dialogue in Psychoanalysis* (New York: Basic Books, 1992), especially chapter 2.

29. See William H. Willimon, *Peculiar Speech: Preaching to the Baptized* (Grand Rapids: Eerdmans, 1992).

30. The critique often leveled against Willimon and Hauerwas, that they are sectarian, is driven by the long-established categories of H. Richard Niebuhr concerning "Christ and Culture." It is now clear that those older categories are no longer adequate for the actual situation of the church in Western culture and that a critique must be made of Niebuhr's typology. See, for example, Robert E. Webber, *The Church in the World: Opposition, Tension, or Transformation?* Academie Books (Grand Rapids: Zondervan, 1986), 261–78 passim.

31. Daniel Smith provides a most discerning study of the letter concerning the "social psychology of a group under stress" (*Religion of the Landless,* 127–38).

32. Karl Barth, *Church Dogmatics* IV.1 (Edinburgh: T&T Clark, 1956) #59, pp. 157–210.

33. Barth, *Church Dogmatics,* 180–83, 188–94.

34. Karl Barth, *Church Dogmatics* IV.2 (Edinburgh: T&T Clark, 1958) #64, pp. 20–154. On the parable of Luke 15:11-32, see pp. 21–25.

35. On the "impossibilities" of the kingdom, see Walter Brueggemann, "'Impossibility' and Epistemology in the Faith Traditions of Abraham and Sarah (Gen. 18:1-15)," *Zeitschrift für die alttestamentliche Wissenschaft* 94 (1982), 615–34.

10. Preaching a Sub-Version

1. Michael J. Buckley, *At the Origins of Modern Atheism* (New Haven: Yale University Press, 1990).

2. For a review of the origins of these intellectual developments, see Paul Hazard, *The European Mind, 1680–1715: The Critical Years* (New York: Fordham University Press, 1990). On the contemporary culmination in "Sheilaism," see Robert N. Bellah et al., *Habits of the Heart: Individualism and Commitment in American Life* (Berkeley: University of California Press, 1985), 221, 235.

3. On the "complete unfamiliarity" of the Bible, see the classic statements of Karl Barth, "The Strange New World within the Bible," in *The Word of God and the*

Word of Man (New York: Harper & Brothers, 1957), 28–50; and Martin Buber, "The Man of Today and the Jewish Bible," in *On the Bible: Eighteen Studies,* edited by Nahum N. Glatzer (New York: Schocken Books, 1968), 1–13. On the *Jewish* "unfamiliarity" of the text, see Susan A. Handelman, *The Slayers of Moses: The Emergence of Rabbinic Interpretation in Modern Literary Theory* (Albany: SUNY Press, 1982).

4. On the relation of *how* and *who* in the text, see Gail R. O'Day, *The Word Disclosed: John's Story and Narrative Preaching* (St. Louis: CBP, 1987).

5. On the relation between Jewish modes of interpretation and Freud, see Handelman, *Slayers of Moses;* Geoffrey H. Hartman and Sanford Budick, eds., *Midrash and Literature* (New Haven: Yale University Press, 1986); and John Murray Cuddihy, *The Ordeal of Civility: Freud, Marx, Levi-Strauss and the Jewish Struggle with Modernity* (New York: Basic Books, 1974).

6. On violence in the character of God, see Renita J. Weems, *Battered Love: Marriage, Sex, and Violence in the Hebrew Prophets* (Minneapolis: Fortress Press, 1995); and Regina M. Schwartz, *The Curse of Cain: The Violent Legacy of Monotheism* (Chicago: University of Chicago Press, 1997).

7. On the power of the myth of scarcity, see the theological critique of M. Douglas Meeks, *God the Economist: The Doctrine of God and Political Economy* (Minneapolis: Fortress, 1989), and the hermeneutical analysis of Regina Schwartz, *Curse of Cain.*

8. Fox Butterfield, *All God's Children: The Bosket Family and the American Tradition of Violence* (New York: Alfred A. Knopf, 1995).

9. On the psalms of complaint and lament, see the comprehensive study of Patrick D. Miller, *They Cried to the Lord: The Form and Theology of Biblical Prayer* (Minneapolis: Fortress Press, 1994).

10. On such practices as "signals of oddity" in the Jewish community, see Jacob Neusner, *The Enchantments of Judaism: Rites of Transformation from Birth through Death* (New York: Basic Books, 1987).

11. Walter Brueggemann, *Cadences of Home: Preaching among Exiles* (Louisville: Westminster John Knox, 1997). See also Frederick Buechner, *The Longing for Home: Recollections and Reflections* (San Francisco: Harper Collins, 1996).

11. Truth-Telling as Subversive Obedience

1. For a parallel consideration of the fourth and tenth commandments, see Walter Brueggemann, *Finally Comes the Poet: Daring Speech for Proclamation* (Minneapolis: Fortress Press, 1989), 79–110; and Brueggemann, "The Commandments and Liberated, Liberating Bonding," in *Interpretation and Obedience: From Faithful Reading to Faithful Living* (Minneapolis: Fortress Press, 1991), 145–58.

2. The literature on the Decalogue is immense. In addition to the magisterial and normative interpretations of Luther and Calvin, see Walter Harrelson, *The Ten Commandments and Human Rights,* Overtures to Biblical Theology 8 (Philadelphia: Fortress Press, 1980); Brevard S. Childs, *Old Testament Theology in a Canonical*

Context (Philadelphia: Fortress Press, 1985), 63–83; Paul Lehman, *The Decalogue and a Human Future: The Meaning of the Commandments for Making and Keeping Human Life Human* (Grand Rapids: Eerdmans, 1994); and Horst Dietrich Preuss, *Old Testament Theology I* (OTL; Louisville: Westminster John Knox, 1995), 100–117.

3. A range of texts is related to this commandment and some perhaps derived from it: Exod. 23:1, 6-8; Lev. 19:11, 16-17; Deut. 19:15ff.; Amos 2:7; 5:15; Mic. 3:11; Prov. 11:9-13; Ps. 12:2; 27:2; 64:8.

4. There is a long-standing critical tradition that situates the judicial provisions of Exodus 18 in the context of Jehoshaphat's reform, on which see 2 Chronicles 19:4-11. While such a critical judgment may be made, the text as it stands makes a claim for Mosaic authorization.

5. See Thomas W. Overholt, *The Threat of Falsehood: A Study in the Theology of the Book of Jeremiah*, Studies in Biblical Theology, Second Series 16 (London: SCM, 1970).

6. The issue of false and true prophecy is an enormously vexed one. While it may be claimed that there is nothing that *formally* distinguishes false and true prophets, it is clear that *in substance* ancient Israel, in its canonizing process, made important distinctions. For representative views of the issue, see James L. Crenshaw, *Prophetic Conflict: Its Effect Upon Israelite Religion*, Beihefte zur Zeitschrift für die alttestamentliche Wissenschaft 124 (Berlin: de Gruyter, 1971); and James A. Sanders, "Canonical Hermeneutics: True and False Prophecy," in *From Sacred Story to Sacred Text: Canon as Paradigm* (Philadelphia: Fortress Press, 1987), 87–105. On the classic case of Jeremiah 27–28, see Henri Mottu, "Jeremiah vs. Hananiah: Ideology and Truth in Old Testament Prophecy," in *The Bible and Liberation: Political and Social Hermeneutics,* edited by Norman K. Gottwald (Maryknoll: Orbis Books, 1983), 235–51.

7. The NRSV renders the first word "ah." That innocuous translation is unfortunate, for the term bespeaks sadness at loss and death. The word indicates a sense of loss that is to come on those who practice deceiving euphemism.

8. Robert J. Lifton, *The Nazi Doctors: Medical Killing and the Psychology of Genocide* (New York: Basic Books, 1986), 202 passim.

9. Noam Chomsky's argument in this regard is stated in many places. See, for example, *Necessary Illusions: Thought Control in Democratic Societies* (Boston: South End, 1989); idem, *What Uncle Sam Really Wants* (Tucson: Odonian, 1992); idem, *The Washington Connection and Third World Fascism* (Boston: South End, 1979). My own references are from a lecture he presented in June 1995.

10. See especially Neil Postman, *Amusing Ourselves to Death: Public Discourse in the Age of Show Business* (New York: Penguin Books, 1986); idem, *Technopoly: The Surrender of Culture to Technology* (New York: Random House, 1993); idem, *How to Watch TV News* (New York: Viking Penguin, 1992).

11. The most important studies of the theme are by Jacques Ellul, *The Humiliation of the Word* (Grand Rapids: Eerdmans, 1991); idem, *Propaganda: The Formation of Men's Attitudes* (New York: Random House, 1973); and idem, *Technological Society* (New York: Random House, 1967).

12. Karl Marx saw this with the greatest clarity and influence. Note his programmatic statement: The criticism of heaven is thus transformed into the criticism of earth, the criticism of religion into the criticism of law, and the criticism of theology into the criticism of politics.

13. On the importance of juridical language in the Fourth Gospel, see Robert V. Moss, "The Witnessing Church in the New Testament," *Theology and Life* 3 (1960): 262–68; Andrew T. Lincoln, "Trials, Plots and the Narrative of the Fourth Gospel," *Journal for the Study of the Old Testament* 56 (1994): 3–30; and more generally A. A. Trites, *The New Testament Concept of Witness*, Society for New Testament Studies Monograph Series 31 (Cambridge: Cambridge University Press, 1977), 78–127. Most remarkably, the Fourth Gospel affirms the Paraclete as a witness to Jesus, on which see Gail R. O'Day, "Excursus: The Paraclete," in "The Gospel of John: Introduction, Commentary, and Reflections," *The New Interpreter's Bible* (Nashville: Abingdon, 1994–2004), 9:774–78.

14. On this text, see the helpful comments of O'Day, "Gospel of John," 815–27, and the shrewd interpretation by Paul Lehmann, *The Transfiguration of Politics* (New York: Harper & Row, 1975), 48–70.

15. See M. Scott Peck, *People of the Lie: The Hope for Healing Human Evil* (New York: Simon & Schuster, 1985).

16. Richard N. Goodwin, "A Three-Party Election Won't Address Issue of Economic Injustice," *Boston Globe,* Friday, July 26, 1996, A17.

Indexes

Passages

Names and Subjects